n hatton@tcd.ie

THE COMPLETE GUIDE
TO CONVERTIBLE
SECURITIES WORLDWIDE

THE COMPLETE GUIDE TO CONVERTIBLE SECURITIES WORLDWIDE

Laura A. Zubulake

Wiley Finance Editions
JOHN WILEY & SONS, INC.
New York • Chichester • Brisbane • Toronto • Singapore

Library of Congress Cataloging in Publication Data:

Zubulake, Laura A.
    The complete guide to convertible securities worldwide /
Laura A. Zubulake.
    p. cm. – (Wiley finance editions)
    Includes index.
    ISBN 0-471-52802-1 (cloth)
    1. Convertible securities.   I. Title.   II. Series.
HG4651.283   1991
332.63'2044–dc20   90-49249

Printed in the United States of America

91 92 10 9 8 7 6 5 4 3

To my parents, Mary and George Zubulake, and my brother Paul.

Preface

Convertible securities have been used as financing vehicles for several decades. Corporations are able to issue convertibles at rates lower than comparable straight debt while also selling equity on a deferred basis at a premium to the current market price. Investors are attracted to the hybrid nature of convertible securities. They participate in equity price appreciation with limited downside risk.

Convertibles are interesting and relatively sophisticated securities. The concepts and theories associated with domestic and international convertibles can be difficult to understand. From the standpoint of a broker, a domestic or foreign equity or fixed-incomes portfolio manager, or an average investor, questions with regard to domestic and international convertible securities are generally quite similar. With this in mind, this book was written using practical examples to ease the learning process.

This book can be divided into four sections, each with different objectives. The first section is a general analysis of a typical U.S. dollar–

denominated Euroconvertible. The use of one example throughout the section to explain the features adds continuity to the book. All terms associated with convertible securities are defined with respect to this example. Practical applications are used extensively to explain the evaluation techniques. This approach combines the practical and theoretical aspects of a convertible security. It is intended to teach investors of all levels.

With the globalization of securities markets, understanding foreign securities is becoming increasingly important. The second section discusses international convertible securities. International convertibles may be denominated in various currencies. These multicurrency bonds often have unique features. Practical examples are used to explain the special characteristics of international convertibles. International convertibles also provide an opportunity to take advantage of currency fluctuations. Foreign currency exposure is explained in great detail under various scenarios. The analysis shows that the total return of international convertibles is a function of the fluctuation in equity prices, interest rates, and foreign currencies.

The analysis of international convertibles is then taken a step further. The characteristics of various domestic convertible markets in the United States, Britain, Japan, France, Australia, and Canada are examined. These markets have some unique features and evaluation methods. Practical examples are used to study these techniques in detail.

Another section discusses convertible hedging. This book explains the rationale behind convertible hedges and uses practical examples to explain hedge ratios, break-even analysis, risk profile, and rate of return, enabling the average investor to understand this sophisticated trading technique.

Overall, the reader will become familiar with the intricacies of various types of convertible securities. Practical examples are combined with theoretical discussions in order to explain the principles of domestic and international convertibles.

This book is the result of many years of involvement in domestic and international convertible markets. I would particularly like to acknowledge the influences of Mike Vacca and Bill Kay. During different stages of my career, they both unselfishly taught me the necessary skills of convertible and foreign security investing. I truly appreciate their time and efforts in editing and critiquing my manuscript. I would also like to thank Jon Singer for his contributions.

Most important, I would like to dedicate this book to my parents, Mary and George Zubulake, and my brother, Paul, for their love, support, and encouragement. Without their efforts, none of what I have accomplished over the years could have been possible.

LAURA A. ZUBULAKE

New York, New York

CONTENTS

List of Figures   **xvii**

Chapter 1 Introduction   **1**

Chapter 2 Convertible Securities   **5**

Convertible Classification 5
Convertible Market Terminology 6
A Hybrid Security 8

Chapter 3 The Equity Component   **11**

Conversion Feature 11
Conversion Value 13

Chapter 4 Options and Warrants   **17**

Options 17
    Equity Cost Basis 18
    Intrinsic Value 19
    Time Value 20
    Factors Affecting Option Premiums 21

Warrants 23

    Intrinsic Value 23

    Warrant Premium 24

    Factors Affecting Warrant Premiums 26

Chapter 5 The Debt Component   29

Investment Value 29

Factors Affecting Investment Value 31

Chapter 6 Redemption   33

Call Feature 33

Sinking Fund 35

Put Feature 36

Chapter 7 Convertible Yield Advantage   41

Percent Method 41

Equity Method 42

Point/Dollar Method 43

Yield-to-Put Method 43

Chapter 8 Premium Over Conversion Value   45

Calculating the Premium over Conversion Value 45

Justification of the Premium over Conversion Value 48

Why Premiums Increase 49

Why Premiums Decrease 51

Costs of the Premium over Conversion Value 52

Chapter 9 Premium Over Investment Value   55

Justification of the Premium over Investment Value 56

Changes in the Premium over Investment Value 57

Chapter 10 Valuation Methods For Convertible Securities   59

  Break-Even Analysis 60

    Equity Method 60

    Point/Dollar Method 61

    Percent Method 62

    Yield-to-Put Method 63

  Discounted Yield Advantage 64

  Fixed Income Plus Option 70

Chapter 11 Alternatives to Traditional Convertible Bonds   73

  Zero-Coupon Convertible Bonds 73

  Equity Bond Units 81

    Synthetic Convertible 82

Chapter 12 International Convertible Securities   87

  International Euroconvertible Conversion Feature 88

  Shares Received upon Conversion 93

  International Convertible Evaluation 94

Chapter 13 Foreign Currency Management and Exposure   97

  Foreign Currency Markets 98

  Foreign Currency Management 102

  Foreign Currency Exposure 109

    Case 1: Convertible bonds denominated in local currency, but different from investor's currency 110

    Currency and Convertible Price Fluctuations 115

    Case 2: Convertible bonds denominated in the currency of the investor but different from the local currency 117

Currency Exposure through Conversion Value 118

The Effect of Currency Fluctuations on Premium 121

Conversion Value as a Function of Currencies and Equity Prices 123

Case 3: Convertible bonds denominated in a currency other than the investor's and local currency 126

Currency Exposure through Conversion Value 126

Currency Exposure through Translation 129

Case 4: Convertible bond denominated in a currency different from both the local currency and investor's currency 132

Cross-Currency Relationship 133

Cross-Currency Effect on Conversion Value 135

Pound Sterling—Based Investor 152

Case 5: Cross-currency translation exposure 153

Case 6: Cross-currency exposure through conversion value 155

Review 158

Chapter 14 Convertible Security Evaluation   165

Chapter 15 Convertible Security Investment Opportunities   173

Convertibles as Equity Alternatives 173

Convertibles as Bond Alternatives 175

Convertibles as Currency Vehicles 177

Chapter 16 Convertible Hedge   179

What Is a Convertible Hedge? 179

Why Establish Convertible Hedges? 181

Bullish Hedge 182

Working the Premium to Zero 186

Bearish Hedge 192

Neutral Hedge 195

Analysis of Hedge Positions 197
    Upside Risk 198
    Downside Risk 199
    Rate of Return 200

Chapter 17 Convertible Bond Indenture　　**205**

Chapter 18 Domestic Convertible Markets　　**209**

U.S. Domestic Convertible Bonds 210
U.S. Convertible Preference Shares 213
British Domestic Convertibles 216
Japanese Domestic Convertibles 223
French Domestic Convertibles 225
Australian Domestic Convertibles 228
Canadian Domestic Convertibles 232

Appendixes　　**235**

Appendix A Examples of Convertible Evaluation　　**237**

Appendix B Glossary　　**277**

Index　　**285**

LIST OF FIGURES

3.1   Conversion Value   15
4.1   Intrinsic Value of a Call Option   21
4.2   Time Value of a Call Option   22
4.3   Intrinsic Value of a Warrant   24
4.4   Warrant Premium   26
5.1   Investment Value   30
5.2   Response of Investment Value to an Increase in Interest Rates   32
5.3   Response of Investment Value to a Decrease in Interest Rates   32
6.1   Redemption   34
8.1   Premium over Conversion Value   48
8.2   Changes in Levels of Premium   50
9.1   Premium over Investment Value   56
9.2   Changes in Level of Premium over Investment Value   57
10.1 Discounted Net Cash Flows   65
10.2 Net Cash Flows—10% Dividend Growth Rate   67
10.3 Net Cash Flows—15% Dividend Growth Rate   67
10.4 Net Cash Flows—20% Dividend Growth Rate   68
10.5 Present Value of Flows to Conversion Date   69
11.1 Call Feature Schedule—Zero-Coupon Convertible   81
13.1 Currency Movements   98
13.2 Changes in Convertible Price and Currency   116
13.3 Conversion Value as a Function of Conversion Ratio, Equity Price, and Currency   124
13.4 Factors Affecting Conversion Value   125
18.1 Discounted Net Cash Flow: 10% Dividend Growth Rate   222
18.2 Discounted Net Cash Flow: 15% Dividend Growth Rate   222

1

Introduction

Convertible securities are hybrid financial instruments that combine equity and debt features. Through convertible securities, the investor participates in an equity's price appreciation with limited downside risk.

Convertible securities come in the form of convertible debentures or preference shares and are generally categorized as equity derivative products. The convertible's equity component is due to its conversion feature. During a specific time period, the investor has the right to exchange the convertible security for a predetermined number of equity shares (or other assets) at a set price. The conversion feature is the most important factor in determining the price of a convertible security. It enables this hybrid security to participate in equity price appreciation.

The convertible security is usually convertible into the equity of the issuer. It may be convertible into the equity of another concern, cash plus equity, a straight bond, gold, silver, or a unit of several securities. A bond convertible into the equity of a company other than the issuer is referred to as an *exchangeable security*.

The debt feature of a convertible security is derived from the convertible's stated coupon and claim to principal. As such, it is subject to changes in interest rates and creditworthiness of the issuer. The debt component provides the convertible with limited downside risk. It protects the investor from a full decline in the equity price.

Convertibles are often viewed as units combining a straight bond with an equity call option. As previously stated, the value of the debt component is derived from the coupon payments and claim to principal. Straight bonds are valued in the same manner. The conversion feature is essentially a call option on the underlying equity. The convertible holder has the right to call the equity from the issuer for a specific time period at a preset price. The act of conversion shortens the time period during which coupons are received and precludes the receipt of the principal. Thus, convertibles are comparable to a package combining a straight bond and call option but do not share all of the same characteristics.

Convertible securities are an attractive financing vehicle. Due to the conversion feature, issuers are able to raise funds at a lower cost than would be paid on comparable straight debt. Investors weigh the loss in yield against the opportunity to benefit from equity price appreciation.

Convertibles add flexibility to the issuer's financial structure. Initially, convertibles appear as debt on the balance sheet. Upon conversion into equity, the debt-to-equity ratio is decreased, and the fixed interest costs are eliminated. All financials are stated on a fully diluted basis when the bonds are issued.

In addition, convertibles sometimes offer tax advantages to the issuer. Unlike equity dividends, fixed interest payments are tax-deductible.

Convertible securities are issued with the intent of having the bonds eventually converted into equity rather than redeemed at maturity. The issuer is raising equity capital on a deferred basis. The dilution of equity ownership is postponed through the mechanics of the deferred conversion process.

Due to their hybrid nature, convertibles are considered to be both bull and bear market instruments. They attract a variety of investors with different financial objectives. Convertibles are attractive investments because of their equity and yield components.

Convertible securities have been used as financing tools for decades. There are convertible markets all over the world, and the size of these markets continues to increase. Since convertible securities are purchased by equity, bond, and convertible investors globally, there are often questions about the best ways to evaluate these securities. The main issues will be addressed in this book from both practical and theoretical standpoints.

This book can be separated into four sections. The first section explains the basics of convertible securities. All of the terms associated with convertibles are explained in detail using practical examples. The methods used in the marketplace to evaluate convertibles are discussed. One representative convertible is used throughout most of the book in practical examples to clarify the theoretical discussions.

International Euroconvertibles sometimes have features different from those of traditional domestic convertibles, and these features will be discussed in the second section. Foreign currency exposure under various scenarios is evaluated from a U.S. dollar perspective.

The equity, debt, and currency features of convertible securities attract various investors. Convertibles are evaluated as equity and debt alternatives and currency vehicles in the third section. Convertible hedge strategies are also presented.

Many countries have domestic convertible markets, some of which are unique. In the final section, the distinguishing features of the U.S., British, Japanese, French, Australian, and Canadian markets are discussed.

The following chapter introduces the reader to some of the fundamental terms associated with convertible securities.

2
Convertible Securities

The *USA Inc. 7.5% of 200X* is a U.S. dollar–denominated Euroconvertible bond; it will be the example used to explain the features and evaluation techniques of convertible securities. This chapter will introduce the reader to some of the terms used throughout the text.

CONVERTIBLE CLASSIFICATION

Convertible bonds are issued in either domestic, foreign, or Eurobond form. *Domestic convertibles* are issued in the home country and are denominated in the local currency (currency of the underlying equity). For example, a British company issues a convertible denominated in pound sterling in the United Kingdom. Domestic convertibles comply with local regulations and are generally sold to domestic investors.

Foreign convertible bonds are issued by a foreign borrower in another country's domestic market and local currency. For example, a Japanese borrower may issue a convertible denominated in Swiss francs in Switzerland. Foreign bonds also include domestic bonds denominated in a foreign currency.

Euroconvertible bonds are (1) simultaneously issued in more than one foreign country, (2) issued by an international syndicate, and (3) denominated in a Eurocurrency (i.e., U.S. dollar, British pound sterling, deutsche mark, Japanese yen, Canadian dollar, Dutch guilder, Danish krone, French franc, Italian lire, Spanish peseta, Austrian schilling, Belgian franc, or ECU). *Eurocurrencies* are liabilities at a bank outside of the country where the currency is legal tender.

Traditionally, during the subscription period, before the bond's terms have been finalized, trading begins on a when-issued basis in the gray market. The *gray market* is a forward market where commitments are made to trade the official bonds (bonds with established terms) in the future at prearranged prices. The gray market brings the potential demand and supply into equilibrium. Gray markets are not always allowed in the issuing of Euroconvertibles. Sometimes the bonds are placed with investors at the issue price, and trading is not allowed until the terms have been finalized.

Euroconvertibles are issued in either bearer or registered form. Ownership of *bearer bonds* is evidenced by physical possession of the bond. *Registered bonds* attach a serial number to the owner. The bond's ownership can be transferred through a reassignment of the registered name.

Interest income paid on Euroconvertibles is generally not subject to withholding tax. Most Euroconvertible bonds pay interest on an annual basis.

Borrowers elect to issue bonds in the Euromarket when international market conditions are more favorable than the domestic market. The Euromarket is more flexible with regard to the size of the issue and disclosure requirements. Eurobonds attract a broader investor base. Borrowers are able to issue in different currencies to match assets with liabilities.

CONVERTIBLE MARKET TERMINOLOGY

Convertible bonds are issued with a *maturity date*. The USA Inc. 7.5% bonds mature on February 20 in 15 years. At maturity, the convertible bonds are redeemed at face value by the issuer.

The *coupon* is the stated rate of interest paid by the issuing company to the holder of the bond. The USA Inc. bonds pay a 7.5% coupon. The convertible's *denomination* is the currency and the minimum amount in which the bonds are traded. The USA Inc. convertibles are denominated in U.S. dollars.

Face value (par value) of the bond is typically $1,000. Upon redemption at maturity, the issuer pays $1,000 per bond for all convertibles redeemed. Face value is used to compute the interest payment. For example, the USA Inc. convertible bonds bear a 7.5% coupon and pay $75 per $1,000 bond annually:

$$\text{Annual interest payment} = \text{Coupon rate} \times \text{Face value}$$
$$= .075 \times \$1,000$$
$$= \$75$$

Interest is paid semiannually or annually on the coupon date. The USA Inc. bonds pay $75 interest per bond annually on February 20. Interest accrues between coupon payment dates. _Accrued interest_ is the amount of interest earned since the last coupon payment date. The interest income accrues daily and is based on the number of months plus days elapsed. For calculating accrued interest, generally a 30-day month/360-day year basis is used:

$$\frac{\text{Accrued interest}}{\text{per bond}} = \frac{\text{Days since last coupon}}{360 \text{ days}} \times \frac{\text{Annual coupon}}{\text{payment}}$$

Assume the investor wants to calculate accrued interest up to April 5:

Calendar		
From	To	Number of Days Elapsed
February 20	February 30*	10
March 1	March 30	1 month = 30
April 1	April 5	5
		45

*A 30-day month is used.

$$\text{Accrued interest per bond} = \frac{45}{360} \times \$75$$
$$= \$9.375$$

If the investor owns 500M bonds (face amount U.S.$500,000), the total accrued interest is $4,687.50:

$$\text{Total accrued interest} = \frac{\text{Days since last coupon}}{360 \text{ days}} \times \frac{\text{Annual coupon payment}}{} \times \frac{\text{Number of bonds}}{}$$

$$= \frac{45}{360} \times \$75 \times 500\text{M}$$

$$= \$4,687.50$$

The accrued interest calculation for a bond that pays semiannually is adjusted for the two payment dates.

$$\frac{\text{Semiannual}}{\text{accrued interest}} = \frac{\text{Days since last coupon}}{180 \text{ days}} \times \frac{\text{Annual coupon}}{2} \times \frac{\text{Number of bonds}}{}$$

The bond purchaser pays the seller the accrued interest to the settlement date of the trade. Upon coupon payment date, the holder of record receives the entire coupon payment. For example, an investor sells the convertible to another investor for settlement date April 5. The buyer will pay the seller the price of the bond plus the $9.375 per bond of accrued interest earned to April 5. On February 20 of next year, the buyer will receive the full $75 coupon payment per bond. The net accrued interest is $65.625.

A HYBRID SECURITY

The USA Inc. convertible bond has both an equity feature and a debt feature. The *conversion feature* is the investor's right to exchange the convertible for the underlying equity for a given period of time at a preset price. The convertible is exchangeable for a certain number of shares. The *conversion period* is the time during which the convertible can be exchanged for the underlying equity. The *conversion price* is the price at which the bond may be exchanged. The *conversion ratio* is the number of shares for which the bond is exchangeable.

The conversion feature is viewed as a long-term call option on the underlying equity. A *call option* gives the holder the right to buy a certain number of shares at a predetermined price for a period of time. The bond's *conversion value* is the current market value of the equity received upon conversion.

The USA Inc. 7.5% bond's *debt component* is its claim to principal (face amount) and interest payments. The *investment value* is the price at which the convertible would trade if it were valued strictly on its debt characteristics.

As previously stated, convertible securities have a final maturity date on which the bonds are redeemed by the issuer at par value. Convertible securities may be redeemed prior to final maturity on either a mandatory (issuer redeems) or voluntary (investor redeems) basis. Mandatory early redemption is through a call feature or a sinking fund. A *call feature* gives the issuer the right to redeem the bonds prior to maturity. Through a *sinking fund*, the issuer retires a portion of the convertible issue before maturity. A convertible may be voluntarily redeemed through a put feature. A *put feature* is the investor's right to tender the bonds back to the issuer before maturity at a predetermined price.

These terms are all important features of convertible securities. They will be discussed in great detail in the subsequent chapters. The USA Inc. 7.5% Euroconvertible bond will be used to illustrate features and evaluation techniques of convertible securities.

3

The Equity Component

A convertible security's conversion feature provides the bond's equity component. The conversion feature, which is in effect a call option on the equity shares at a preset price, gives the investor the right to exchange a convertible security during a specific time period for a predetermined number of equity shares at a preset price. Like a call option, the conversion feature provides the opportunity to benefit from the equity's price appreciation. The value of the equity component is dependent on the perceived capital appreciation of the underlying equity and the perceived creditworthiness of the issuer. The conversion feature is the most important factor in the evaluation of a convertible security.

CONVERSION FEATURE

Conversion is the exchange of the convertible security for a predetermined number of equity shares. Investors exercise their conversion right by delivering the bond certificates to the conversion agent. Upon receipt of the shares, the investors must pay any tax and stamp duty incurred. Fractional shares are generally not issued upon conversion; however, cash adjustments are sometimes made.

Conversion usually occurs at the discretion of the investor (see Chapter 6). Conversion rights extend for a specified period of time. In most cases, they extend approximately from the time of issue to maturity. In these instances, the conversion feature is an American-style call option. An *American-style option* allows for the exercise into the underlying equity at any time up to the date of the option expiry. A *European-style option* allows for the exercise into the equity only on expiration. Some issues have deferred and/or periodic conversion dates. Deferred conversion dates decrease the value of the conversion feature.

Upon issuance, convertible bonds are set with features that define the bond's debt and equity component. The pricing of a new convertible entails setting a coupon level and a conversion price. The level of the coupon is a function of the current level of interest rates, the issuer's credit rating, general market conditions, and the demand/supply curve for convertible paper. Some issues have provisions to reset the coupon on a specific date to a level where the convertibles will trade at par. This feature protects against adverse interest rate movements.

The conversion price is the price of the equity at which the bond may be exchanged. The conversion price is set at a percentage premium above the current equity price. The initial premium depends on the equity's growth projection, dividend payout, and volatility, and on general market conditions.

Through the conversion feature, the issuer is actually selling equity at a premium above the current equity price (i.e., conversion price) at a future, unknown date. The conversion price is adjusted for capital distributions, stock splits, stock dividends, and rights issues. Some issues have a provision to reset the conversion price at a certain date to maintain a certain premium level. This feature protects against a decline in equity prices.

The *conversion price* represents the amount of par value exchangeable for one share. The *conversion ratio* is the number of shares received upon conversion. It is stated as a number of shares per face value amount of bond. The conversion ratio may be computed by dividing the par value of the convertible security by the conversion price.

USA Inc. 7.5% Feb. 20, 200X

Par value:	U.S.$1,000
Conversion ratio:	28.369 shares/U.S.$1,000 bond
Conversion price:	U.S.$35.25

$$\text{Conversion ratio} = \frac{\text{Par value}}{\text{Conversion price}}$$

$$= \frac{\text{U.S.\$1,000}}{\text{U.S.\$35.25}}$$

$$= 28.369 \text{ equity shares}$$

$$\text{Conversion price} = \frac{\text{Par value}}{\text{Conversion ratio}}$$

$$= \frac{\text{U.S.\$1,000}}{28.369 \text{ shares}}$$

$$= \text{U.S.\$35.25}$$

The conversion ratio is an indication of the leverage of the convertible bond. The convertible security with a larger conversion ratio will fluctuate more for a given move in the underlying equity. This point will be expanded upon in the following discussion.

CONVERSION VALUE

Conversion value is the market value of the shares received upon conversion. It can be viewed as the amount of money received if the shares received upon conversion were immediately sold at the current market price. Assuming conversion, it is often referred to as the equity value of the bond. Conversion value is quoted as either a percentage of par value or in dollar terms. Net conversion value is the conversion value less the accrued interest. In general, bonds are converted when conversion value exceeds the bond price.

USA Inc. 7.5% Feb. 20, 200X

Conversion ratio:	28.369 shares
Conversion price:	U.S.$35.25
Current equity price:	U.S.$32.50
Par value:	U.S.$1,000

$$\text{Conversion value} = \text{Conversion} \times \text{Current equity}$$
$$\text{(Parity)} \qquad \text{ratio} \qquad \text{price}$$
$$= 28.369 \text{ shares} \times \text{U.S.\$32.50}$$
$$= \text{U.S.\$921.99}$$
$$= 92.199$$

$$\text{Conversion value} = \frac{\text{Equity price}}{\text{Conversion price}} \times 100$$
$$\text{(Parity)}$$
$$= \frac{\text{U.S.\$32.50}}{\text{U.S.\$35.25}} \times 100$$
$$= 92.199$$
$$= \text{U.S.\$921.99}$$

The conversion price is the level at which the equity must trade in order for conversion value to be equal to par value.

$$\text{Conversion value} = \text{Conversion ratio} \times \text{Equity Price}$$
$$\text{Par value} = \text{Conversion ratio} \times \text{Conversion price}$$
$$\$1,000 = 28.369 \text{ shares} \times \text{U.S.\$35.25}$$
$$\$1,000 = \$1,000$$

Parity is the price at which the convertible security must trade to be equivalent to the market value of the equity received upon conversion. Parity is expressed as a percentage of par value. (For trading purposes, par value is assumed to be 1,000.) The monetary values of conversion value and parity are equivalent. For instance, if the conversion value of a bond and the bond price are both 105, the convertible is said to be trading at parity. The terms *conversion value* and *parity* are often used interchangeably.

Conversion value is the prime factor affecting the convertible bond price. Due to the conversion feature, a convertible security is considered an equity derivative. The equity component is mainly responsible for convertible price fluctuations.

It is possible to graph a linear relationship between conversion value and the equity price based on the following equation.

why?

$$Y = mX + b$$

where Y = Conversion value
         m = Conversion ratio
         X = Equity price
         b = 0

The conversion ratio is the slope of the line and remains constant at 28.369 shares. For a given change in the equity price, the conversion value changes by a multiple of 28.369.

For example, in Figure 3.1, point *A* represents an equity price of $25 and a resulting conversion value of $709.225 ($25 × 28.369 shares). At point *B*, the equity price is $40, and the conversion value is $1,134.76. When the equity price equals the conversion price of $35.25, conversion value is par.

As previously stated, the conversion ratio is an indication of the leverage of the convertible bond. If the conversion ratio of the USA Inc. bonds were 50 shares rather than 28.369 shares, a $1 increase in the equity

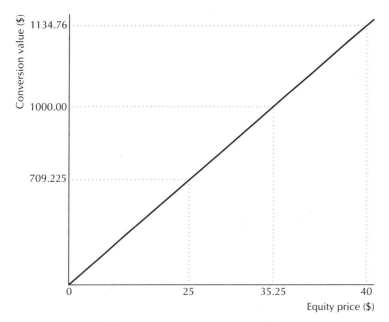

Figure 3.1   Conversion Value.

price would increase the conversion value by $50 rather than $28.369. Higher conversion ratios lead to greater moves in conversion value for a given move in the underlying equity.

Conversion value provides the convertible security with a theoretical price floor; it is a level through which the convertible security usually does not trade. This occurs because of the opportunity to arbitrage between two securities. *Arbitrage* is the purchase and sale of similar or identical securities simultaneously with the intent to profit upon conversion of one of the securities. If the convertible bond's price fell below net conversion value, arbitrageurs would purchase the convertible bond, convert the security into equity, and simultaneously sell the deliverable shares.

For example, assume a bond is trading at U.S.$1,310.00 and the equity is at U.S.$47.00. Assume there is no accrued interest and no expenses. Net conversion value is U.S.$1,333.34 (28.369 shares × U.S.$47.00). Arbitrageurs buy the bond for U.S.$1,310.00 and sell the equivalent number of shares embodied in the convertible bond for U.S.$1,333.34. The bond is converted into the equity, and the shares received upon conversion are delivered versus the short equity position. The arbitrageur earns a risk-free profit of U.S.$23.34 per bond (U.S.$1,333.34 − U.S.$1,310.00).

Through this procedure, arbitrageurs cause convertibles at risk of call (see Chapter 6) to trade close to net conversion value. The investor is able to benefit from the conversion feature without actually converting the bond. The arbitrageur will purchase the bond from the investor at net conversion value less expenses and convert the bond.

Conversion value does not reflect some costs and adjustments. The investor may incur minor fees resulting from the exchange of the convertible security for the underlying equity. The convertible position must be financed until the actual day of conversion. Accrued interest is almost always forfeited upon conversion.

A convertible bond's conversion feature provides it with the equity component. The conversion feature is a call option on the underlying equity. Like a call option, the conversion feature gives the investor the right to call (i.e., exchange a convertible for equity) the equity from the issuer, during a specific time period, for a predetermined number of shares at a preset price. Through this feature, the convertible participates in equity price appreciation. It is the most important factor in the evaluation of a convertible bond.

4

Options and Warrants

Convertible bonds incorporate, in essence, a straight bond with an equity call option or a longer-term equity warrant. Thus, concepts and theory used for call options and warrants can be applied to the convertible's conversion feature. Since the conversion feature is basically a call option, the call option, rather than a put option, will be the focus of the options discussion.

OPTIONS

An *option* contract grants the right to buy or sell a certain number of equity shares at a predetermined price for a period of time. A *call option* gives the owner the right to buy the underlying equity. A *put option* gives the holder the right to sell the equity at a given price for a specific period of time. In general, the contract covers 100 shares. Unlike a warrant, an option is not issued by the corporation into whose shares the option is exercisable.

An option contract is exercised when the holder of a call option decides to call or buy the equity from the seller of the option, or when a put holder decides to put or sell the equity to the put seller at the predetermined price. The *exercise price* (strike price) is the predetermined price at which the option may be exercised.

Call Option

Equity price:	$45
Exercise price:	$40
Shares/contract:	100

The contract may be exercised up to the expiration date. American-style options can be exercised at any time up to expiration, whereas European-style options are exercisable at expiration.

Options are usually issued in cycles. The three cycles are as follows.

1. January, April, July, October
2. February, May, August, November
3. March, June, September, December

In general, the period to expiration can be no longer than nine months. Thus, at any one time, an option cannot have more than three expiration dates outstanding.

Equity Cost Basis

The price of the option is the *option premium*. A seller (writer) of a call option is obligated to sell the equity to the call owner at the exercise price when the call option is exercised. In return, the writer of the call receives the option premium.

Premium: $8

$$\text{Total premium/contract} = \text{Shares/contract} \times \text{Premium}$$
$$= 100 \text{ shares} \times \$8$$
$$= \$800$$

The writer of a put option is obligated to buy the equity from the put owner at the exercise price.

The cost basis of the equity purchased via a call option is the premium plus the exercise price. Upon exercise of the call option, cash equal to the exercise price must be paid for the equity to be received. In the present example, the $800 premium was paid upon purchase of the call option. Upon exercise, the call option owner must pay $4,000:

$$\text{Payment upon exercise} = \text{Exercise price} \times \text{Shares/contract}$$
$$= \$40 \times 100 \text{ shares}$$
$$= \$4,000$$

The total cost of the 100 shares is $4,800 or $48 per share:

$$\text{Total cost of equity} = \text{Payment upon exercise} + \text{Premium}$$
$$= \$4,000 + \$800$$
$$= \$4,800$$

In the writing of a call option, the sale price of the equity through the option is the exercise price plus premium. Upon sale of the call option, the $800 premium is received. When the equity is called away from the option seller, the call buyer must pay the exercise price, $4,000, to receive the shares. The effective equity sale price is $4,800 or $48 per share.

To the buyer of a put option, the effective equity sale price is the total exercise price received ($4,000) upon exercise less the premium ($800) paid for the put option contract. The sale price is $3,200, or $32 per share. Likewise, the cost of the equity via the sale of a put option is the exercise price paid upon exercise ($4,000) less the premium ($800) received from the sale of the put option.

Intrinsic Value

The option premium is a function of intrinsic value and time value:

$$\text{Option premium} = \text{Intrinsic value} + \text{Time value}$$

The *intrinsic* (or tangible) *value* is the difference between the equity price and the exercise price:

$$\text{Intrinsic value} = \text{Equity price} - \text{Exercise price}$$
$$= \$45 - \$40$$
$$= \$5$$

Assuming immediate exercise of the option, the intrinsic value is the money value of the option. An option is trading at parity when the premium equals the intrinsic value.

In the case of a call option, an equity trading above the exercise price is *in the money*. (This concept is sometimes applied to convertibles. A convertible is in the money when the equity price exceeds the conversion price.) When the premium plus exercise price is less than the current equity price, it is economic to buy the option, exercise it into the equity, and sell the equity at the current price. A call option is *out of the money* when the equity price is less than the exercise price. The intrinsic value for an out-of-the-money call option is zero. Intrinsic value cannot be a negative number.

An option's in-the-money value is measured as the percentage amount by which the equity price exceeds the exercise price:

$$\text{In the money} = \left(\frac{\text{Equity price}}{\text{Exercise price}} - 1 \right) 100$$
$$= \left(\frac{\$45}{\$40} - 1 \right) 100$$
$$= 12.5\%$$

Intrinsic value can be graphed (Figure 4.1). A call option's intrinsic value is zero when the equity price is less than or equal to the exercise price. When the equity exceeds the exercise price, intrinsic value increases point for point with the equity.

A put option is in the money when the equity price is below the exercise price. The right to sell the stock at a higher price than the current market level gives the put option its value.

Time Value

The second component of the option premium is *time value*, which is a function of the amount of time to expiration. The longer the life of the

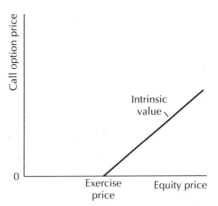

Figure 4.1 Intrinsic value of a call option.

option, the more time the equity has to move to a level where the option becomes profitable. Once intrinsic value is calculated, time value can be derived.

$$\text{Time value} = \text{Option premium} - \text{Intrinsic value}$$
$$= \$8 - \$5$$
$$= \$3$$

The investor pays $3 to have a call on the equity until the expiration date. Time value can be graphed as the difference between the option premium and the intrinsic value (Figure 4.2). Intrinsic value represents the option's downside value. Time value (the shaded area in Figure 4.2) decays over time. Time value is greatest when the equity price equals the exercise price.

Factors Affecting Option Premiums

An option's premium is a function of several factors. The most important factor is the relationship between the equity price and the exercise price. The intrinsic value represents the actual dollar value of the option. The percentage by which the option is in the money greatly affects the premium. At very high and low levels of the equity price, intrinsic value

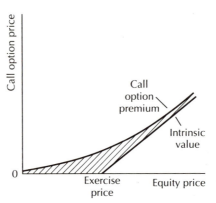

Figure 4.2   Time value of a call option.

is of most importance. At expiration, the option is worth its intrinsic value.

Time value is another factor affecting the option premium. Time value is directly related to the amount of time to expiration and decreases as expiration approaches.

The underlying equity's volatility also affects the option premium. Volatility is the standard deviation of the equity price, often expressed on an annual basis. Historical volatility is derived from past, actual data, and implied volatility is based on iterations using current option prices (assuming efficient markets). Implied volatility is based on expectations. Higher rates of volatility increase the premium. Volatile stocks are more likely to trade at levels where the option becomes profitable.

In addition, higher levels of interest rates promote greater premiums. Equities paying high dividends imply lower premiums. Also, general market sentiment affects premium levels.

Options are attractive investments because of their leverage and limited downside. Options are used to control a certain number of shares at a lower cost than a direct investment in the equity. For a given move in the equity, options will have a greater percentage shift because of their low cost. A loss in a long option investment is limited to the total amount of the premium. A long call option position provides a leveraged means to enjoy equity appreciation with limited downside risk.

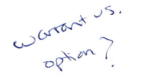

warrant us. option?

WARRANTS

A *warrant* gives the right to buy a certain number of shares at a predetermined price. This right generally extends from 3 to 10 years. Warrants are long-term call options usually issued by the corporation into which whose equity the warrant is exercisable.

A convertible's conversion feature is viewed more as a warrant than as a call option because a warrant has a longer life and is usually issued by the corporation. Since a warrant is issued by the corporation, it is dilutive but is not entitled to equity dividends, confers no voting rights, and is not backed by corporate assets. Warrants are often included in financings as an equity "kicker" to provide an additional incentive for investors.

Warrants have much in common with call options. Warrants are exercisable into a certain number of equity shares. The conversion feature is usually American-style. Conversion is sometimes deferred for a period after issuance. Warrants have an exercise price, which is the amount of cash the investor must pay to exercise the warrant and receive the underlying equity. The warrant's exercise price can increase or "step up" over time.

The following will serve as an example for a warrant evaluation.

Expiration date:	2 years
Exercise price:	$45
Shares/warrant:	1:1
Equity price:	$58
Warrant price:	$16

Intrinsic Value

A warrant's intrinsic value corresponds to that of an option: it is the difference between the equity price and the exercise price. Intrinsic value represents the dollar value of the warrant if it were immediately exercised (Figure 4.3).

$$\text{Intrinsic value} = \text{Equity price} - \text{Exercise price}$$
$$= \$58 - \$45$$
$$= \$13$$

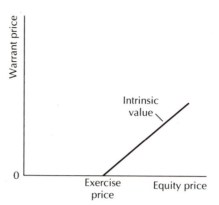

Figure 4.3   Intrinsic value of a warrant.

As in the case of an option, intrinsic value represents the warrant's downside value.

A warrant is in the money when the equity price exceeds the exercise price. The percentage by which a warrant is in the money affects its price.

$$\text{In the money} = \left(\frac{\text{Equity price}}{\text{Exercise price}} - 1 \right) 100$$

$$= \left(\frac{\$58}{\$45} - 1 \right) 100$$

$$= 29\%$$

Warrant Premium

An option's premium is its price. This is not the case with warrants. A warrant has a price and a premium. A warrant's premium represents the additional cost of the equity when purchased through the warrant compared with a direct investment in the equity. The premium compares the cost of the equity via the warrant (warrant price plus exercise price) to the current equity price. This concept of premium applies to convertible securities. Several approaches to calculate the premium follow. (The examples assume a warrant is exercisable into one share.)

$$\text{Premium} = \frac{\begin{array}{c}\text{Cost of equity} \\ \text{via warrant}\end{array} - \text{Equity price}}{\text{Equity price}} \times 100$$

$$= \frac{\left(\begin{array}{c}\text{Warrant} \\ \text{price}\end{array} + \begin{array}{c}\text{Exercise} \\ \text{price}\end{array}\right) - \begin{array}{c}\text{Equity} \\ \text{price}\end{array}}{\text{Equity price}} \times 100$$

$$= \frac{(\$16 + \$45) - \$58}{\$58} \times 100$$

$$= 5.17\%$$

$$\text{Premium} = \left(\frac{\text{Warrant price} + \text{Exercise price}}{\text{Equity price}} - 1\right) 100$$

$$= \left(\frac{\$16 + \$45}{\$58} - 1\right) 100$$

$$= 5.17\%$$

$$\text{Premium} = \frac{\text{Warrant price} - \text{Intrinsic value}}{\text{Equity price}} \times 100$$

$$= \frac{\$16 - \$13}{\$58} \times 100$$

$$= 5.17\%$$

When a warrant is exchangeable into more than one share, the warrant price must reflect the per-share cost.

$$\text{Premium} = \left[\frac{\left(\dfrac{\text{Warrant price}}{\text{Shares/warrant}}\right) + \begin{array}{c}\text{Exercise} \\ \text{price}\end{array}}{\text{Equity price}} - 1\right] 100$$

The premium indicates the equity appreciation required for the intrinsic value to equal the warrant price. There is an inverse relationship between the premium and the intrinsic value.

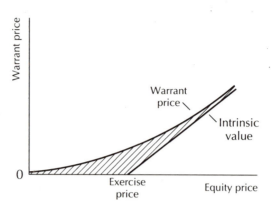

Figure 4.4 Warrant premium.

Factors Affecting Warrant Premiums

Premium is affected by the amount the warrant is in the money, the volatility of the equity, time value, leverage, interest rates, yield of common stock, and general market conditions.

The premium is dynamic. It changes with the relationship between the equity price and the exercise price (Figure 4.4). The premium increases to the point where the equity equals the exercise price. As the equity increases above the exercise price, the premium decreases. The premium declines because as the warrant price increases, downside risk rises. Thus, as the equity becomes more in the money, the premium declines.

Higher equity volatility promotes higher premium levels. A volatile equity price is more likely to reach a level where the warrant becomes profitable.

The amount of time to expiration also affects the premium. Investors are willing to pay a larger premium for warrants with a longer time to expiration, since this increases the likelihood of the warrant becoming profitable.

Assume the issuer of the two-year warrant also issued a six-year warrant with equivalent terms. The six-year warrant trades at a larger premium.

Expiration date: 6 years
Exercise price: $45
Shares/warrant: 1:1
Equity price: $58
Warrant price: $21
Intrinsic value: $13

$$\text{Premium} = \left[\frac{\left(\begin{matrix} \text{Warrant} \\ \text{price} \end{matrix} + \begin{matrix} \text{Exercise} \\ \text{price} \end{matrix} \right) - \begin{matrix} \text{Equity} \\ \text{price} \end{matrix}}{\text{Equity price}} \right] 100$$

$$= \frac{(\$21 + \$45) - \$58}{\$58} \times 100$$

$$= \frac{\$66 - \$58}{\$58} \times 100$$

$$= 13.79\%$$

	Price	Premium
Two-year warrant	$16.00	5.17%
Six-year warrant	$21.00	13.79%

The only difference between the warrants is the time to expiration. The investor pays an additional 8.63% in premium for the additional time to expiration.

Investors are willing to pay a premium for the warrant's leverage. Like an option, a warrant controls equity at a lower cost than a direct investment in the equity. For a given move in the equity price, the warrant moves more on a percentage basis.

Gearing is a measure of the leverage. It relates the equity price to the warrant price because they both have comparable equity exposure.

$$\text{Gearing} = \frac{\text{Equity price}}{\text{Warrant price share}}$$

Gearing assumes the warrant's premium remains constant and is applicable only when a warrant is trading at its intrinsic value.

Warrants are long-term call options. The major feature shared by warrants and call options is the ability to participate in equity price appreciation. As stated earlier, warrants more aptly reflect the convertible's equity component. Like the conversion feature, a warrant is a long-term call on the equity. A warrant's premium is like a convertible's premium: the premium is the cost of the warrant or convertible bond in return for the benefits each kind of security provides.

5

The Debt Component

A convertible security's *debt component* is derived from its stated coupon and claim to principal. The debt component protects the convertible from a full decline in the price of the equity. The convertible's bond value is a function of interest rates and the creditworthiness of the issuer.

INVESTMENT VALUE

Investment value is the price at which a convertible security would trade if it were valued strictly on its debt characteristics. A convertible bond's claim to interest and principal provides straight bond value. The investment value is calculated by applying a yield to maturity from a straight bond of similar quality and maturity.

USA Inc. 7.5% Feb. 20, 200X

Current bond price:	103
Coupon payment date:	Annually on Feb. 20
Current yield to maturity:	7.16%

Assuming the yield to maturity on comparable straight debt is 10.15%, the convertible's implicit investment value is 80. In other words, a comparable straight bond would trade at 80 (Figure 5.1).

It is often difficult to find a straight bond with a comparable maturity and credit rating. In such cases, investment value can be estimated with the model used to value straight bonds. Straight bonds are valued by taking the net present value of the cash flows. Coupon payment and redemption value are discounted to the present.

$$\text{Investment value} = \sum_{i=1}^{m} \frac{C}{(1+d)^i} + \frac{P}{(1+d)^m}$$

where m = Years to maturity
i = Number of interest payments
C = Coupon
P = Principal
d = Discount rate

The discount rate must be assumed for the life of the bond. The rate used should reflect the bond's maturity and credit rating. This model values

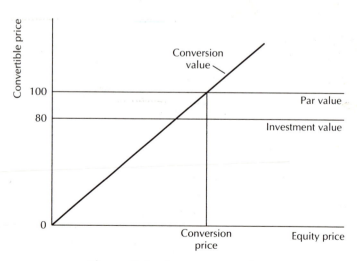

Figure 5.1   Investment value.

the debt component from the present value of the cash flows over the life of the convertible.

Investment value provides downside protection for the convertible security against adverse equity moves. Assuming constant interest rates and creditworthiness of the issuer, investment value is a theoretical price floor below which a convertible will not usually trade as the price of the equity declines. As the equity price declines, the convertible will begin to trade off the investment value. The convertible will trade at a yield of comparable straight debt.

Due to its straight bond feature, a convertible bond may be valued on the basis of its investment value. The value of a convertible's equity feature, namely, the premium of the call option on the underlying equity, increases the value of the convertible bond relative to comparable straight debt. The relatively higher convertible price lowers the yield of the convertible with respect to straight debt of comparable quality and maturity.

FACTORS AFFECTING INVESTMENT VALUE

Investment value is affected by changes in interest rates, changes in the fundamentals of the issuer, and the passage of time. Investment value increases with a decrease in the market level of interest rates or with improved creditworthiness of the issuer. It is more sensitive to changes in long-term interest rates.

For example, if the general level of interest rates increased so that a comparable straight bond's yield increased to approximately 12%, the convertible's implicit investment value would decrease to 69.25 (Figure 5.2). Thus, there is an inverse relationship between interest rates and bond prices. An increase in interest rates reduces the convertible's downside protection. Ceteris paribus, an increase in interest rates decreases investment value.

On the other hand, assume that a fall in the general level of interest rates decreases a comparable straight bond's yield to approximately 8%. If the yield to maturity of the comparable straight bond is applied to the convertible, the resultant investment value increases to 95.75 (Figure 5.3). A decrease in interest rates thus increases the investment value. At

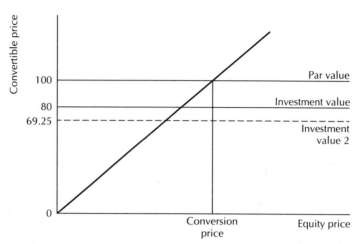

Figure 5.2 Response of investment value to an increase in interest rates.

relatively lower interest rates, the convertible's debt component provides greater downside protection.

Investment value is a difficult concept to apply. It is a particularly important parameter when the equity price is declining. The debt component's contribution to the overall value of a convertible is due to the downside protection and cash flows it provides.

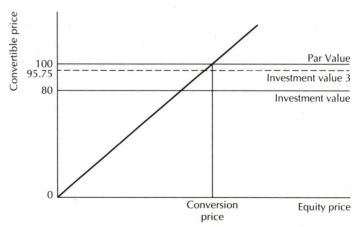

Figure 5.3 Response of investment value to a decrease in interest rates.

6

Redemption

Convertible bonds have a final maturity date at which they are redeemed *always that figure)* by the issuer at par value. The USA Inc. 7.5% of 200X bonds mature on February 20. On this date, holders receive $1,000 per bond.

However, convertible bonds are not always held to the final maturity date. From the investor's standpoint, early redemption may be mandatory or voluntary (Figure 6.1). Mandatory redemption is the result of the issuer exercising a call feature or a sinking fund. Investors can voluntarily redeem convertibles by exercising a put feature.

CALL FEATURE

A call feature gives the issuer the right to redeem the bonds prior to maturity. The act of calling a convertible bond reduces the life of the conversion feature. The *call price* is the price at which the bonds may be redeemed by the issuer before maturity. In general, the call price is highest in early years and declines to par value.

Call protection is the period during which the convertible cannot be called. Convertible bonds offer two types of call protection. Absolute call protection prohibits the issuer from calling the bond before a certain date. Longer periods of absolute call protection extend the probable life of the conversion feature and increase the relative value of the bond. Provisional

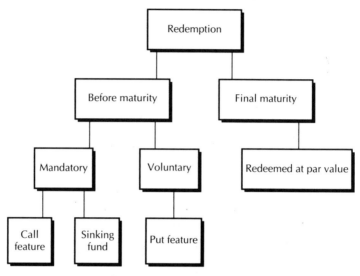

Figure 6.1   Redemption

call protection is contingent upon the performance of the underlying equity. The convertible bond becomes callable when the equity trades at or above a certain percentage (usually 130%–150%) of the conversion price for a specified number of days.

For example, the USA Inc. 7.5% of 200X convertible bond has both absolute and provisional call protection.

Call Protection
USA Inc. 7.5% Feb. 20, 200X

Absolute: Callable in 3 years on or after February 20 at the following call prices

Year Beginning February 20		Year Beginning February 20	
3 years	103.00	6 years	101.50
4 years	102.50	7 years	101.00
5 years	102.00	8 years	100.50
		Thereafter at par	

Provisional: Noncallable before five years on February 20, unless the average closing middle market quote of the equity share for 30 days is at least 130% of the conversion price

Companies generally issue convertible bonds with the intention of having the issue converted into equity before maturity. Convertible bonds are called with the intention of forcing conversion rather than redemption for cash (unless it is economically feasible for the issuer to refinance). If the call protection period has elapsed, the rise of conversion value above call price enables the issuer to force conversion by calling the convertible bonds. Upon notice of call redemption, the investor would opt to convert and receive the conversion value in equity rather than redeem the convertible bond at the lower call price. In this instance, the decision to convert the bond is based on actions of the issuer (i.e., calling the convertible issue) rather than being a voluntary process. The issuer has forced conversion.

The volatility of the underlying equity affects the issuer's decision to call a convertible. The issuer wants the convertible to trade at a cushion above the call price sufficient to prevent a decline in the equity from pulling conversion value below the call price and making redemption attractive.

Upon notice of call, if the convertible is redeemed, accrued interest is added to the call price. Upon conversion, accrued interest is almost always forfeited. Therefore, a convertible bond with call risk usually trades at a discount to conversion value equal to the loss of accrued interest.

Occasionally, an issuer will call a convertible for early redemption to lower the debt/equity ratio or to refinance at a lower interest rate. A call is less likely during periods of rising interest rates, as the issuer would have to refinance at higher rates. Call protection is less valuable in an environment of higher interest rates.

SINKING FUND

Sinking funds require early redemption. Through a sinking fund, the issuer retires a portion of the issue before maturity. The bonds are redeemed at a preset price regardless of the current price of the convertible bond. The sinking fund states the amount of the bonds to be redeemed as a dollar amount or as a percentage of the total issue.

The most common types of sinking funds are through open-market purchases and by lottery. The issuer redeems the convertible bonds on prearranged dates. The issuer may either draw the bonds through a random lottery and redeem them at the redemption price or purchase them in the open market and cancel the bonds. The issuer will purchase the bonds in the open market when they are trading below the redemption price. When the bonds are redeemed by lottery, they can be selected at random. For example, the issuer draws 20% of the issue on coupon dates for five consecutive years. The bonds drawn through the lottery are redeemed at face value.

Another system is through a serial sinking fund. For example, the issuer may draw 25% of the issue on coupon dates over a four-year period. Bondholders have 25% of their positions drawn in each of these four years. From the investor's standpoint, this method is more predictable.

Sinking funds reduce the likelihood of the issuer having to redeem the entire convertible issue at maturity. As sinking fund dates approach, sinking funds tend to support bond prices. They also reduce the life of the conversion feature.

PUT FEATURE

A put feature is the investor's right to tender the bonds to the issuer before maturity at a predetermined price. The date the bonds can be tendered is referred to as the *put exercise date*. The predetermined price is the *put strike price*. Typically, a bond with a put feature is issued at par but is putable in five to seven years at a premium above par.

Since most put exercise dates are deferred, the value of a put feature is the net present value of the cash flows. The equation used to calculate the yield to put is similar to the one used to determine the investment value (see Chapter 5). The yield to put is the discount rate that equates the present value of the cash flows to the current bond price. The cash flows consist of coupon payments and the put strike price.

$$\text{Convertible price} = \sum_{i=1}^{m} \frac{C}{(1 + d)^i} + \frac{P}{(1 + d)^m}$$

$$\begin{aligned}
\text{where } C &= \text{Coupon} \\
P &= \text{Put strike price} \\
m &= \text{Put exercise date} \\
i &= \text{Interest payment} \\
d &= \text{Discount rate}
\end{aligned}$$

For example, the USA 7.5% of 200X convertible bond has a put feature. Holders may opt to have their convertible bonds redeemed on Feb. 20 in year 3 at 123% of par value.

USA 7.5% Feb. 20, 200X

Exercise date:	Year 3 on Feb. 20
Current bond price:	103
Put strike price:	123
Current yield to put:	9.48%

An investor purchasing a bond below the put price and holding it to the exercise date is guaranteed to earn the yield to put. The yield to put assumes the issuer is financially able to pay the put price at the exercise date. The put feature is a means to protect the investor from a lessening of credit quality.

When a convertible is trading below the put strike price, the yield to put becomes the effective yield to maturity. The difference between the current convertible price and the put price is continuously accreted. The convertible bond with a put feature may be considered a short-dated bond maturing on the put date with an equity call option.

In theory, convertible bonds should not trade below a level where the yield to put approximately equates the straight debt yield of comparable quality and time to maturity. Like investment value, the put feature provides downside protection. The put feature reduces downside risk by accreting the discount between the convertible price and put price and skewing the bond's market price toward the put price on exercise dates.

The put feature of a bond trading below the put strike price is more valuable the higher the put price, the greater the frequency of exercise dates, and the earlier the first exercise date. In periods of declining interest rates, the value of a put feature decreases. Put values increase with longer bond maturities because there is more sensitivity to changes in interest rates.

There is an inverse relationship between interest rates and bond prices. As interest rates decline, bond prices increase. In periods of declining interest rates, the convertible's investment value increases. The increase in the convertible price reduces the value of the put feature because it makes it less likely to be exercised.

Borrowers are able to issue convertibles with put features at relatively lower coupon rates. A convertible bond with a put feature is priced off its yield to put. The 5–7 year yield to put will be comparable to 5–7 year rates with similar credit rating. A 30-year convertible with a 5-year put feature is sometimes considered a 5-year bond with a call option on a 25-year bond and an equity call option. Issuers trade off lower current interest payments for future potential put payments.

The borrower may also issue the convertible bond with a put feature at a higher conversion premium. Through a higher conversion price, the issuer is able to sell equity in the future at a higher price.

Issuers sometimes include multiple put dates, or a *rolling put feature*. In general, the rolling put dates will occur on the same month and day over consecutive years. The put strike prices are set at levels so that for each additional year, the yield to put remains constant. The convertible should trade at the maximum level possible by pricing the convertible to the yield at the appropriate put exercise date.

For example, if the USA Inc. 7.5% of 200X initial yield to put is 9.93%, the subsequent put strike prices will increase each year to result in a 9.93% yield to put annually. The increase in the put strike price compensates for the additional time until the next put date.

USA Inc. 7.5% Feb. 20, 200X
Convertible Price at Issue: 100

Put Date, Feb. 20	Put Strike Price	Yield to Put
Year 3	123.00	9.93%
Year 4	127.75	9.93%
Year 5	132.875	9.93%

The rolling put feature reduces the likelihood of the bonds' being put back to the company on the first put date; the bonds are more likely to serve as long term financing. Rolling puts give the equity more time to appreciate to a level where converting into equity is more attractive than exercising the put feature.

The belief that put features indicate financial weakness of the issuer is incorrect. Borrowers do not expect the put feature to be exercised. They expect growth over the next five to seven years to be reflected as an increase in the equity price. The increase in the equity price above conversion price will cause the bond's conversion value to surpass the put price, discouraging exercise of the put option.

7

Convertible Yield Advantage

Convertible securities generally offer a current income advantage over the equity into which they are convertible. The incremental yield of the convertible over the underlying equity is referred to as the *yield advantage*. The current interest income of the bond accrues daily, whereas the current dividend income of preferred and common shares pays periodically and is declared. A greater degree of yield advantage increases the relative value of the bond.

USA Inc. 7.5% Feb. 20, 200X

Conversion ratio:	28.369 shares
Coupon frequency:	Annually on Feb. 20
Bond coupon income:	U.S.$75/U.S.$1,000 bond
Annual equity dividend:	U.S.$0.95/share
Current bond price:	103, or U.S.$1030
Current equity price:	U.S.$32.50
Current yield to put:	9.48%

PERCENT METHOD

Yield advantage is expressed using either the percent method, the equity method, or the point/dollar method. The percent method defines the current income of the bond and the equity with respect to the current bond price and equity price, respectively.

$$\text{Current bond yield} = \frac{\text{Bond coupon income}}{\text{Bond price}} \times 100$$

$$= \frac{\text{U.S.\$75}}{\text{U.S.\$1030}} \times 100$$

$$= 7.28\%$$

$$\text{Current equity yield} = \frac{\text{Equity dividend}}{\text{Equity price}} \times 100$$

$$= \frac{\text{U.S.\$0.95}}{\text{U.S.\$32.50}} \times 100$$

$$= 2.92\%$$

$$\begin{array}{c}\text{Yield advantage}\\ \text{(Percent method)}\end{array} = \begin{array}{c}\text{Current bond}\\ \text{yield}\end{array} - \begin{array}{c}\text{Current equity}\\ \text{yield}\end{array}$$

$$= 7.28\% - 2.92\%$$

$$= 4.36\%$$

EQUITY METHOD

The equity method measures the difference between the dollar income from the bond and the annual dividend income from the equivalent number of equity shares embodied in the bond. The conversion ratio represents the equivalent equity embodied in the bond. The equity method assumes that the number of shares controlled through a purchase of a convertible equals the original equity investment. The equity dividend income forgone is based on the number of shares controlled by a convertible bond.

$$\begin{array}{c}\text{Yield advantage}\\ \text{(Equity method)}\end{array} = \begin{array}{c}\text{Bond coupon}\\ \text{income}\end{array} - \begin{array}{c}\text{Equivalent equity}\\ \text{dividend income}\end{array}$$

$$= \frac{\text{Bond coupon}}{\text{income}} - \left(\frac{\text{Conversion}}{\text{ratio}} \times \frac{\text{Equity}}{\text{dividend}} \right)$$

$$= \text{U.S.\$75.00} - (28.369 \times \text{U.S.\$0.95})$$

$$= \text{U.S.\$75.00} - \text{U.S.\$26.95}$$

$$= \text{U.S.\$48.05}$$

$$= 4.805 \text{ points/U.S.\$1,000}$$

POINT/DOLLAR METHOD

The point/dollar method measures the difference between the coupon income and the dividend income from the number of equity shares that could have been purchased with a direct investment in the equity rather than the convertible bond. In the case of a bond trading at a premium to conversion value, the number of shares that could have been purchased, for a given dollar investment, is greater than the conversion ratio (see Chapter 9). Relative to the equity method, the point/dollar method assumes that greater dividend income is forgone with an alternative investment in the convertible bond.

$$\frac{\text{Yield advantage}}{\text{(Point/dollar method)}} = \frac{\text{Bond coupon}}{\text{income}} - \left(\frac{\text{Bond price}}{\text{Equity price}} \times \frac{\text{Equity}}{\text{dividend}} \right)$$

$$= \text{U.S.\$75.00} - \left(\frac{\text{U.S.\$1,030.00}}{\text{U.S.\$32.50}} \times \text{U.S.\$0.95} \right)$$

$$= \text{U.S.\$75.00} - (31.692 \times \text{U.S.\$0.95})$$

$$= \text{U.S.\$75.00} - \text{U.S.\$30.11}$$

$$= \text{U.S.\$44.89}$$

$$= 4.489 \text{ points/U.S. \$1,000}$$

YIELD-TO-PUT METHOD

The yield-to-put method is a variation on the percent method. When the yield to put dominates the current bond yield, it is substituted in the calculation. This method assumes that the bond is held to the put date.

$$\begin{array}{l} \text{Yield advantage} \\ \text{(Yield-to-put method)} \end{array} = \begin{array}{c} \text{Current yield} \\ \text{to put} \end{array} - \text{Current equity yield}$$

$$= 9.48\% - 2.92\%$$

$$= 6.56\%$$

The convertible's yield advantage calculated under the various methods is reviewed in the following table.

Method	Yield Advantage
Percent	4.36%
Equity	4.805 pts.
Point/dollar	4.489 pts.
Yield to put	6.56%

The percent method is a quick and simple approach to calculating yield advantage. The equity and point/dollar methods measure yield advantage in terms of cash flow. The equity method is appropriate when the bond is viewed as an alternative to the equivalent equity embodied in the bond. The point/dollar method is used when the dollar investment in the equity would equal the dollar investment in the convertible. The yield-to-put method is appropriate when the yield to put dominates the current yield.

8

Premium Over Conversion Value

Premium over conversion value is the difference between the convertible security's market price and its conversion value. The premium indicates the equity appreciation required for the conversion value to equal the convertible's market price. Bonds trading below conversion value are said to be trading at a discount to conversion value.

Premium over conversion value is expressed either in points or as a percentage of conversion value. Stated as a percentage, it provides a relative measurement of the upside potential and downside risk of a convertible security.

Premium over conversion value is a function of the underlying equity's volatility, the convertible's yield advantage, the probability of call, and general demand/supply factors. Wider premiums are associated with a volatile underlying equity, a greater degree of yield advantage, a lower probability of call, and a greater demand for and lower supply of convertible issues.

CALCULATING THE PREMIUM OVER CONVERSION VALUE

The USA Inc. 7.5% of 200X are trading at a premium over conversion value.

USA Inc. 7.5% Feb. 20, 200X

Conversion ratio:	28.369 shares
Current bond price:	U.S.$103 or U.S.$1,030
Current equity price:	U.S.$32.50

$$\text{Conversion value} = \text{Equity price} \times \text{Conversion ratio}$$
$$= \text{U.S.\$32.50} \times 28.398 \text{ shares}$$
$$= \text{U.S. \$921.99}$$
$$= 92.199$$

Premium over
conversion value = Bond price − Conversion value
(Point/dollar
method)

$$= \text{U.S.\$1,030.00} - \text{U.S.\$921.99}$$
$$= \text{U.S.\$108.01}$$

or

$$= 103.00 - 92.199$$
$$= 10.801 \text{ points/U.S.\$1,000}$$

Premium over
conversion value $= \dfrac{\text{Bond price} - \text{Conversion value}}{\text{Conversion value}} \times 100$
(Percent method)

$$= \dfrac{\text{U.S. \$1030.00} - \text{U.S. \$921.99}}{\text{U.S. \$921.99}} \times 100$$

$$= \dfrac{\text{U.S. \$108.01}}{\text{U.S. \$921.99}} \times 100$$

$$= 11.71\%$$

The percent method displays the importance of the relationship between the bond price and the equity price to the premium over conversion value.

$$\begin{aligned}
\frac{\text{Premium over}}{\substack{\text{conversion value}\\ \text{(Percent method)}}} &= \frac{\text{Bond price} - \text{Conversion value}}{\text{Conversion value}} \times 100 \\[2mm]
&= \left(\frac{\text{Bond price}}{\text{Conversion value}} - 1\right) 100 \\[2mm]
&= \left[\left(\frac{\text{Bond price}}{\text{Equity price}} \times \frac{1}{\text{Conversion ratio}}\right) - 1\right] 100
\end{aligned}$$

Another method of calculating the premium over conversion value is through the equity price. Here the premium is expressed on a per-share basis. First, the cost of the equity as realized through the purchase of the convertible is calculated.

USA Inc. 7.5% Feb. 20, 200X

Conversion ratio:	28.369 shares
Convertible price:	U.S.$1,030
Equity price:	U.S.$32.50

$$\begin{aligned}
\text{Equity price via convertible} &= \frac{\text{Convertible bond price}}{\text{Conversion ratio}} \\[2mm]
&= \frac{\text{U.S.}\$1,030}{28.369 \text{ shares}} \\[2mm]
&= \text{U.S.}\$36.31
\end{aligned}$$

The premium over conversion value is computed with respect to the equity price.

$$\begin{aligned}
\frac{\text{Premium over}}{\text{conversion value}} &= \frac{\substack{\text{Equity price}\\ \text{via convertible}} - \text{Equity price}}{\text{Equity price}} \times 100 \\[2mm]
&= \frac{\text{U.S.}\$36.31 - \text{U.S.}\$32.50}{\text{U.S.}\$32.50} \times 100 \\[2mm]
&= 0.117 \times 100 \\[2mm]
&= 11.7\%
\end{aligned}$$

JUSTIFICATION OF THE PREMIUM OVER CONVERSION VALUE

Convertible securities usually trade above conversion value (Figure 8.1). The premium over conversion value is justified by the advantages inherent in the hybrid nature of convertible securities.

Convertible securities offer the equity investor yield advantage over the underlying shares (see Chapter 7). The investor pays a premium over conversion value for the incremental income. A direct relationship exists between the degree of yield advantage and the size of the premium. The premium is a function of the safety of the coupon and dividend income, and of the period of time in which the yield advantage is expected to be realized.

The bond feature provides the convertible with downside protection against adverse equity moves (see the discussion of investment value in Chapter 5). The investor pays a premium over conversion value for

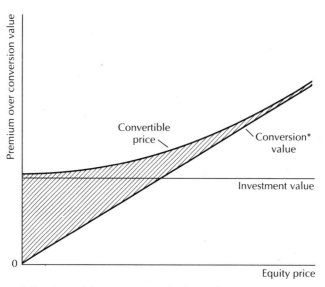

* The slope of the conversion value line is the conversion ratio.

Figure 8.1   Premium over conversion value.

this additional safety. The debt feature protects the investor from the full extent of a decline in the price of the underlying equity. As the price of the equity declines, the bond is valued more on its investment value.

The level of the premium over conversion value is directly related to the volatility of the underlying equity. Volatile equities are associated with higher premiums because the safety feature is of greater value. Also, as is the case with options, volatile equities have a greater chance of trading at levels where they become profitable (i.e., more in the money).

Premium over conversion value is not the same as the premium of an option, which refers to the price of the option. Premium over conversion value has two components. Like a standard option, the premium over conversion value has time value. Unlike an option, as the equity falls, the premium over conversion value increases as the convertible bond tends to trade more on its investment value.

The following relationship exists between the level of the equity price and the premium over conversion value.

Equity Price	Premium over Conversion Value
Decreases	Increases
Increases	Decreases

WHY PREMIUMS INCREASE

Premium over conversion value increases (widens) as the price of the equity declines. In Figure 8.2, as the equity price declines from point B to point A, the convertible security increasingly trades off its investment value rather than its equity feature. The equity continues to decline while the convertible is supported by its investment value. The difference between the convertible's market price and its conversion value is greatest at very low equity prices.

For example, assume the USA Inc. equity price declines from U.S. $32.50 to U.S.$25.00, and the convertible declines from 103 to 94. An

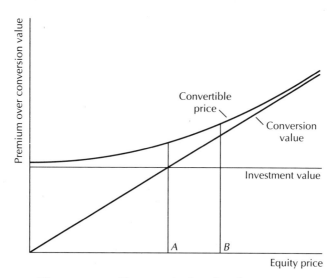

Figure 8.2   Changes in levels of premium.

investor holding a comparable number of equity shares rather than the convertible would have underperformed:

Position	Price 1	Price 2	Percent Decline	Dollar Loss
Convertible 1,000M	103	94	8.74	90,000
Equity 28,369	U.S.$32.50	U.S.$25.00	23.08	212,767
Premium	11.71%	32.54%		

As the equity price declined, the bond traded off its investment value. The expansion of the premium over conversion value thus protects the equity investor from a full decline in the equity price.

A *busted* or *broken convertible* is one in which the equity has substantially declined below the conversion price and the premium over conversion value has expanded. Due to the high premium, it is not feasible to exercise the conversion feature of a busted convertible. The bond trades primarily with fluctuations in interest rates rather than equity prices. Busted convertibles are analyzed as straight bonds with cheap equity call options.

At very low equity prices, busted convertibles have little call risk. They trade at high yields to maturity, put, and sink (sinking funds). Through busted convertibles, investors are able to purchase a claim to assets at a discount to par value.

WHY PREMIUMS DECREASE

Premium over conversion value decreases (narrows) with a rise in the equity price. As the equity price rises (from point A to B in Figure 8.2) and approaches the conversion price, the value of the convertible bond is increasingly controlled by the equity characteristics (conversion value). The convertible security will trade off its equity feature rather than its debt component. Downside risk becomes greater as the price of the convertible bond increases above its investment value. The premium over conversion value declines as the convertible bond's safety feature diminishes.

Premium over conversion value also declines as the equity price rises because the risk of call increases (see Chapter 6). Investors will not pay a premium over conversion value for a convertible bond with call risk. Upon notice of call, the convertible price tends to trade at net conversion value. The bond will trade at the market value of the total number of shares received upon conversion, less accrued interest and costs. Any premium paid for a called convertible is lost.

At higher levels of equity price and lower premiums over conversion value (point B in Figure 8.2), the convertible's value will increase in proportion to the rise of the equity. At higher equity prices, the convertible's value is determined mainly by the equity and less so by its investment value. The convertible may assume characteristics of an in-the-money option, trading dollar for dollar. It is often said that the future market value of the convertible and the equity will theoretically be the same.

The level at which the conversion premium disappears is a function of the yield advantage, the volatility of the underlying equity, and the risk of call. Greater degrees of yield advantage, higher equity volatility, and lower risk of call promote relatively higher conversion premiums for longer periods of time.

COSTS OF THE PREMIUM OVER CONVERSION VALUE

Investors purchasing a convertible security trading at a premium to conversion value forfeit some of the advantages of a direct investment in the equity. Convertible securities trading at a premium will appreciate more slowly than the underlying equity. Theoretically, the price of the convertible increases at a rate equal to the appreciation of the equity embodied in the bond less the decrease in the premium. The price of a convertible trading at parity will increase in proportion to a rise in the underlying equity.

An investor purchasing a convertible trading at a premium forfeits some of the equity appreciation in return for the yield advantage and downside protection. The USA Inc. 7.5% of 200X bonds are trading at a 21% premium. The equity would have to move from U.S.$30.00 to U.S.$36.30 for the conversion value to equal the price paid for the bond.

USA Inc. 7.5% Feb. 20, 200X

Conversion ratio:	28.369 shares
Convertible price:	U.S.$1,030

$$\frac{\text{Equity cost}}{\text{basis}} = \frac{\text{Convertible price}}{\text{Conversion ratio}}$$

$$= \frac{\text{U.S.}\$1,030}{28.369 \text{ shares}}$$

$$= \text{U.S.}\$36.31$$

When the equity reaches U.S.$36.31, conversion value is equivalent to the price paid for the bond. The U.S.$36.31 price level represents the price at which the investor is purchasing the equity through the convertible. The investor could have purchased the equity outright at U.S.$32.50. The equity move from U.S.$32.50 to U.S.$36.31 is an 11.7% increase. The 11.7% premium represents the potential equity appreciation forgone with a purchase of the convertible.

As in the case of a called convertible, there are certain instances (e.g., a takeover) where the premium paid over conversion value may be lost.

That is, the convertible position may be less profitable than a direct investment in the underlying equity.

For a given investment, the buyer of the convertible trading at a premium to conversion value controls fewer shares compared with a direct investment in the equity. For example, see the following figures for an investment in the USA Inc. 7.5% of 200X.

USA Inc. 7.5% Feb. 20, 200X

Conversion ratio:	28.369 shares/bond
Conversion premium:	10.801 points

Assume an investment of U.S.$1,000,000.

	Purchase Price	Amount Purchased	Number of Shares Controlled
Convertible bond	U.S.$1,030	970M bonds	27,517 (970M bonds × 28.369)
Equity	U.S.$32.50	30,769 shares	30,769

Given a U.S.$1 million investment, a direct equity purchase of 30,769 shares exceeds the 27,517 shares controlled through the convertible investment. An investor purchasing the USA Inc. 7.5% of 200X benefits from the convertible's yield advantage and downside protection. Due to the premium paid over conversion value, some of the attributes of a direct equity investment are forfeited.

In summary, premium over conversion value is the difference between the convertible security's market price and its conversion value. It measures the equity appreciation needed to equate conversion value to the convertible bond price. The premium decreases with an increase in the underlying equity and increases with a decrease in the equity price. The premium is the cost for the advantages inherent in convertible securities.

9

Premium Over Investment Value

Convertible securities generally trade at a level above investment value. The difference between the convertible's market price and its investment value is referred to as the *premium over investment value* and is expressed as a percentage of investment value.

USA Inc. 7.5% Feb. 20, 200X

Current bond price:	U.S.$1,030
Investment value:	U.S.$800*

$$\begin{aligned}\text{Premium over investment value (Percent method)} &= \frac{\text{Bond price} - \text{Investment value}}{\text{Investment value}} \times 100 \\[2mm] &= \frac{\text{U.S.\$1,030} - \text{U.S.\$800}}{\text{U.S.\$800}} \times 100 \\[2mm] &= 28.75\%\end{aligned}$$

* See Chapter 5 for a discussion of investment value.

JUSTIFICATION OF THE PREMIUM OVER INVESTMENT VALUE

As shown in Figure 9.1, convertible securities usually trade above investment value. The premium over investment value is justified by the advantages inherent in the hybrid nature of convertible securities. In addition to the debt component, convertible securities incorporate an equity call option. The investor pays a premium over investment value for the potential appreciation of the underlying equity. The premium is a measurement of stock market risk.

Convertible bonds trading at a premium over investment value offer a lower yield relative to comparable straight debt. The equity call option increases the value of the convertible relative to comparable straight debt, thus decreasing the convertible's yield.

Premium over investment value provides a relative measurement of downside risk of a convertible security. Larger premiums over investment value are commensurate with higher levels of equity risk. Convertible bonds trading well above investment value have greater downside potential. Convertible bonds with a small premium over investment value are less susceptible to a decline in the equity price.

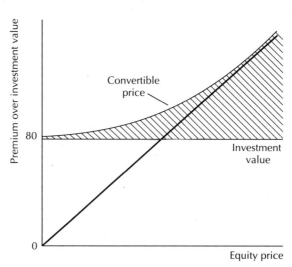

Figure 9.1   Premium over investment value.

CHANGES IN THE PREMIUM OVER INVESTMENT VALUE

The following relationship exists between the level of the equity price and premium over investment value.

| | Premium over |
Equity Price	Investment Value
Increases	Increases
Decreases	Decreases

Premium over investment value decreases as the price of the equity declines. A decrease in the equity price from point *B* to point *A* in Figure 9.2 causes the convertible to assume characteristics of a debt instrument. The investment value protects the investor from a full decline in the price of the equity share. The price of the convertible drops to a level where investment value provides a theoretical price floor, while the price of the equity continues to decline. At equity price *A*, the convertible

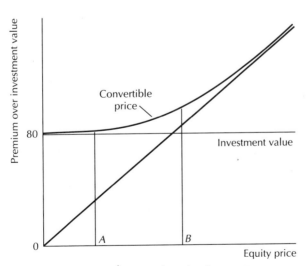

Figure 9.2   Changes in level of premium over investment value.

is trading close to investment value but well above conversion value. Convertibles trading at a relatively small premium to investment value have less downside risk.

Premium over investment value increases with an increase in the equity price. As the equity price increases from point A to point B, the convertible trades off of its equity value. The convertible progressively loses its bond characteristics and assumes more speculative traits of the equity. At equity point B, the convertible is susceptible to declines in the equity.

Assuming the convertible and equity prices trade in the same direction, the premium over investment value is inversely related to the premium over conversion value. An increase in the premium over investment value is associated with an increase in the equity price. At higher equity prices, the bond is exposed to greater downside risk, reducing the premium over conversion value. A decrease in the premium over investment value is associated with a decline in the equity. The bond is less susceptible to declines in the equity price, and the premium over conversion value increases to reflect the value of this downside protection.

10

Valuation Methods
For Convertible Securities

Valuing convertible securities can be an involved process. The hybrid nature of the security often makes it difficult to evaluate the equity component with respect to the investment value. Valuation methods range from the simple to the complex and tend to be oriented toward either income advantage, discounted cash flows, options evaluation, or fixed-income evaluation.

The valuation methods to be discussed in this chapter include break-even analysis, discounted yield advantage (discounted cash flow), and a theoretical fixed-income-plus-option model.

Break-even analysis will be presented using the equity, point/dollar, percent, and yield-to-put methods. All of the techniques are deviations from a general analytical method.

The discounted cash flow method initially compares conversion value adjusted for the discounted yield advantage to the conventional conversion value. Second, the model discounts the yield advantage to maturity and compares it with the premium paid over conversion value. A discount rate and dividend growth rate are assumed.

The fixed-income-plus-option method combines the theoretical valuation of the debt component with the equity component. The value of the bond is added to the value of the call option.

Each method has its advantages and disadvantages, and each makes assumptions as to important elements in the valuation process. The appropriate method must be selected for valuing convertible securities.

BREAK-EVEN ANALYSIS

The *break-even period* is the amount of time required for the convertible's yield advantage to recoup the premium paid over conversion value. Break-even analysis assumes a constant level of interest rates and equity dividend. Break-even time, expressed in years, is measured using either the equity, point/dollar, percentage, or yield-to-put method. Each method produces slightly different results. The equity and point/dollar methods are popular.

The USA Inc. 7.5% of 200X are trading at a premium to conversion value and offer a yield advantage over USA Inc. equity shares. The break-even period is calculated using the following information.

USA Inc. 7.5% Feb. 20, 200X

Conversion ratio:	28.369 shares
Coupon frequency:	Annual
Bond coupon income:	U.S.$75.00
Annual equity dividend:	U.S.$0.95

Current market data:

Convertible bond price:	103 or U.S.$1,030
Equity price:	U.S.$32.50
Conversion value:	U.S.$921.99*
Premium:	10.801 points
	11.71%

Equity Method

The equity method is useful when the number of shares of a security sold is equal to the number purchased. That is, the equity method should be used if the number of shares sold to purchase a convertible is equivalent to the conversion ratio. The investor's interest in the equity remains the same. The break-even period is calculated as follows.

*See chapters 2 and 8.

$$\text{Break-even period (Equity method)} = \frac{\text{Dollar premium}}{\text{Bond coupon} - \left(\dfrac{\text{Conversion}}{\text{ratio}} \times \dfrac{\text{Equity}}{\text{dividend}}\right)}$$

$$= \frac{\text{U.S.\$108.01}}{\text{U.S.\$75.00} - (28.369 \text{ shrs} \times \text{U.S.\$0.95})}$$

$$= \frac{\text{U.S.\$108.01}}{\text{U.S.\$75.00} - \text{U.S.\$26.95}}$$

$$= \frac{\text{U.S.\$108.01}}{\text{U.S.\$48.05}}$$

$$= 2.25 \text{ years}$$

The equation takes the premium (in dollar terms) and divides it by the yield advantage as calculated by the equity method (see Chapter 7). In the denominator, the conversion ratio is used to represent the number of shares controlled either through the convertible or the equity investment. The conversion ratio represents the number of shares on which the equity dividend is forgone. The equity method does not reflect the opportunity cost of paying more for the equity via the convertible.

Point/Dollar Method

The point/dollar method measures the time required to recoup the total convertible investment. For a given investment, the purchase of a convertible bond trading at a premium to conversion value controls less shares than a direct investment in the equity. For the USA Inc. 7.5% of 200X,

$$\text{Number of shares controlled via direct purchase} = \frac{\text{Total convertible investment}^*}{\text{Equity price}}$$

$$= \frac{\text{U.S.\$1,030.00}}{\text{U.S.\$32.50}}$$

$$= 31.69 \text{ shares}$$

If the dollars invested in the convertible security were used to purchase equity, a total of 31.69 shares could be purchased per one convertible

*Often includes accrued interest.

bond. This number exceeds the conversion ratio of 28.369 shares controlled through the convertible.

In computing the break-even period, the point/dollar method takes into account the number of shares that could have been purchased with a direct investment in the equity and assumes that greater dividend income is forgone with alternative investment in the convertible bond than does the equity method.

$$
\begin{aligned}
\text{Break-even period} \\
\text{(Point/dollar} \\
\text{method)}
\end{aligned}
=
\frac{\text{Dollar premium}}{\text{Bond coupon} - \left(\dfrac{\text{Bond price}}{\text{Equity price}} \times \begin{array}{c}\text{Annual equity} \\ \text{dividend}\end{array} \right)}
$$

$$
= \frac{\text{U.S.\$108.01}}{\text{U.S.\$75.00} - \left(\dfrac{\text{U.S.\$1,030.00}}{\text{U.S.\$32.50}} \times \text{U.S.\$0.95} \right)}
$$

$$
= \frac{\text{U.S.\$108.01}}{\text{U.S.\$75.00} - (31.69 \text{ shrs} \times \text{U.S.\$0.95})}
$$

$$
= \frac{\text{U.S.\$108.01}}{\text{U.S.\$75.00} - \text{U.S.\$30.11}}
$$

$$
= \frac{\text{U.S.\$108.01}}{\text{U.S.\$44.89}}
$$

$$
= 2.41 \text{ years}
$$

The dollar premium is divided by the yield advantage as expressed by the point/dollar method. In the denominator, the use of the bond price/equity price ratio in lieu of the conversion ratio reflects the additional shares that could be purchased by the amount of dollars spent on the premium over conversion value. The point/dollar method better reflects the opportunity cost of paying more for the equity via the convertible. This method is appropriate when the dollar investment is the same for the security sold and the security purchased.

Percent Method

The percent method is used often because of its simplicity and convenience. However, the concept is inconsistent in that premium percentage is defined with regard to conversion value whereas the yield advantage percentage is defined in terms of the bond and equity price.

Conversion value:	U.S.$921.99
Premium over conversion value:	11.71%
Current bond yield:	7.28%
Current equity yield:	2.92%
Yield advantage:	4.36%

$$\frac{\text{Break-even period}}{\text{(Percent method)}} = \frac{\text{Premium}}{\text{Yield advantage}}$$

$$= \frac{11.71\%}{4.36\%}$$

$$= 2.69 \text{ years}$$

Yield-to-Put Method

Break-even period based on the yield to put is used when the yield to put dominates the current bond yield. This method assumes that the bond is held to the put date and the issuer is financially able to pay the put strike price on the put date.

$$\frac{\text{Break-even period}}{\text{(Yield-to-put method)}} = \frac{\text{Premium}}{\text{Yield-to-put advantage}}$$

$$= \frac{\text{Premium}}{\text{Yield to} - \text{Current equity}}_{\text{put} \quad \text{yield}}$$

$$= \frac{11.78\%}{9.48\% - 2.92\%}$$

$$= \frac{11.78\%}{6.56\%}$$

$$= 1.80 \text{ years}$$

Each break-even method yields a different result. The investor's objectives will determine the appropriate method. The USA Inc. 7.5% of 200X break-even analysis is reviewed in the following chart.

Break-even Method	Years
Equity	2.25
Point/dollar	2.41
Percent	2.69
Yield to put	1.80

Convertible securities with break-even periods of less than 2–3 years are generally deemed reasonable. A convertible bond with a long break-even period must be evaluated with regard to the issue's probability of being called. The concept of break-even is less important for convertibles with little risk of call. A convertible with a long break-even period may be superior to the underlying equity if payment of the common dividend is questionable.

Break-even analysis is static in nature. It does not consider future dividend growth nor the time value of money. It also does not include the value of the convertible's equity call option. In volatile markets, the value of the option increases and is an important consideration. Break-even analysis is a popular concept and is a basic means for determining relative value.

DISCOUNTED YIELD ADVANTAGE

In valuing the convertible security, the *discounted yield advantage* (discounted cash flow) method considers the convertible's excess income over the underlying equity. The convertible's yield advantage is discounted from the date of maturity to the present. There are different applications of this method. Throughout this discussion, for simplicity, it is assumed that there is an even number of coupon payments. These calculations can be adjusted for partial period payments.

The discounted yield advantage can be used to adjust conversion value. To begin, the present value of the net cash flows (interest income less dividend flow) over the life of the bond is calculated (Figure 10.1).

	Year						
	1	2	3	4	5	6	7
Coupon/share	$2.64	$2.64	$2.64	$2.64	$2.64	$2.64	$2.64
Dividend/share	0.95	1.09	1.26	1.44	1.66	1.91	2.20
Net cash flow (NCF)	1.69	1.55	1.39	1.20	0.98	0.73	0.45
Discounted NCF	1.54	1.28	1.04	0.82	0.61	0.41	0.23

	Year						
	8	9	10	11	12	13	14
Coupon/share	$2.64	$2.64	$2.64	$2.64	$2.64	$2.64	$2.64
Dividend/share	2.53	2.91	3.34	3.84	4.42	5.08	5.85
Net cash flow (NCF)	0.12	−0.26	−0.70	−1.20	−1.78	−2.44	−3.20
Discounted NCF	0.05	−0.11	−0.27	−0.42	−0.57	−0.71	−0.84

Differences due to rounding.
Even period payments assumed.

Figure 10.1   Discounted net cash flows.

USA Inc. 7.5% Feb. 20, 200X

Conversion ratio:	28.369 shares
Coupon payment/share:	U.S.$2.64
Equity price:	U.S.$32.50
Equity dividend/share:	U.S.$0.95

Assumptions:

Dividend growth rate:	15%
Discount rate:	10%
Total net cash flow	−U.S.$1.47
Total discounted net cash flow	U.S.$3.07

Next, the sum of the net present value of the yield advantage is added to the current equity price. This amount is multiplied by the conversion ratio to arrive at the conversion value.

$$
\begin{aligned}
\text{Adjusted conversion} \atop \text{value} \quad &= \left(\begin{matrix} \text{Current} \\ \text{equity} \\ \text{price} \end{matrix} + \begin{matrix} \text{Discounted} \\ \text{yield} \\ \text{advantage} \end{matrix} \right) \times \begin{matrix} \text{Conversion} \\ \text{ratio} \end{matrix} \\
&= (\text{U.S.}\$32.50 + \text{U.S.}\$3.07) \times 28.369 \text{ shares} \\
&= \text{U.S.}\$1,009.09
\end{aligned}
$$

This adjusted conversion value is the price that should be paid for the convertible given its equity value and the present value of the additional income earned over the life of the bond. This conversion value does not consider the value of the call option incorporated in the convertible bond. A premium level must be applied to take account of the option and other attributes of convertible securities.

The investor should analyze the convertible price with regard to the adjusted conversion value. Unlike break-even analysis, this method takes future dividend growth and the time value of money into consideration. The premium paid over conversion value is a function of the yield advantage as well as the equity component.

The discounted yield advantage method is subjective in that a dividend growth rate and discount rate must be assumed for the life of the bond. This method does not consider either a call feature or a put feature. Early redemption would decrease the amount of the yield advantage received over the life of the bond.

Another approach to the discounted yield advantage method views the net yield advantage as a determinant of the optimal conversion date. Also, it views the present value of the net cash flows as a representative value for the premium over conversion value.

The procedure is similar to the preceding evaluation. Assuming a dividend growth rate, the convertible's net income advantage (convertible income less equity dividend) over the life of the bond is calculated. The last year in which the convertible yield exceeds the equity yield is considered the optimal year for conversion. In essence, at this time there is no longer an economic advantage to holding the convertible rather than the equity. The convertible investor would be forfeiting any potential equity dividend growth.

The charts in Figures 10.2–10.4 illustrate this approach for the USA Inc. 7.5% of 200X bond and assume 10%, 15%, and 20% dividend

	Year						
	1	2	3	4	5	6	7
Coupon/share	$2.64	$2.64	$2.64	$2.64	$2.64	$2.64	$2.64
Dividend/share	0.95	1.05	1.15	1.26	1.39	1.53	1.68
Net cash flow (NCF)	1.69	1.60	1.49	1.38	1.25	1.11	0.96

	Year						
	8	9	10	11	12	13	14
Coupon/share	$2.64	$2.64	$2.64	$2.64	$2.64	$2.64	$2.64
Dividend/share	1.85	2.04	2.24	2.46	2.71	2.98	3.28
Net cash flow (NCF)	0.79	0.61	0.40	0.18	0.07	−0.34	−0.64

Figure 10.2   Net cash flows—10% dividend growth rate.

growth rates, respectively. For a 10% dividend growth rate, the dividend income exceeds the convertible income in year 13. Under this assumption, up to year 12 the net cash flow is positive. After this point, it is no longer economic to maintain a position in the convertible. To benefit

	Year						
	1	2	3	4	5	6	7
Coupon/share	$2.64	$2.64	$2.64	$2.64	$2.64	$2.64	$2.64
Dividend/share	0.95	1.09	1.26	1.44	1.66	1.91	2.20
Net cash flow (NCF)	1.69	1.55	1.39	1.20	0.98	0.73	0.45

	Year						
	8	9	10	11	12	13	14
Coupon/share	$2.64	$2.64	$2.64	$2.64	$2.64	$2.64	$2.64
Dividend/share	2.53	2.91	3.34	3.84	4.42	5.08	5.85
Net cash flow (NCF)	0.12	−0.26	−0.70	−1.20	−1.78	−2.44	−3.20

Figure 10.3   Net cash flows—15% dividend growth rate.

	Year						
	1	2	3	4	5	6	7
Coupon/share	$2.64	$2.64	$2.64	$2.64	$2.64	$2.64	$2.64
Dividend/share	0.95	1.14	1.37	1.64	1.97	2.36	2.84
Net cash flow (NCF)	1.69	1.50	1.28	1.00	0.67	0.28	−0.19

	Year						
	8	9	10	11	12	13	14
Coupon/share	$2.64	$2.64	$2.64	$2.64	$2.64	$2.64	$2.64
Dividend/share	3.40	4.08	4.90	5.88	7.06	8.47	10.16
Net cash flow (NCF)	−0.76	−1.44	−2.26	−3.24	−4.41	−5.83	−7.52

Figure 10.4   Net cash flows—20% dividend growth rate.

from future dividend growth, the investor should convert the bond into the equity. Higher dividend growth rates accelerate the process. For 15% and 20% dividend growth rate, the years to convert are the eighth and the sixth years, respectively.

An alternative approach discounts the net income advantage over the life of the bond to the present. In Figure 10.5 a discount rate of 10% and a dividend growth rate of 15% are assumed.

In this scenario, year 8 is the year to convert into equity. At this point, the convertible yield still exceeds the equity yield. In year 9, the net cash flow turns negative, and it is no longer economic to maintain a position in the convertible. The sum of the present value of the positive net cash flows is $5.98. This can be viewed as the amount that should be paid for the convertible's yield advantage and it can be compared to the dollar premium paid over conversion value ($10.801 premium). In this context, a convertible bond with a dollar premium less than the present value of the yield advantage is considered reasonable; the investor will be paying less than the current value of the convertible's yield advantage. A premium exceeding this amount must be evaluated with regard to the convertible's other attributes.

This method is limited in that it ignores the call option features of the convertible. A convertible may be deemed expensive based on the

	Year						
	1	2	3	4	5	6	7
Coupon/share	$2.64	$2.64	$2.64	$2.64	$2.64	$2.64	$2.64
Dividend/share	0.95	1.09	1.26	1.44	1.66	1.91	2.20
Net cash flow (NCF)	1.69	1.55	1.39	1.20	0.98	0.73	0.45
Discounted NCF	1.54	1.28	1.04	0.82	0.61	0.41	0.23

	Year						
	8	9	10	11	12	13	14
Coupon/share	$2.64	$2.64	$2.64	$2.64	$2.64	$2.64	$2.64
Dividend/share	2.53	2.91	3.34	3.84	4.42	5.08	5.85
Net cash flow (NCF)	0.12	−0.26	−0.70	−1.20	−1.78	−2.44	−3.20
Discounted NCF	0.05	−0.11	−0.27	−0.42	−0.57	−0.71	−0.84

Differences due to rounding.
Even period payments assumed.

Figure 10.5 Present value of flows to conversion date—10% discount rate, 15% dividend growth rate.

discounted yield advantage method, when in actuality it is fairly priced due to the value of the conversion feature.

The discounted net cash flow method also does not consider call or put features. A voluntary or involuntary early redemption will decrease the net cash flow projections. In a scenario of early redemption, a convertible once considered reasonable may become expensive.

In general, the discounted yield advantage method is attractive in that it places a value on the convertible's yield advantage over the underlying equity. It does not consider early redemption, which may lead to an overvaluation of the convertible based on its yield advantage. This method does not value the equity call option, the most important factor affecting the convertible price. It is a subjective valuation method in that it assumes a dividend growth rate and a discount rate.

This approach should be used in instances where the convertible is purchased more for its debt component than its equity component. It is also more applicable when there are neither call nor put features involved.

FIXED INCOME PLUS OPTION

A convertible security is defined as a hybrid financial instrument, combining an equity feature and a debt feature, that allows the investor to participate in the equity's upside potential with limited downside risk. The hybrid nature of a convertible allows it to be viewed as a fixed-income security (straight bond) with an equity call option. The convertible's investment value, its claim to coupon payments and principal, is the straight bond portion. The conversion feature, the right to exchange the convertible for the underlying equity, is in essence a call option. As such, it is reasonable to analyze the fixed-income portion and add it to the value of the call option.

The investment value can be estimated by analyzing a comparable straight bond. However, it is often difficult to find a bond with a similar maturity and credit rating. The straight bond component can be valued by calculating the net present value of the coupons and principal received at maturity (see the discussion of investment value in Chapter 5). A simple formula can be used that assumes full coupon payments or that can be adjusted for partial payments. A discount rate for the life of the bond must be assumed. In this way, the bond component of a convertible can be estimated by calculating the present value of cash flows from maturity.

The equity call option of a convertible can be evaluated with an option model. In general, conversion features are long-term; therefore, the option may more aptly be valued with a longer-term warrant model than with an option model.

A theoretical option or warrant model is a sophisticated means of placing a value on the right to buy an equity at a price over a stated period of time. There are various inputs to the model, and estimations of any of these inputs can affect results. These inputs include (in no particular order) the current date, expiration date, conversion period, current equity price, exercise price, volatility of the underlying equity, equity dividend information, and current level of interest rates. Each input contributes some aspect to the total value of the call on the underlying equity.

The current date and expiration date are included to account for the option's time value. Longer times to expiration are more valuable because there is more time for the equity price to trade at a level that is profitable. The conversion period (i.e., continuous versus periodic conversion rights) indicates when the option can be exercised; continuous, or American-style, options are more valuable. The current equity price and exercise price indicate whether the option is in or out of the money. Equities with higher volatilities are more valuable because the equity is more likely to trade at profitable levels. The amount and timing of the equity dividend is important because it is an opportunity cost of holding a call option. Call option holders forfeit the underlying equity's dividend; thus, larger and closer (referring to the timing of the payment) dividends adversely affect the value of the option. Interest rates are important because options are a leveraged instrument, so the financing cost of holding an equity is not incurred. All these inputs affect the resulting value of the call option.

Once values for the straight bond and call option are estimated, it is commonly thought that the two values should be combined. Unfortunately, it is not as simple as adding the values together. The values of the bond and option were estimated assuming that the components were independent securities. However, the bond and call option components of a convertible cannot be separated. Straight bonds and call options are freely traded and are subject to their own demand/supply curves. There is also a difference between an equity call option and the call option embodied in the convertible. An equity call option is exercised by paying the amount of the exercise price. A convertible's conversion feature (call option) is exercised by exchanging the bonds for the underlying equity.

The covariance between interest rates and the underlying equity price must be taken into account. The convertible price may not realize the total effect a change in the level of interest rates has on the investment value and equity value. The sum of the parts (i.e., investment value plus equity component) may not be reflected in the price of the whole (i.e., convertible bond).

Assuming there is no early redemption, a convertible bond can be redeemed at maturity or be converted into the underlying equity. If the convertible is redeemed at maturity, the investor receives all of the coupons and principal. The price of the convertible's call option is forfeited and is a cost of owning the convertible. The value of the convertible is mainly determined by the debt component.

If the investor opts for early conversion, future coupons and the principal are forgone. This loss becomes a cost of exercising the call option. During earlier years of the life of the convertible, the cost is greater because more coupon payments are forfeited. Thus, the cost of the equity via the convertible is in essence greater because of this opportunity cost and will vary based on the timing of the conversion.

Throughout this discussion, it has been assumed that there were no call or put features to be considered in valuing the convertible. A call feature may reduce the life of a convertible, which is usually called to force conversion rather than redemption at the call price. A call feature tends to decrease the number of coupon payments received and diminish the likelihood of receipt of the principal. A potential call also reduces the life of the equity call option. Thus, a call feature tends to decrease the value of a convertible and must be accounted for in a theoretical model. A put feature also tends to shorten a convertible's life. The theoretical value of a convertible should be compared to the value of a put.

The fixed-income-plus-option method is useful in that it includes a value for the conversion feature as well as the debt component. It may not be accurate in that the straight bond and call option are valued separately and subsequently combined. The conversion feature of a convertible bond cannot be separated from the bond. The model may overstate the value of the convertible.

The model needs to allow for early redemption. Call and put features would shorten the life of the call option and also decrease the value of the cash flows from the debt component. The model also needs to account for the covariance between interest rates and the equity price.

The bond-plus-option method is one of the few that attempt to evaluate the hybrid nature of the convertible. It is a complex and time-consuming process. This method is also subject to the various assumption made to value the bond and option features.

11

Alternatives to Traditional Convertible Bonds

Convertible securities are financing alternatives to equity and debt. Through convertible securities, the issuer sells equity at a premium to its current level and defers the dilution of the equity. Relative to the cost of comparable straight debt, the issuer is able to finance at a lower cost through a convertible bond.

Zero-coupon convertible bonds and equity bond units are variations on the standard convertible bond. All of these alternatives offer participation in the equity accompanied with a debt feature. Zero-coupon convertibles and equity bond units have unique characteristics that make them attractive financial instruments to both issuers and investors.

ZERO-COUPON CONVERTIBLE BONDS

Zero-coupon bonds pay no coupon interest and are issued at deep discounts to par value. Zero-coupon bonds are generally issued at a 70–80% discount to par value (i.e., a price of $200–$300). The bonds generate no annual cash flow stream (i.e., bonds pay a 0% coupon) but provide a yield to maturity. Since the bonds are issued at deep discounts to face value and mature in 15–20 years at par, zero-coupon bonds provide attractive yields to maturity.

From the issuer's standpoint, zero-coupon bonds are attractive alternatives to issuing equity or straight debt. The issuer receives financing without diluting equity interests and does not incur current interest payments. Zero-coupon bonds, however, generate only a small amount of financing while appearing as a liability on the balance sheet at the principal amount.

Zero-coupon convertible bonds combine the attributes of zero-coupon bonds and convertible securities. They are issued at deep discounts, pay no coupons, and are convertible into equity. The inclusion of the conversion feature enables issuers to sell zero-coupon convertibles at relatively higher prices (lower discounts to par value) than straight zero-coupon bonds. Zero-coupon convertibles defer equity dilution. Although the premiums on zero-coupon convertibles are less than those of traditional convertibles, upon conversion the equity is sold at a premium to the current equity price.

Zero-coupon convertible bonds are priced differently than traditional convertible bonds. Initially, a competitive yield to maturity is selected based on the current level of interest rates, the bond's maturity, and credit rating. The principal ($1,000 face value) is discounted over the life of the bond at the yield to maturity to arrive at the discounted issue price.

Assume that the semiannual yield to maturity is 8%. The 15-year zero-coupon convertible issue price is 30.832, or $308.32. Zero-coupon convertible bonds are quoted as a percentage of par value.

Zero-Coupon Convertible Bond

Maturity date:	15 yrs
Yield to maturity:	8.0%
Face amount:	$1,000.00
Issue price	30.832 or $308.32

Given market conditions, the premium is set at a competitive level. The conversion price is derived by multiplying the percent premium by the current equity price. Assume the premium is 15%.

Current equity price:	$40.00
Premium:	15%

$$\text{Conversion price} = \text{Current equity price} \times (1 + \text{Premium})$$
$$= \$40.00 \times (1 + 0.15)$$
$$= \$46.00$$

The conversion ratio is derived by dividing the issue price by the conversion price. This is different from traditional convertibles, whose conversion ratio is derived with respect to face value.

Issue price:	$308.32
Conversion price:	$46.00

$$\text{Conversion ratio} = \frac{\text{Issue price}}{\text{Conversion price}}$$
$$= \frac{\$308.32}{\$46.00}$$
$$= 6.703 \text{ shares}$$

The conversion ratio is 6.703 shares per $1,000 face amount of bonds. The conversion ratio is used in calculating the conversion value and premium.

At an equity price of $40.00, the conversion value is $268.12:

$$\text{Conversion value} = \text{Equity price} \times \text{Conversion ratio}$$
$$= \$40.00 \times 6.703 \text{ shares}$$
$$= \$268.12 \text{ or } 26.812$$

Given the zero convertible price of $308.32, the 15% premium (as earlier indicated) can be backed out of the equation:

$$\frac{\text{Premium}}{\text{(Percent method)}} = \frac{\text{Convertible price} - \text{Conversion value}}{\text{Conversion value}} \times 100$$
$$= \frac{\$308.32 - \$268.12}{\$268.12} \times 100$$
$$= 15\%$$

The zero-coupon convertible's premium usually behaves similarly to that of the traditional convertible. The zero-coupon convertible bond participates with equity movement and provides some downside protection. The actual behavior of the premium will be discussed later.

Zero-coupon convertible bonds have unique qualities. As previously stated, they pay no coupon but are priced at a discount to face value to provide a yield to maturity. If the bond is purchased at 30.832 and held 15 years to maturity, the investor earns an 8% return.

It is unlikely that the investor would have to hold the convertible to maturity to earn an 8% return. If interest rates remain constant, a zero-coupon convertible will yield 8% next year; the convertible's price will increase to compensate for the passage of one year. Assuming constant interest rates, the zero-coupon convertible price will increase each year by a certain amount to maintain a constant yield to maturity. The amount by which the convertible increases is called the *original issue discount*.

The price at which the bond should trade in one year, assuming no change in interest rates, can be calculated. The cash flows are discounted over the life of the bond at 8% semiannually to the next year. Assuming constant interest rates, in order for the zero-coupon convertible to yield 8% in years 1 and 2, the bond price would have to increase to $333.48 and $360.69, respectively. In both years, the bond price would have to increase approximately 8% (difference due to rounding) to maintain the 8% yield to maturity. Therefore, assuming constant interest rates, the convertible price can be expected to increase by the percentage amount of the yield to maturity each year.

Year	Issue Price	Original Issue Discount	Price	Yield to Maturity	Percent Change in Price
Issue date	$308.32	$0	$308.32	8%	—
1	$308.32	$25.16	$333.48	8%	8.16%
2	$308.32	$52.37	$360.69	8%	8.16%

Zero-coupon convertible bonds generally trade at low premiums relative to traditional convertibles. Convertibles trading at low premiums usually participate in equity price movements. This is not always the case with zero-coupon convertible bonds.

As previously stated, assuming constant interest rates, the zero-coupon convertible bond price should increase over time. Assuming both a constant interest rate environment and a constant equity price, the increase in the convertible's price over time will increase the premium. For example, if the convertible price increases to $333.48 from $308.32 and the equity price remains at $40.00, the premium will expand:

$$\text{Conversion value} = \$268.12$$

$$\frac{\text{Premium}}{\text{(Percent method)}} = \frac{\text{Convertible price} - \text{Conversion value}}{\text{Conversion value}} \times 100$$

$$= \frac{\$333.48 - \$268.12}{\$268.12} \times 100$$

$$= 24.38\%$$

Assuming constant interest rates, the bond should increase by the amount of the yield to maturity. The equity price must increase by as much as the convertible price on a percentage basis to maintain the current level of the premium. At a convertible price of $333.48, the equity would have to rise to $43.26 (an 8.16% increase) to maintain a 15% premium.

	Price 1	Price 2	Increase
Convertible price	$308.32	$333.48	8.16%
Equity price	$ 40.00	$ 43.26	8.16%

$$\text{Conversion value} = \text{Equity price} \times \text{Conversion ratio}$$

$$= \$43.26 \times 6.703 \text{ shares}$$

$$= \$289.97$$

$$\frac{\text{Premium}}{\text{(Percent method)}} = \frac{\text{Convertible price} - \text{Conversion value}}{\text{Conversion value}} \times 100$$

$$= \frac{\$333.48 - \$289.97}{\$289.97} \times 100$$

$$= 15\%$$

For the equity to have an impact on the zero-coupon convertible, it must increase by more than the bond's yield to maturity. The equity must be volatile to give value to the conversion feature.

For instance, in the previous example, under a constant interest rate scenario, both the convertible price and equity price increased by 8.16%. To show the effect on the premium, a sensitivity analysis is conducted with respect to the equity price. Assume that, due to constant interest rates, the convertible price increases by 8.16%, from $308.32 to $333.48, and the equity price increases by 6%, from $40.00 to $42.40.

$$\text{Conversion value} = \text{Equity price} \times \text{Conversion ratio}$$

$$= \$42.40 \times 6.703 \text{ shares}$$

$$= \$284.21$$

$$\begin{array}{l} \text{Premium} \\ \text{(Percent method)} \end{array} = \frac{\text{Convertible price} - \text{Conversion value}}{\text{Conversion value}} \times 100$$

$$= \frac{\$333.48 - \$284.21}{\$284.21} \times 100$$

$$= 17.34\%$$

Assuming constant interest rates, when the equity price increases by less than the yield to maturity, the premium expands. Theoretically, as with traditional convertibles, an increase in the equity price is accompanied by a decrease in premium. Although they have low premiums, zero-coupon convertibles do not always participate in equity price appreciation.

Now assume that the convertible price increases by 8.16% and the equity price increases 10%, from $40.00 to $44.00.

$$\text{Conversion value} = \text{Equity price} \times \text{Conversion ratio}$$

$$= \$44.00 \times 6.703 \text{ shares}$$

$$= \$294.93$$

$$\text{Premium} \atop \text{(Percent method)} = \frac{\text{Convertible price} \ - \ \text{Conversion value}}{\text{Conversion value}} \times 100$$

$$= \frac{\$333.48 \ - \ \$294.93}{\$294.93} \times 100$$

$$= 13.07\%$$

The preceding analysis is reviewed in the following chart. This analysis has assumed constant interest rates. The convertible's original premium was 15%.

	Price 1	Price 2	Percent Change	Premium
Convertible price	$308.32	$333.48	8.16	—
Equity price	$ 40.00	$ 43.26	8.16	15.00%
	$ 40.00	$ 42.40	6.00	17.34%
	$ 40.00	$ 44.00	10.00	13.07%

The convertible price increases each year by the amount of the yield to maturity when interest rates are constant. The equity's annual performance must exceed the convertible's yield to maturity in order for the conversion feature to be of value.

Zero-coupon convertibles are very sensitive to changes in interest rates. Relative to straight bonds, the zero-coupon convertible's price will fluctuate more given a move in interest rates. Given an increase in rates, on a percentage basis, the zero-coupon convertible's price will decrease more compared with a straight bond. A decrease in rates will result in a greater increase in price.

For example, compare a 15-year zero-coupon convertible bond yielding 8% with a 15-year 8% coupon bond. When interest rates are 8%, the zero-coupon convertible's price is $308.32 and the 8% bond's price is $1,000. An increase in the general level of interest rates to 10% results in a zero-coupon convertible price of $231.38 and an 8% bond price of $846.28. The zero-coupon convertible price and the 8% bond price decrease by 25% and 15.4%, respectively.

A decrease in interest rates to 6% increases the zero-coupon convertible price and the 8% bond price to $411.99 and $1,196.00, respectively. The zero-coupon convertible price increases by 33.6%, and the 8% bond price increases by 19.6%.

Interest Rates	Zero-Coupon Convertible Price	8% Bond Price	Percent Change	
			Zero	8% Bond
8%	$308.32	$1,000.00		
10%	$231.38	$ 846.28	−25.0	−15.4
6%	$411.99	$1,196.00	+33.6	+19.6

Clearly, zero-coupon convertible bonds are more sensitive to changes in interest rates than straight bonds and traditional convertible bonds. The traditional convertible's investment value lends stability and provides more downside protection.

Zero-coupon convertible bonds have call features. Typically the call protection is a provisional feature and is contingent upon the performance of the underlying equity. For instance, the convertibles cannot be called unless the equity trades at 150% of the conversion price. In this instance, the equity would have to trade at $69 (150% of $46) for a certain period of time.

The schedule of prices at which the zero-coupon convertibles can be called reflects the bond's price action under the assumption of constant interest rates. The call price increases annually until it reaches par value at the date of maturity. Each call price equates the convertible's yield to maturity to the yield to call. The difference between the call price and the issue price is the original issue discount. The schedule in Figure 11.1 displays the call prices that produce an 8% semiannual yield to maturity. Issuers may want to call a zero-coupon convertible to reduce the liability on the balance sheet.

Zero-coupon convertible bonds may also have put features. The put feature usually starts in 4–5 years and follows the concept behind the call feature. The put price will be set at levels that reflect the yield to maturity. In this instance, the put exercise date is in year 5 at a price of U.S.$456.39. An investor purchasing the bond at issue date will realize an 8% return if the put is exercised.

Date	Issue Price	Original Issue Discount	Call Price
Issue date	$308.32	0	$ 308.32
1	308.32	$ 25.16	333.48
2	308.32	52.37	360.69
3	308.32	81.80	390.12
4	308.32	113.64	421.96
5	308.32	148.07	456.39
6	308.32	185.31	493.63
7	308.32	225.59	533.91
8	308.32	269.16	577.48
9	308.32	316.28	624.60
10	308.32	367.24	675.56
11	308.32	422.37	730.69
12	308.32	481.99	790.31
13	308.32	546.48	854.80
14	308.32	616.24	924.56
Maturity	308.32	691.68	1,000.00

Figure 11.1   Call feature schedule—zero-coupon convertible.

The put feature lends stability to the zero-coupon convertible. It guarantees a yield to put regardless of the performance of the equity or interest rates. Even if the put is exercised, the issuer has received financing over a short period of time at a relatively low cost.

Zero-coupon convertible bonds are issued at discounts to face value and provide no current income. They are volatile instruments in that they are very sensitive to movements in interest rates and equity prices. They are low-cost, provide attractive yields, and can participate in equity price appreciation. The tax consequences of purchasing a zero-coupon convertible, however, can detract from their appeal. After tax, they often result in an annual negative cash flow and thus should be evaluated with respect to tax laws.

EQUITY BOND UNITS

Equity bond units are issued as packages combining a straight bond with equity warrants. The bond and warrants can trade as three different vehicles. The securities can trade as a unit (bond cum warrants), or the units can be stripped to trade separately as bonds alone (bonds ex warrants) and as warrants.

From the issuer's standpoint, bond units provide 5–10-year financing. The investor has a shorter call on the underlying equity than is the case with traditional convertible bonds. The addition of the warrant enables the pricing of the bond's coupon to be below that of comparable straight bonds. The warrant's premium is usually set at a relatively high level, allowing the issuer to sell equity in the future at a higher premium to current levels.

The ability to separate the unit attracts a wider variety of investors. Income-oriented investors can strip the units of the warrants and retain the bond. Equity-oriented investors are likely to sell off the bond component and maintain exposure in the equity through the warrant. Investors wanting to generate income and participate in equity appreciation will retain the unit. Unit holders anticipating increases in interest rates or falling equity prices can avoid losses by selling the bond or warrants, respectively.

Synthetic Convertible

A variation on bond units are usable bonds plus warrants. To exercise a warrant, cash in the amount of the exercise price is needed to receive the equity. A usable bond's principal can be given up at par value to pay for the act of exercising the warrants. In lieu of cash, the bond's par value is used to pay the exercise price.

A usable bond plus warrant is referred to as a *synthetic convertible*. As with the convertible bond, the usable bond is surrendered in return for the equity, or the number of shares embodied in the bond.

In addition to the interest payment and the claim to principal, the usability feature provides another source of demand for the bond. Due to the additional demand, usable bonds provide more support against rises in interest rates than comparable straight bonds.

As previously stated, a usable bond can be given up at par value to exercise the warrant. If the bond is purchased below par value, the effect is to lower the effective exercise price of the warrant. The cost of exercising the warrant is decreased by using a bond purchased below par value and surrendering it at par value. The following analysis will explain this concept.

9.5% Usable Bond plus Warrants

Usable bond price:	$850, or 85% of par value
Par value:	$1,000
Warrant exercise price:	$9.50
Warrant price:	$4.00
Equity price:	$10.50
Equity dividend:	$0

The number of warrants to purchase per bond is calculated by dividing par value by the warrant's exercise price.

$$\begin{aligned} \text{Number of warrants to purchase} &= \frac{\text{Par value}}{\text{Warrant exercise price}} \\ &= \frac{\$1,000}{\$9.50} \\ &= 105 \end{aligned}$$

A synthetic convertible is equal to one bond plus 105 warrants. The result of 105 warrants is equivalent to a conversion ratio. The price of the synthetic convertible is the sum of the parts, or $1,270.

$$\begin{aligned} \text{Synthetic convertible price} &= \text{Usable bond price} + \left(\text{Number of warrants} \times \text{Warrant price} \right) \\ &= \$850 + (105 \times \$4) \\ &= \$1,270 \end{aligned}$$

The synthetic convertible's current yield is 7.48%. To arrive at this value, the coupon is divided by the synthetic convertible's price.

$$\begin{aligned} \text{Current yield} &= \frac{\text{Coupon}}{\text{Synthetic convertible price}} \times 100 \\ &= \frac{\$95}{\$1,270} \times 100 \\ &= 7.48\% \end{aligned}$$

The usable bond purchased at $850 is given up at $1,000 to exercise the 105 warrants at $9.50 per warrant. Since the bond cost 85% of par value, the effective exercise price of the warrants is 85% of $9.50.

$$\text{Effective exercise price} = \frac{\text{Bond price as a}}{\text{percentage of par}} \times \frac{\text{Exercise}}{\text{price}}$$

$$= 0.85 \times \$9.50$$

$$= \$8.075$$

The exercise of 105 warrants at an effective exercise price of $8.075 costs $850, the price of the bond.

The warrant's intrinsic value is the amount by which the equity price exceeds the effective exercise price. Thus the warrant is in the money by $2.425.

$$\text{Intrinsic value} = \text{Equity price} - \text{Effective conversion price}$$

$$= \$10.50 - \$8.075$$

$$= \$2.425$$

The cost of the equity (referred to as parity) via the usable bond is the sum of the effective exercise price and the warrant price. The cost of the equity is $12.075.

$$\begin{array}{l}\text{Equity price} \\ \text{via bond} \\ \text{(Parity)}\end{array} = \text{Effective exercise price} + \text{Warrant price}$$

$$= \$8.075 + \$4.00$$

$$= \$12.075$$

The synthetic convertible's investment value is $850, the price of the usable bond. Unlike a traditional convertible, a synthetic convertible's investment value can be quantified. The synthetic convertible's conversion value is $1,102.50. Conversion value is calculated using a method similar to that for a traditional convertible.

$$\text{Conversion value} = \text{Number of warrants} \times \text{Equity price}$$

$$= 105 \times \$10.50$$

$$= \$1,102.50$$

The synthetic convertible's premium is 15%. It can be calculated using any of several methods.

$$\begin{aligned}\text{Premium}\atop\text{(Percent)} &= \left(\frac{\text{Synthetic bond price}}{\text{Conversion value}} - 1\right) \times 100\end{aligned}$$

$$= \left(\frac{\$1,270.00}{\$1,102.50} - 1\right) \times 100$$

$$= 15\%$$

$$\begin{aligned}\text{Premium}\atop\text{(Percent)} &= \frac{\text{Parity} - \text{Equity price}}{\text{Equity price}} \times 100\end{aligned}$$

$$= \frac{\$12.075 - \$10.50}{\$10.50} \times 100$$

$$= 15\%$$

$$\begin{aligned}\text{Premium}\atop\text{(Percent)} &= \frac{\substack{\text{Synthetic convertible} \\ \text{price}} - \substack{\text{Conversion} \\ \text{value}}}{\text{Conversion value}} \times 100\end{aligned}$$

$$= \frac{\$1,270.00 - \$1,102.50}{\$1,102.50} \times 100$$

$$= 15\%$$

The synthetic convertible's yield advantage is 7.48%. The synthetic convertible's current yield is 7.48%, whereas the equity pays no dividend. The break-even period is 2.03 years.

$$\text{Break-even period} = \frac{\text{Premium percent}}{\text{Yield advantage}}$$

$$= \frac{15\%}{7.48\%}$$

$$= 2.03 \text{ years}$$

Usable bonds plus warrants are quite similar to traditional convertible securities. They combine a debt with an equity feature, thus participating in equity appreciation with limited downside risk. The benefit of synthetic convertibles is the ability to separate the components and trade them as individual securities, permitting more flexibility with regard to one's investment orientation.

12

International Convertible Securities

International convertible securities are issued in either domestic, foreign, or Eurobond form. They provide investors with the opportunity to realize greater overall current returns while maintaining equity and currency exposure.

Euroconvertibles issued by foreign borrowers and denominated in Eurocurrencies will be the focus of the following chapters. It should be noted that the concepts and calculation methods of some domestic and foreign convertibles differ from those of Euroconvertible issues. Domestic issues will be addressed in a subsequent chapter.

The mechanics of international Euroconvertible securities are similar to those of the U.S. Euroconvertible discussed in previous chapters. The concepts and calculation methods of conversion value, premium, yield advantage, and break-even period are applicable. International Euroconvertibles differ from other convertible issues in that they may be denominated in a currency other than the local currency (the currency of the underlying equity). For this reason, foreign Euroconvertibles have special conversion features and currency exposure.

INTERNATIONAL EUROCONVERTIBLE CONVERSION FEATURE

International Euroconvertibles are generally convertible into a predetermined number of ordinary shares. The bond participates in the potential price appreciation of ordinary shares. An international Euroconvertible's conversion value is the market value of the ordinary shares received upon conversion. As with U.S. Euroconvertibles, conversion value is the prime factor affecting the bond price.

The conversion feature of an international Euroconvertible is similar to that of a U.S. Euroconvertible. When the convertible is denominated in the local currency, the evaluation procedures are identical. The conversion feature differs when the bond is denominated in a currency other than the local currency. For instance, if a French company (local currency is the French franc) issues a U.S. dollar–denominated convertible bond, adjustments are made so that the U.S. dollar bond is evaluated with regard to a U.S. dollar conversion price. In order to evaluate the bond with respect to the equity, the conversion price is translated into the bond currency.

The *effective conversion price* is the bond's conversion price in terms of the local currency. At issue date, the bond's effective conversion price is set at a percentage premium above the current ordinary price. The effective conversion price is the price of the equity at which the bond may be exchanged. It is usually used for the provisional call feature. The effective conversion price is used for calculations (i.e., conversion ratio, conversion value) when the currency of the bond is the local currency. For example, for a French company that issues a convertible denominated in French francs, the effective conversion price is the conversion price set at issue date expressed in French francs.

Convertible bonds denominated in a currency other than the local currency are usually set with a fixed exchange rate between the two currencies. The fixed exchange rate is the exchange rate, set at bond issue date, used to express the effective conversion price in terms of the equivalent bond currency. For example, a U.S. dollar–denominated convertible issued by a British company is set with a U.S. dollar/sterling fixed exchange rate. In this case, the U.S. dollar is the bond currency, and the pound sterling is the local currency. The fixed exchange rate is the current rate at the time of issue and is fixed for the life of the bond.

The *equivalent conversion price* is the effective conversion price expressed in the bond currency. The fixed exchange rate translates the effective conversion price into the equivalent conversion price. For example, suppose a Spanish company issues a convertible denominated in U.S. dollars. At issue date, the bond is set with a fixed peseta/U.S. dollar rate and an effective conversion price specified in pesetas. The fixed exchange rate translates the conversion price into the U.S. dollar equivalent conversion price. The equivalent conversion price is used in the calculations for a bond not denominated in the local currency.

The equivalent conversion price is arrived at by either dividing or multiplying the effective conversion price by the fixed exchange rate. The following examples clarify the difference in techniques.

Singapore Inc. 4% Dec. 17, 200X

Local currency:	Singapore dollar
Denomination:	U.S. dollar
Par value:	U.S.$1,000
Effective conversion price:	S$9.05
Fixed exchange rate:	S$2.1810/U.S.$1.0000

In this case, the fixed exchange rate is expressed in units of local currency (Singapore dollar) per one unit of the bond currency (U.S. dollar). Adjust the effective conversion price to U.S. dollar terms by dividing by the fixed exchange rate.

$$\text{Equivalent conversion price} = \frac{\text{Effective conversion price}}{\text{Fixed exchange rate}}$$

$$= \frac{\text{S\$9.05}}{\text{S\$2.1810/U.S.\$1.0000}}$$

$$= \text{U.S.\$4.1495}$$

The following fixed exchange rate is expressed in units of the bond currency (U.S. dollar) per one unit of the local currency (New Zealand dollar). The effective conversion price is adjusted to U.S. dollar terms by multiplying by the fixed exchange rate.

New Zealand Co. 5.25% July 21, 200X

Local currency:	New Zealand dollar
Denomination:	U.S. dollar
Par value:	U.S.$1,000
Effective conversion price:	N.Z.$3.94
Fixed exchange rate:	U.S.$0.5965/N.Z.$1.0000

$$\text{Equivalent conversion price} = \begin{matrix} \text{Effective} \\ \text{conversion} \\ \text{price} \end{matrix} \times \begin{matrix} \text{Fixed} \\ \text{exchange} \\ \text{rate} \end{matrix}$$

$$= \text{N.Z.}\$3.94 \times \text{U.S.}\$0.5965/\text{N.Z.}\$1.0000$$

$$= \text{U.S.}\$2.3502$$

The equivalent conversion price is needed to calculate the conversion ratio when the bond is not denominated in the local currency. To derive a conversion ratio, a U.S. dollar par value, for example, can only be divided by a U.S. dollar conversion price. By setting an equivalent conversion price, the fixed exchange rate guarantees that the bond may be converted into a certain number of shares.

Singapore Inc. 4% December 17, 200X

$$\text{Conversion ratio} = \frac{\text{Par value}}{\text{Equivalent conversion price}}$$

$$= \frac{\text{U.S.}\$1,000}{\text{U.S.}\$4.1495}$$

$$= 240.99 \text{ ordinary shares (U.S. dollar cost basis)}$$

The absence of a fixed exchange rate would subject the investor to a fluctuating conversion ratio; the investor would not be certain as to the number of shares to be received upon conversion. The conversion ratio would be a function of the then-current local currency rate versus the bond currency. To illustrate, if the Singapore Inc. 4% of 200X were not set with a fixed exchange rate, the equivalent conversion price would be derived using the current Singapore dollar/U.S. dollar rate. The conversion ratio of the Singapore Inc. 4% of 200X would be a function of the current Singapore dollar/U.S. dollar rate.

$$\text{Conversion ratio} = \frac{\text{Par value}}{\text{Equivalent conversion price}}$$

$$= \frac{\text{Par value}}{\left(\begin{array}{c}\text{Effective conversion}\\\text{price}\end{array}\right) \div \left(\begin{array}{c}\text{Current}\\\text{S\$/U.S.\$}\end{array}\right)}$$

Several convertible bond issues not denominated in the local currency are set with a conversion ratio rather than an effective conversion price and fixed exchange rate. The equivalent conversion price may be derived by dividing par value by the conversion ratio. A fixed exchange rate is implied between the derived equivalent conversion price and the equity price (in local currency) at issue date.

The following example compares two tranches of convertible bonds issued by the same Australian company. The tranches have different bond denominations. Tranche A is denominated in the local currency, and tranche B is not. Both issues were set with conversion ratios, from which a fixed exchange rate for tranche B can be inferred. This example illustrates the features of foreign convertible bonds.

	Tranche A	Tranche B
Coupon	9.75%	6.5%
Maturity	June 10, 200X	June 10, 200X
Country of issuer	Australia	Australia
Bond denomination	A$1,000	U.S.$1,000
Local currency	Australian dollar	Australian dollar
Bond currency	Australian dollar	U.S. dollar
Conversion ratio	316	438*
Effective conversion price	Not stated	Not stated
Fixed exchange rate	NA	Not stated
Equivalent conversion price	NA	Not stated
Equity price at issue	A$2.58	A$2.77
Premium at issue (percent)	22.67	14.44

*Investor receives ordinary shares with a U.S. dollar cost basis. In effect, the shares are received at a fixed U.S. dollar price.

Tranche A was set with a conversion ratio of 316 shares/A\$1,000 bond. The effective conversion price can be derived as follows.

$$\text{Tranche A effective conversion price} = \frac{\text{Par value}}{\text{Conversion ratio}}$$

$$= \frac{A\$1,000}{316 \text{ shares}}$$

$$= A\$3.1645$$

Tranche B was set with a conversion ratio of 438 shares/U.S.\$1,000 bond, from which the equivalent U.S. dollar conversion price can be derived.

$$\text{Tranche B equivalent conversion price} = \frac{\text{Par value}}{\text{Conversion ratio}}$$

$$= \frac{U.S.\$1,000}{438 \text{ shares}}$$

$$= U.S.\$2.283$$

At issue date, the effective conversion price is usually set at a premium to the equity price. In this instance, the effective conversion price can be derived from the equity price and premium at issue date. The fixed exchange rate is implied in the effective and equivalent conversion prices.

$$\text{Tranche B effective conversion price} = \frac{\text{Equity price at issue}}{} \times (1 + \text{Premium})$$

$$= A\$2.77 \times (1 + 0.1444)$$

$$= A\$3.17$$

The fixed exchange rate is derivable from the equivalent and effective conversion prices.

$$\frac{\text{Tranche B implied}}{\text{U.S. dollar/Australian dollar}} = \frac{\text{Equivalent conversion price}}{\text{Effective conversion price}}$$

$$= \frac{\text{U.S.\$2.283}}{\text{A\$3.17}}$$

$$= 0.7202$$

The inferred results can now be added to the table.

	Tranche A	Tranche B
Coupon	9.75%	6.5%
Maturity	June 10, 200X	June 10, 200X
Country of issuer	Australia	Australia
Bond denomination	A$1,000	U.S.$1,000
Local currency	Australian dollar	Australian dollar
Bond currency	Australian dollar	U.S. dollar
Conversion ratio	316	438*
Effective conversion price	A$3.1645	A$3.17
Fixed exchange rate	NA	U.S.$/A$ = 0.7202
Equivalent conversion price	NA	U.S.$2.283
Conversion price used for		
provisional call test price	A$3.1645	A$3.17
Equity price at issue	A$2.58	A$2.77
Premium at issue (percent)	22.67	14.44

*Investor receives ordinary shares with a U.S. dollar cost basis.

SHARES RECEIVED UPON CONVERSION

Upon conversion of a bond not denominated in the local currency, the investor receives ordinary shares with a cost basis in terms of the bond currency. The cost basis is derived from the total original investment.

Suppose an investor purchases 1,000M Singapore Inc. 4% of 200X at U.S.$1,050 net (assume no accrued interest). The local currency is the Singapore dollar, and the bond currency is the U.S. dollar. Assume the bonds become callable, and the investor decides to convert the bonds into equity. The investor receives the ordinary shares with a cost basis in U.S. dollars. The Singapore dollar shares are received with a fixed Singapore dollar/U.S. dollar exchange rate. The cost basis of the ordinary shares (in Singapore dollars) received upon conversion is derived from the total original investment in the convertible bond position (U.S. dollar purchase price plus accrued interest).

$$\text{Equity cost basis} = \frac{\text{Total original investment}}{\substack{\text{Number of shares received} \\ \text{upon conversion}}}$$

$$= \frac{\left(\substack{\text{Purchase} \\ \text{price}} \times \substack{\text{Number} \\ \text{of bonds}} \right) + \substack{\text{Accrued} \\ \text{interest}}}{\substack{\text{Number of} \\ \text{bonds}} \times \text{Conversion ratio}}$$

$$= \frac{\text{U.S.\$1,050} \times \text{1,000M}}{\text{1,000M} \times 240.99 \text{ shares}}$$

$$= \frac{\text{U.S.\$1,050,000}}{240,990}$$

$$= \text{U.S.\$4.357/share}$$

Upon sale of the 240,990 ordinary shares, the investor receives Singapore dollars as payment. Profit/loss is calculated by translating the Singapore dollar proceeds into equivalent U.S. dollar terms (i.e., selling the Singapore dollars for U.S. dollars at the current Singapore dollar/U.S. dollar exchange rate). The U.S. dollar proceeds are compared to the U.S.\$4.357/share cost basis.

INTERNATIONAL CONVERTIBLE EVALUATION

For purposes of calculating conversion value and yield advantage, the current equity price and equity dividend must be expressed in the currency of the bond. The equity price and dividend are adjusted by the current exchange rate between the local currency and the bond currency.

For example, the conversion value of the Singapore 4% of 200X bond must be expressed in terms of the bond currency. A U.S. dollar bond price can only be evaluated relative to a U.S. dollar conversion value.

Singapore Inc. 4% Dec. 17, 200X

Local currency:	Singapore dollar
Denomination:	U.S. dollar
Equivalent conversion price:	U.S.$4.1495
Conversion ratio:	240.99 shares
Current equity price:	S$8.00
Current S$/U.S.$ rate:	S$2.0375/U.S.$1.0000
Equity dividend:	S$0.07

$$\text{Conversion value} = \frac{\text{Conversion}}{\text{ratio}} \times \frac{\text{Equivalent equity}}{\text{price}}$$

$$= \frac{\text{Conversion}}{\text{ratio}} \times \left(\frac{\text{Current equity price}}{\text{Current S\$/U.S.\$}} \right)$$

$$= 240.99 \text{ shares} \times \left(\frac{\text{S\$8.00}}{\text{S\$2.0375/U.S.\$1.0000}} \right)$$

$$= \text{U.S.\$946.22}$$

$$\text{Premium} = \text{Bond price} - \text{Conversion value}$$

$$= \text{U.S.\$1,050.00} - \text{U.S.\$946.22}$$

$$= \text{U.S.\$103.78}$$

The yield advantage of the Singapore Inc. 4% of 200X over the equity must be evaluated in U.S. dollar terms. The bond and equity yields must be compared on the same interest rate term structure.

$$\begin{matrix} \text{Yield} \\ \text{advantage} \\ \text{(Percent} \\ \text{method)} \end{matrix} = \left(\begin{matrix} \text{Current} \\ \text{bond} \\ \text{yield} \end{matrix} - \begin{matrix} \text{Equivalent} \\ \text{current equity} \\ \text{yield} \end{matrix} \right) \times 100$$

$$= \left(\frac{\text{Coupon}}{\text{Bond price}} - \frac{\text{Equity dividend} \div (\text{S\$/U.S.\$})}{\text{Equity price} \div (\text{S\$/U.S.\$})} \right) \times 100$$

$$= \left(\frac{\text{U.S.\$40.00}}{\text{U.S.\$1,050.00}} - \frac{\text{S\$0.07} \div (\text{S\$2.0375/U.S.\$1})}{\text{S\$8.00} \div (\text{S\$2.0375/U.S.\$1})} \right) \times 100$$

$$= (0.0381 - 0.00875) \times 100$$
$$= 2.935\%$$

The currency rate appears in the numerator and denominator of the equivalent current equity yield equation. The Singapore dollar/U.S. dollar rate cancels out. In this instance, the inclusion of the currency rate is of no consequence. In essence, the equity price and dividend can remain in the local currency.

Euroconvertibles denominated in a currency other than the local currency have special conversion features. At issue date, the bonds are set at an effective conversion price and a fixed exchange rate. The fixed exchange rate provides for an equivalent conversion price and a constant conversion ratio. The special conversion features allow for the analysis of the convertible with regard to the ordinary share.

When a convertible is not denominated into the local currency, it is very important to translate all variables into the bond currency. A U.S. dollar bond price can only be evaluated with regard to a U.S. dollar equity price, conversion price, and conversion value. Bond and equity yields must be compared on the same interest rate term structure. It is this aspect of international Euroconvertibles that is most confusing, but it is important for evaluation purposes.

13

Foreign Currency Management and Exposure

Convertible securities denominated in foreign currencies or convertible into the shares of a foreign company have currency exposure. Currency exposure is typically categorized into translation, transaction, and economic currency exposure. Currency exposure arises when the future values of cash inflows, translated into the local currency for accounting purposes, are uncertain.

Translation exposure arises from the uncertainty of converting foreign-denominated assets and liabilities into the local currency. *Transaction exposure* refers to the effect of fluctuating exchange rates on revenues, expenses, and profitability. *Economic exposure* relates to the effect of fluctuating exchange rates on long-term macroeconomics (e.g., price competition, exports/imports).

From a U.S. dollar perspective, investments in convertibles denominated in the foreign (local) currency are usually exposed to currency fluctuations through the translation of foreign currency proceeds into the investor's currency. In other words, when the convertible position is sold, the foreign currency proceeds must be translated back into the investor's currency (in this case, the U.S. dollar) for accounting purposes.

Convertibles not denominated in the local currency (i.e., where the bond currency is different from the local currency) are exposed to currencies through the mathematics of conversion value. Convertibles are exposed to transaction and economic currency risk as they are vulnerable to the underlying equity's price fluctuations.

Currency fluctuations can affect the value of the convertible as much as changes in the equity price and the level of interest rates. Total expected returns on convertibles are a function of relative movements and future expectations of currency values. Through translation currency fluctuations can negate any capital gain realized in the convertible price in terms of the bond currency. In other words, capital gains, in U.S. dollar terms, will fluctuate with a given move in the currency rate.

Foreign currency exposures under various scenarios and the management of these exposures are detailed in the following section. The analysis is from a U.S. dollar perspective. A brief explanation of currency markets precedes the analysis.

FOREIGN CURRENCY MARKETS

Foreign currency markets are expressed with respect to the U.S. dollar. Most currencies are quoted as the amount of foreign currency per one U.S. dollar (e.g., number of Japanese yen per one U.S. dollar). The British pound sterling is an example of a currency that is quoted in number of U.S. dollars per one sterling (Figure 13.1).

Currency	Level 1	Level 2	Result
Yen/U.S. dollar	125	150	U.S. dollar appreciates vs. yen: receive more yen per one dollar.
Yen/U.S. dollar	125	100	U.S. dollar depreciates vs. yen: receive less yen per one dollar.
U.S. dollar/sterling	1.7000	1.5000	U.S. dollar appreciates vs. sterling: receive less sterling per one dollar.
U.S. dollar/sterling	1.7000	1.9000	U.S. dollar depreciates vs. sterling: receive more sterling per one dollar.

Figure 13.1   Currency movements.

A movement in the yen/U.S. dollar rate from ¥125/U.S.$1 to ¥150/ U.S.$1 indicates an appreciation of the dollar relative to the yen (or a depreciation of the yen versus the dollar). The investor now receives more yen per one dollar. The opposite is true of a depreciation of the U.S. dollar versus the yen. When the dollar depreciates, fewer yen are received per one dollar.

A movement in the U.S. dollar/sterling rate from U.S.$1.7000/£1 to U.S.$1.5000/£1 represents an appreciation of the U.S. dollar versus the pound sterling (or a depreciation of the sterling versus the dollar). At a rate of U.S.$1.5000/£1, fewer dollars are received per sterling. Another interpretation is that fewer dollars are needed to buy one sterling. When the dollar depreciates versus the sterling, more dollars are needed to buy one sterling.

Foreign exchange spot rates (cash market) are determined by the demand and supply for the foreign currency relative to the U.S. dollar. The demand and supply are a function of trade and capital investment cash flows.

Cross-currency rates do not directly involve the U.S. dollar. The deutsche mark/sterling rate is a cross-currency rate derived from the U.S. dollar/sterling and deutsche mark/U.S. dollar rates. Fluctuations in either the U.S. dollar/sterling or deutsche mark/U.S. dollar rate affect the deutsche mark/sterling rate. Knowledge of two of the currency rates at any time allows derivation of the third value.

$$\text{Deutsche mark/£} = \text{Deutsche mark/U.S. dollar} \times \text{U.S. dollar/£}$$

$$\text{U.S. dollar/£} = \text{Deutsche mark/£} \div \text{Deutsche mark/U.S. dollar}$$

$$\text{Deutsche mark/U.S. dollar} = \frac{\text{Deutsche mark/£}}{\text{U.S. dollar/£}}$$

Forward exchange rates are prices at which contracts are made for the eventual exchange of currencies. They are usually determined with regard to spot rates. Unlike the standardized futures contract, forward contracts are tailored to specific needs. They can vary as to volume and timing.

Forward exchange rates are a function of interest rate differentials. The forward rate's premium/discount is related to the interest rate term structure of the associated currencies. Currencies associated with a relatively higher interest rate will trade in the forward market at a discount to the spot rate. The discount exists because the currency in the higher-interest-rate environment can be invested in higher yielding financial instruments. The return on domestic and covered foreign financing assets is equivalent. Similarly, currencies in a lower-interest-rate environment trade at a premium to the spot rate.

For example, domestic U.S. interest rates are higher than Dutch interest rates. Forward domestic currency rates trade at a discount to the spot rate. The following example is a very basic calculation of a forward rate.

30-day Dutch interest rate	6.60%
30-day U.S. interest rate	8.90%
Interest rate differential	−2.30%
Dutch guilder/U.S. dollar spot rate	2.1070

$$\substack{\text{Difference} \\ \text{between} \\ \text{30-day spot} \\ \text{and forward} \\ \text{rates}} = \frac{\substack{\text{Guilder/U.S. dollar} \\ \text{spot rate}} \times \substack{\text{Interest rate} \\ \text{differential}} \times \substack{\text{Number of} \\ \text{days}}}{360 \text{ days}}$$

$$= \frac{2.1070(-0.023)30}{360}$$

$$= -0.0040$$

$$\substack{\text{30-day} \\ \text{forward} \\ \text{guilder/} \\ \text{U.S. dollar} \\ \text{rate}} = \text{Spot rate} + (-0.0040)$$

$$= 2.1070 + (-0.0040)$$

$$= 2.1030$$

The currency in the higher-interest-rate environment sells in the forward market at a discount to the spot rate. The spot rate is Dfl2.1070/U.S. $1, and the 30-day forward rate is Dfl2.1030/U.S.$1. This implies that one dollar receives fewer guilders at the 30-day forward rate than at the spot rate. In other words, the U.S. dollar sells at a discount in the forward market to the spot rate, or the forward Dutch guilder rate trades at a premium to the spot rate.

The forward rate is quoted as the difference between the spot and forward rates. In this example, the forward rate might be quoted as 40/30. This indicates that 0.0040 is subtracted from the spot bid rate to derive the 30-day forward bid rate (i.e., 2.1070 - 0.0040 = 2.1030), and 0.0030 is subtracted from the spot offer rate to derive the 30-day forward offer rate. In the case of a forward rate quote of 20/30, 0.0020 is added to the spot bid rate, and 0.0030 is added to the spot offer rate. When the forward rate is quoted as larger/smaller, the ratio numerator and denominator are subtracted from the spot bid and offer rates, respectively. If the forward rate is quoted in the form smaller/larger, these values are added to the spot rates.

The rate of return on an investment of one U.S. dollar at the 30-day U.S. interest rate is equal to the return on investing one U.S. dollar's worth of Dutch guilders (i.e., purchase guilders with one dollar at the spot rate) at the 30-day Dutch interest rate and simultaneously selling the Dutch guilders forward for U.S. dollars (guaranteeing a Dutch guilder/U.S. dollar sale price) at the 30-day forward rate.

To illustrate, one U.S. dollar can be invested for 30 days at 8.9%. In 30 days, U.S.$1.0074 is received.

$$\text{Future U.S. dollar value} = 1 + \left(0.089 \times \frac{30}{360} \right)$$

$$= 1 + 0.0074$$

$$= 1.0074$$

One U.S. dollar can purchase 2.1070 Dutch guilders at the spot rate. The Dutch guilders can be invested for 30 days at 6.6%. In 30 days, Dfl2.1186 is received.

$$\text{Future Dutch guilder value} = 2.1070 \times \left(1 + 0.066 \times \frac{30}{360}\right)$$

$$= 2.1186$$

In 30 days, the Dfl2.1186 received must be translated into U.S. dollars at an uncertain rate. The simultaneous 30-day forward sale of Dutch guilders for U.S. dollars at 2.1030 eliminates the uncertainty. In 30 days, US$1.0074 is received.

$$\text{Future U.S. dollar value} = \frac{2.1070 \times (1 + 0.066 \times 30/360)}{2.1030}$$

$$= 1.0074$$

In theory, forward rates trade (through arbitrage forces) at levels where an investor would be indifferent to investing U.S. dollars at 30-day U.S. interest rates versus buying spot Dutch guilders, investing them at the 30-day Dutch rate, and simultaneously selling the guilders forward 30 days for dollars. The rate of return on domestic and covered foreign financial assets is equivalent.

FOREIGN CURRENCY MANAGEMENT

A U.S. dollar–based investor purchasing an international convertible is usually subject to foreign exchange risk. Currency exposure may be managed in several ways including the use of foreign exchange contracts.

In deciding whether or not to translate a position into another currency, it is important to analyze the issuer's transaction and economic exposure. It is likely that a U.S. dollar–based investor purchasing a company's sterling-denominated security may decide not to translate if the issuer's revenues and costs are generated in U.S. dollars. The currencies in which earnings are generated will affect the equity price. Transaction and economic currency exposure are more applicable in the long term. In the short term, currency contracts are often used to manage exposure.

The following sections analyze foreign currency management from a U.S. dollar perspective. For simplicity, assume that transaction and economic exposure will not affect the equity price. The purpose of the following exercise is to explain the use of foreign currency contracts.

A U.S. dollar–based investor purchases an international Euroconvertible bond denominated in the currency of the underlying equity (local currency). Payment must be made on settlement date using the local currency. The investor either:

1. Receives the bond in the foreign currency. The investor already owns foreign currency.
2. Receives the bonds in the foreign currency and enters into a foreign exchange contract to translate the trade into U.S. dollars.
3. Has the bonds delivered in U.S. dollars. The bond dealer effects the currency transaction on behalf of the investor.

Technically, it might be argued that all three scenarios are equivalent. In the first alternative, at some point the foreign currency must have been purchased by the U.S. dollar–based investor. For illustrative purposes, assume that, in the first alternative, the investor delivers the foreign currency to settle the trade; there is no foreign exchange contract. A foreign exchange contract is transacted in both the second and third alternatives. These trades are settled in the investor's currency.

T-accounts will be used for illustrative purposes. The transactions are entered as follows.

Debit	Credit
Long security	Short security
Short cash balance	Long cash balance

The U.S. dollar–based investor purchases 1,000M New Australia International 9% of 200X at 105 net. The bond is convertible into New Australia International ordinary shares and is denominated in Australian dollars. Assume there is no accrued interest.

Investor's Currency	Local Currency	Bond Currency
U.S. dollar	Australian dollar	Australian dollar

Alternative 1: Convertible received in Australian dollars. No foreign exchange contract transacted.

The investor purchasing 1,000M New Australia International 9% of 200X at 105 net does not enter into a foreign exchange contract. The trade is settled in Australian dollars. The transaction is represented as follows. The broker/customer account is included to illustrate offsetting entries.

Transaction a: Bought 1,000M New Australia International 9% of 200X at 105 net from a broker/customer. Total investment: A$1,050,000.

Australian Security

a. Long security A$1,050M	

Broker/Customer

	a. Short security A$1,050M

Australian dollars must be borrowed to settle the trade. In essence, the investor is short the Australian dollar to the seller of the bonds. The investor's assets (convertible bond) and liabilities (loan) are in Australian dollars.

Assume the price of the bond increases to 110 net. The investor decides to liquidate the convertible position.

Transaction b: Sold 1,000M New Australia International 9% of 200X at 110 net. Total proceeds: A$1,100,000.

Australian Security

a. Long security A$1,050M	b. Sold security A$1,100M

Profit: A$50M

Broker/Customer

b. Bought security A$1,100M	a. Short security A$1,050M

Loss: A$50M

A profit results in Australian dollar terms. For accounting purposes, the profit must be translated into the investor's currency. The resulting profit of A$50,000 is subject to U.S. dollar/Australian dollar exchange rate risk until the cash balance is translated into U.S. dollars. Notice that movements in the U.S. dollar/Australian dollar rate are not considered until the position is closed.

Alternative 2: Convertibles are translated into U.S. dollars. Foreign exchange contract transacted.

Assume the preceding trade must be translated into U.S. dollars on the settlement date. The trade is settled in U.S. dollars rather than Australian dollars. From a trading standpoint, the Australian security/dollar and U.S. dollar accounts are important. The broker/customer account illustrates only offsetting entries.

Transaction a: Bought 1,000M New Australia International 9% of 200X at 105 net from a broker/customer. Total investment: A$1,050,000.

Australian Security
Australian Dollar

a. Long security A$1,050M	

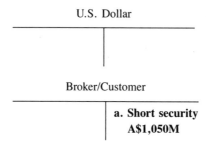

U.S. Dollar

Broker/Customer

a. Short security
A$1,050M

The trade is not complete. The U.S. dollar–based investor needs Australian dollars to settle the trade and enters into a foreign exchange contract to buy Australian dollars with U.S. dollars for settlement date. The Australian dollars are used to pay for the total investment (principal plus accrued interest). The current rate is U.S.$0.8000/A$1.

Transaction b: Bought A$1,050,000 worth of Australian dollars and sold U.S. dollars at 0.8000.

Australian Security
Australian Dollar

| a. Long security A$1,050M | b. **Long cash** **A$1,050M** |

U.S. Dollar

| b. **Short cash** **U.S.$840M*** | |

Broker/Customer

| | a. Short security A$1,050M |

*The U.S. dollar equivalent price of the Australian dollar–denominated bond is calculated as follows:

U.S. dollar equivalent = A$1,050,000 × U.S.$0.8000/A$1
= U.S.$840,000

In essence, the investor is long the Australian bond in U.S. dollar terms. The process is often referred to as "dollarizing" (U.S. dollar) the position.

Assume the price of the bond increases from 105 to 110 and the U.S. dollar/Australian dollar rate remains at 0.8000. Upon sale of the position, the investor will receive Australian dollars.

Transaction c: Sold 1,000M New Australia International 9% of 200X at 110 net. Total proceeds: A$1,100,000.

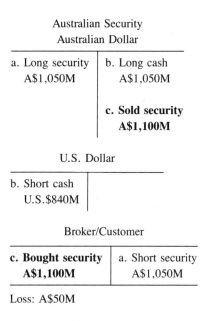

Australian Security
Australian Dollar

| a. Long security
A$1,050M | b. Long cash
A$1,050M |
| | **c. Sold security
A$1,100M** |

U.S. Dollar

| b. Short cash
U.S.$840M | |

Broker/Customer

| **c. Bought security
A$1,100M** | a. Short security
A$1,050M |

Loss: A$50M

The A$1,100,000 dollar proceeds must be translated back into the investor's base currency. The investor reverses the original foreign exchange contract by selling the Australian dollars for U.S. dollars at the current U.S. dollar/Australian dollar exchange rate.

Transaction d: Sold A$1,100,000 worth of Australian dollars and bought U.S. dollars at 0.8000.

Australian Security
Australian Dollar

a. Long security A$1,050M	b. Long cash A$1,050M
d. Sold cash A$1,100M	c. Sold security A$1,100M

–0–

U.S. Dollar

b. Short cash U.S.$840M	**d. Bought cash U.S.$880M**

Profit: U.S.$40M

Broker/Customer

c. Bought security A$1,100M	a. Short security A$1,050M

Loss: A$50M

The profit of U.S.$40,000 is reflected in the credit balance of the U.S. dollar account.

The need to translate the trade into U.S. dollars creates currency exposure. Technically, the U.S. dollar/Australian dollar rate risk arises daily when positions are priced (marked to market). Assuming positions are not marked daily, the U.S. dollar/Australian dollar rate risk arises upon the liquidation of the convertible position. At that time, the investor must sell the Australian dollar proceeds for U.S. dollars. The difference between the currency rate at the trade's origination and liquidation is realized.

Rather than wait for liquidation of the position to reverse the original foreign exchange contract (transaction d), the investor may simultaneously buy Australian dollars with U.S. dollars for settlement date and reverse the contract for a future date. To settle the trade, Australian dollars are purchased with U.S. dollars through a forward contract for settlement date. To reverse the contract, the Australian dollars are sold forward to guarantee a U.S. dollar/Australian dollar rate. Both contracts cover the principal plus accrued interest. Profits and additional accrued interest are not covered by the forward contracts. The investment time horizon must be estimated for the forward sale (e.g., two weeks, three months). Timing can be adjusted by rolling the contract backward or forward.

Inasmuch as the timing of liquidation is unknown, the contractual purchase (for settlement date) and forward sale of Australian dollars has the effect of limiting the U.S. dollar/Australian dollar risk and profit potential. The forward sale of the Australian dollar guarantees a certain U.S. dollar/Australian dollar rate for the ultimate translation of the Australian dollar proceeds (from the sale of the convertible) into U.S. dollars. Proceeds in excess of the original investment (principal plus accrued interest) are translated at the then-current U.S. dollar/Australian dollar rate.

The analysis becomes more complex when the U.S. dollar is not directly involved. The investor is then subject to cross-currency exposure. For example, if a sterling-based investor purchases the New Australia International 9% of 200X, there is Australian dollar/sterling cross-currency rate translation exposure. Profitability in sterling terms is a function of the U.S. dollar/sterling and U.S. dollar/Australian dollar rates. The demand and supply for these currencies affect the Australian dollar/sterling rate. Cross-currency exposure from the perspective of a non–U.S. dollar–based investor is briefly addressed later in this chapter. The mathematics are presented from a sterling-based investor's perspective.

In the cases discussed in this section, the currency remained constant. A fluctuation in the currency rate may offset any gain or loss in the Australian dollar bond price when it is translated into U.S. dollars. Fluctuations in foreign currencies are addressed in the following section.

FOREIGN CURRENCY EXPOSURE

Convertible securities denominated in foreign currencies and convertible into foreign shares usually have currency exposure. The currency exposure is a function of the investor's base currency, the local currency, and the bond currency. The risk is either translation exposure or exposure through the mathematics of conversion value. The bonds are exposed to transaction and economic currency exposure as they are reflected in the underlying equity price.

Currency exposure will now be investigated under various assumptions. In each case, in order to isolate the effect of currency fluctuations on the convertible, it is assumed that only the currency relationship changes. Once again, for simplicity, do not consider the possibility of transaction or economic currency exposure. The analysis is from a U.S. dollar perspective.

	Investor's Currency	Local Currency	Bond Currency
Case 1	x	y	y
Case 2	x	y	x
Case 3	x	x	y
Case 4	x	y	z

Case 1: Convertible Bonds Denominated in Local Currency, but Different from Investor's Currency

	Investor's Currency	Local Currency	Bond Currency
Case 1	U.S. dollar	French franc	French franc

A U.S. dollar–based investor purchases the France S.A. 6% of 200X at 98 net. The convertibles are denominated in French francs.

The investor must ultimately translate the transaction into the investor's currency. The currency exposure is through the translation from French francs to U.S. dollars. The investor may or may not enter into foreign currency contracts (see the preceding section). The profitability of the convertible position in U.S. dollar terms is affected by currency fluctuations.

The translation exposure can be exhibited through T-account entries. In order to isolate the effect of the currency movement, assume that only the currency relationship changes, all else remaining constant.

Since the bond price remains constant, the purchase and sale of the convertible at FF98 net will not result in a trading gain or loss. Profits/losses will be the result of currency fluctuations. The currency exposure is through the translation of the trade into U.S. dollars. To show the translation exposure, assume the investor enters into foreign currency contracts. There is no accrued interest.

U.S. Dollar Appreciates

Transaction a: Bought 1,000M France S.A. 6% of 200X at 98 net. Total investment: FF980,000.

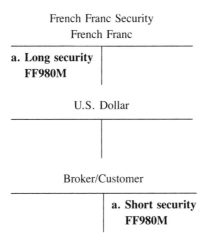

The U.S. dollar–based investor enters into a contract to buy French francs with U.S. dollars for settlement date. The current rate is FF6.3000/ U.S.$1. The French francs are used to pay for the total investment. The contract covers the principal and accrued interest. The transaction is entered in the accounts as cash entries.

Transaction b: Bought FF980,000 worth of French francs and sold U.S. dollars at 6.3000.

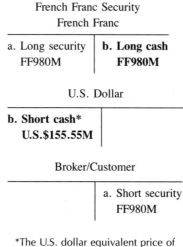

French Franc Security
French Franc

a. Long security FF980M	**b. Long cash FF980M**

U.S. Dollar

b. Short cash* U.S.\$155.55M	

Broker/Customer

	a. Short security FF980M

*The U.S. dollar equivalent price of the French franc–denominated bond is calculated as follows:

$$\text{U.S. dollar equivalent} = \frac{FF980}{FF6.3000/\text{U.S.\$1}}$$
$$= \text{U.S.\$155.55}$$

In essence, the investor owns the French franc–denominated convertible in U.S. dollar terms.

The investor decides to liquidate the position. Assume the bond price has not changed, but the U.S. dollar has appreciated against the French franc from FF6.3000/U.S.\$1 to FF7.000/U.S.\$1.

Transaction c: Sold 1,000M France S.A. 6% of 200X at 98 net. Total proceeds: FF980,000.

French Franc Security
French Franc

a. Long security FF980M	b. Long cash FF980M
	c. Sold security FF980M

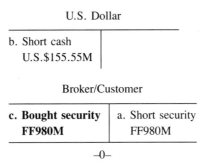

U.S. Dollar

b. Short cash U.S.$155.55M	

Broker/Customer

c. **Bought security** **FF980M**	a. Short security FF980M

–0–

The French franc proceeds are sold for U.S. dollars at FF7.000/U.S.$1. The original foreign exchange contract is reversed.

Transaction d: Sold FF980,000 worth of French francs and bought U.S. dollars at 7.000.

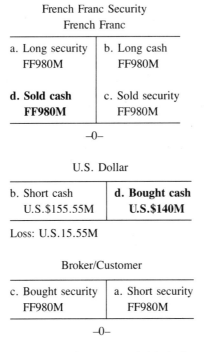

French Franc Security
French Franc

a. Long security FF980M	b. Long cash FF980M
d. **Sold cash** **FF980M**	c. Sold security FF980M

–0–

U.S. Dollar

b. Short cash U.S.$155.55M	d. **Bought cash** **U.S.$140M**

Loss: U.S.15.55M

Broker/Customer

c. Bought security FF980M	a. Short security FF980M

–0–

A loss of U.S.$15.55M is realized as a debit balance in the U.S. dollar account. Ceteris paribus, an appreciation of the U.S. dollar versus the French franc (a relative depreciation of the French franc) will decrease the price of the bond in U.S. dollar terms. The fluctuation from FF6.3000/U.S.$1 to FF7.000/U.S.$1 indicates that it takes more French francs to purchase one U.S. dollar today than it did when the position was assumed. Upon sale of the bond, the investor receives fewer U.S. dollars per one French franc.

French Franc/U.S. Dollar rate	U.S. Dollars received per 1 French Franc
6.3000	0.1587*
7.0000	0.1428

*1 ÷ 6.3000

U.S. Dollar Depreciates. Assume that, upon liquidation, the U.S. dollar has depreciated against the French franc rather than appreciated. The rate has gone from FF6.3000/U.S.$1 to FF5.6000/U.S.$1. The preceding transaction would be as follows.

Transaction d: Sold FF980,000 worth of French francs and bought U.S. dollars at 5.6000.

French Franc Security
French Franc

a. Long security FF980M	b. Long cash FF980M
d. Sold cash **FF980M**	c. Sold security FF980M

–0–

U.S. Dollar

b. Short cash U.S.$155.55M	**d. Bought cash** **U.S.$175M**

Profit: U.S.$19.45M

Broker/Customer

c. Bought security	a. Short security
FF980M	FF980M

–0–

A profit of U.S.$19.45M is realized as a credit balance in the U.S. dollar account. A depreciation of the U.S. dollar versus the French franc (a relative appreciation of the French franc) results in an increase in the price of the bond in U.S. dollar terms. A move from FF6.3000/U.S.$1 to FF5.6000/U.S.$1 means that it takes fewer French francs to purchase one U.S. dollar. Upon sale of the bonds, the investor receives more U.S. dollars per one French franc.

U.S. Dollar versus Foreign Currency	U.S. Dollar Equivalent Security Price
U.S. dollar depreciates/ Foreign currency appreciates	Increase
U.S. dollar appreciates/ Foreign currency depreciates	Decrease

Currency and Convertible Price Fluctuations

The preceding analysis assumed there was no change in the convertible price. Simultaneous movements in the convertible price and the French franc/U.S. dollar rate will affect the profitability of the position in U.S. dollar terms. From a U.S. dollar perspective, an increase in the convertible price coupled with a depreciation in the U.S. dollar against the French franc will increase the dollar-denominated security with a multiplier effect. It is possible to incur a loss in the French franc–denominated bond and have a gain in U.S. dollar terms because of the movement of the currency. The relative percentage movements in the bond price compared with the percentage move of the U.S. dollar versus the French franc will determine the profitability of the convertible. The following scenarios will clarify the relationship between profitability and fluctuations in convertible prices and currencies.

Assume that one of the scenarios reviewed in Figure 13.2 exists. The analysis is from a U.S. dollar investor's perspective. Remember that an appreciation of the U.S. dollar versus the foreign currency results in a decrease in the bond price in U.S. dollar terms.

Scenarios 3–6 assume a 15% increase in the French franc bond price. Scenario 3 indicates that it is possible to have an initial gain in the French franc–denominated bond and have a loss in U.S. dollar terms because of the movement of the currency. The 19% appreciation of the U.S. dollar versus the French franc offset the 15% increase in the French franc bond price. The percent change in the bond price relative to the percent change in the currency relationship determines the extent of the gain/loss in U.S. dollar terms.

In scenario 4, the 15% increase in the French franc bond price was not totally offset by the 11.1% appreciation of the U.S. dollar. In U.S. dollar terms, the appreciation of the U.S. dollar versus the French franc reduced the French franc bond's total increase.

Scenario	French Franc Bond Price	Bond Percent Change	French Franc/ U.S. Dollar Rate	French Franc/ U.S. Dollar Percent Change	Bond Price, U.S. Dollar Equivalent	Bond Percent Change
Original	980	—	6.3000	—	155.55	—
1	980	0	7.0000	+11.1*	140.00	−10.0
2	980	0	5.6000	−11.1	175.00	+12.5
3	1,127	+15.0	7.5000	+19.0	150.27	−3.4
4	1,127	+15.0	7.0000	+11.1	161.00	+3.5
5	1,127	+15.0	5.6000	−11.1	201.25	+29.4
6	1,127	+15.0	5.1000	−19.0	220.98	+42.0
7	833	−15.0	7.5000	+19.0	111.07	−28.6
8	833	−15.0	7.0000	+11.1	119.00	−23.5
9	833	−15.0	5.6000	−11.1	148.75	−4.4
10	833	−15.0	5.1000	−19.0	163.33	+5.0

*Appreciation of the U.S. dollar versus the French franc.

Figure 13.2   Changes in convertible price and currency.

Scenarios 5 and 6 are examples of the multiplier effect. In both in-stances, an increase in the bond price coupled with a depreciation of the U.S. dollar versus the French franc resulted in an increase in the bond price in U.S. dollar terms with a multiplier effect.

In scenarios 7–10 the French franc bond price decreases by 15%. Scenarios 7 and 8 represent the negative multiplier effect. A decline in the French franc bond price coupled with an appreciation of the U.S. dollar versus the French franc results in a decrease in the bond price in U.S, dollar terms with a multiplier effect. Scenario 9 shows that an 11% depreciation of the U.S. dollar versus the French franc combined with a 15% decline in the bond price reduces the ultimate loss in U.S. dollar terms. Scenario 10 represents the converse to scenario 3. A decrease in the French franc–denominated bond can result in a gain in U.S. dollar terms due to currency movements. A 19% depreciation of the U.S. dollar has more than offset the loss in the French franc bond price.

A U.S. dollar–based investor purchasing a bond denominated in its local currency is always subject to equity risk. The translation from the foreign currency proceeds into the investor's currency exposes the bond to fluctuations in the currency. An appreciation of the foreign currency relative to the U.S. dollar increases the bond price in U.S. dollar terms. Profit/loss in the bond price in local currency terms can be offset by fluctuations in the U.S. dollar/local currency exchange rate.

Case 2: Convertible Bonds Denominated in the Currency of the Investor but Different from the Local Currency

	Investor's Currency	Local Currency	Bond Currency
Case 2	U.S. dollar	Peseta	U.S. dollar

A U.S. dollar–based investor purchases the Spain S.A. 4% of 200X. The convertibles are denominated in U.S. dollars. Principal and ac-crued interest are paid in U.S. dollars. Investors restricted to U.S. dollar investments may participate in the appreciation of foreign equities and markets through international convertibles denominated in U.S. dollars. The bond is usually convertible into the registered shares and will be affected by the local currency.

Currency Exposure through Conversion Value

A U.S. dollar–based investor purchasing the bonds will be subject to equity risk. There is no translation exposure because the bonds are denominated in the investor's currency. The convertible is implicitly exposed to peseta/U.S. dollar risk. The exposure is expressed through the mathematics of conversion value.

The ordinary price in U.S. dollar terms (i.e., equivalent equity price) is needed to compute conversion value. A U.S. dollar bond price can only be evaluated with respect to a U.S. dollar conversion value. The current exchange rate is used to express the ordinary share price in terms of the bond's currency.

Spain S.A. 4%   July 27, 200X

Effective conversion price:	Pta 1,130.0
Fixed peseta/U.S. dollar rate:	121.4153
Equivalent conversion price:	U.S.$9.3069
Convertible bond price:	U.S.$1,060
Equity price:	Pta970
Current peseta/U.S. dollar rate:	130.0000

$$\text{Equivalent equity price} = \frac{\text{Current equity price}}{\text{Current Pta/U.S.\$ rate}}$$

$$= \frac{\text{Pta970}}{\text{Pta130/U.S.\$1}}$$

$$= \text{U.S.\$7.460}$$

$$\text{Conversion value} = \frac{\text{Equivalent equity price}}{\text{Equivalent conversion price}} \times 100$$

$$= \frac{\text{Current equity price} \div \left(\begin{array}{c} \text{Current} \\ \text{Pta/U.S.\$ rate} \end{array} \right)}{\text{Effective conversion price} \div \left(\begin{array}{c} \text{Fixed} \\ \text{Pta/U.S.\$ rate} \end{array} \right)} \times 100$$

$$= \frac{\text{Pta}970 \div (\text{Pta}130/\text{U.S.}\$1)}{\text{Pta}1,130 \div (\text{Pta}121.4153/\text{U.S.}\$1)} \times 100$$

$$= \frac{\text{U.S.}\$7.460}{\text{U.S.}\$9.3069} \times 100$$

$$= 80.16$$

$$\text{Premium} = \text{Bond price} - \text{Conversion value}$$

$$= \text{U.S.}\$1,060 - \text{U.S.}\$801.60$$

$$= \text{U.S.}\$258.40$$

Transaction a: Bought 1,000M Spain S.A. 4% of 200X at 106 net. Total investment: U.S.$1,060,000.

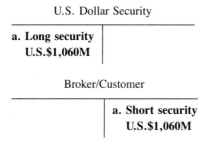

U.S. Dollar Security

a. Long security U.S.$1,060M	

Broker/Customer

	a. Short security U.S.$1,060M

Assume that only the currency value changes: the U.S. dollar depreciates versus the peseta from 130.0000 to 124.0000. Ceteris paribus, a depreciation of the U.S. dollar versus the peseta (or a strengthening of the peseta) increases the equivalent equity price. A higher equivalent equity price results in a higher conversion value.

Original peseta/U.S. dollar rate: 130.0000

Current peseta/U.S. dollar rate: 124.0000

Convertible bond price: U.S.$1060

Equity price: Pta970

Original equivalent equity price: U.S.$7.46

$$\text{Conversion value} = \frac{\text{Current equity price} \div \left(\begin{array}{c} \text{Current} \\ \text{Pta/U.S.\$ rate} \end{array} \right)}{\text{Equivalent conversion price}} \times 100$$

$$= \frac{\text{Pta970} \div (\text{Pta124/U.S.\$1})}{\text{Pta1,130} \div (\text{Pta121.4153/U.S.\$1})} \times 100$$

$$= \frac{\text{U.S.\$7.822}}{\text{U.S.\$9.3069}} \times 100$$

$$= 84.04$$

Conversion value went from 80.16 to 84.04 solely on the basis of the currency movement. Theoretically, premium levels change for a given move in conversion value (see Chapter 8). In order to isolate the currency exposure, assume a constant premium of 25.84 points. The total increase in the bond price is a function of both the conversion value and the premium.

$$\begin{aligned} \text{Convertible bond price} &= \text{Conversion value} + \text{Premium} \\ &= \text{U.S.\$840.40} + \text{U.S.\$258.40} \\ &= \text{U.S.\$1,098.80} \end{aligned}$$

Since the premium remained constant, the increase in conversion value caused the increase in the bond price. The increase in the bond price from U.S.$1,060 to U.S.$1,098.80 was caused by the depreciation of the U.S. dollar versus the peseta. A change in the currency affected conversion value, as would fluctuations in the equity price.

The investor sells the convertibles at U.S.$1,098.80.

Transaction b: Sold 1,000M Spain S.A. 4% of 200X at 109.88 net. Total proceeds: U.S.$1,098,800.

U.S. Dollar Security

a. Long security	**b. Sold security**
U.S.$1,060M	**U.S.$1,098.80M**

Profit: U.S.$38.8M

Broker/Customer

b. Bought security	a. Short security
U.S.$1,098.8M	U.S.$1,060M

Loss: U.S.$38.8M

A depreciation of the U.S. dollar versus the peseta resulted in a profit of U.S.$38.8M. The investor benefits from the relative strengthening of the peseta through the mathematics of conversion value. A depreciation of the bond currency relative to the local currency increased conversion value. U.S. dollar–based investors favorable toward the peseta can benefit from its appreciation through a Spanish issuer's U.S. dollar–denominated convertible.

The Effect of Currency Fluctuations on Premium

Another approach to analyzing the effect of currency fluctuations on a convertible is watching the effect the currency movement has on the premium. To isolate the effect of the currency on the premium, assume a constant bond price rather than a constant premium. Ceteris paribus, a change in the currency affects the level of the premium.

Spain S.A. 4% July 27, 200X

Effective conversion price:	Pta 1,130.0
Fixed peseta/U.S. dollar rate:	121.4153
Equivalent conversion price:	U.S.$9.3069
Convertible bond price:	U.S.$1,060
Equity price:	Pta970
Original peseta/U.S. dollar rate:	130.0000
Conversion value:	U.S.$801.60

$$\frac{\text{Premium}}{\text{(Percent method)}} = \frac{\text{Bond price} - \text{Conversion value}}{\text{Conversion value}} \times 100$$

$$= \frac{\text{U.S.\$1,060} - \text{U.S.\$801.60}}{\text{U.S.\$801.60}} \times 100$$

$$= 32.23\%$$

The U.S. dollar depreciates versus the peseta from 130.0000 to 124.0000. As previously calculated, conversion value increases to U.S.\$840.40. Assuming a constant bond price of U.S.\$1,060, the premium over conversion value changes.

$$\frac{\text{Premium}}{\text{(Percent method)}} = \frac{\text{Bond price} - \text{Conversion value}}{\text{Conversion value}} \times 100$$

$$= \frac{\text{U.S.\$1,060} - \text{U.S.\$840.40}}{\text{U.S.\$840.40}} \times 100$$

$$= 26.13\%$$

The appreciation of the peseta versus the U.S. dollar from Pta130/U.S.\$1 to Pta124/U.S.\$1 is reflected in the bond through the increase in conversion value from U.S.\$801.60 to U.S.\$840.40. To isolate the currency effect, it has been assumed that there was no change in the bond price. A constant bond price and increasing conversion value decreases the conversion premium from 32.23% to 26.13%.

The relationship of the current exchange rate to the fixed exchange rate is important. A stronger foreign currency (or a weaker U.S. dollar) has the effect of decreasing premiums. The bondholder benefits from an appreciation of the peseta through a higher conversion value and a lower premium. There is an unrealized currency benefit.

Likewise, a depreciation of the peseta versus the U.S. dollar results in a decrease in conversion value. A depreciation of the local currency relative to the bond currency decreases conversion value. Assuming a constant bond price, the conversion premium increases. Ceteris paribus, the bondholder is adversely affected by a weaker local currency.

The results of case 2 provide an interesting observation.

	Original Value	Future Value	Percent Change
Peseta/U.S. dollar rate	130.0000	124.0000	−4.8*
Conversion value	80.16	84.04	+4.6

*Peseta appreciated/U.S. dollar depreciated.

Since the Spain S.A. 4% of 200X are denominated in U.S. dollars, it would seem that a U.S. dollar–based investor purchasing the bonds would be exposed only to equity risk. This is not the case. Assuming no change in the equity price, it has been proven that conversion value will move with fluctuations in the bond currency relative to the local currency.

Conversion Value as a Function of Currencies and Equity Prices

Conversion value in U.S. dollar terms increases with a depreciation of the U.S. dollar versus the peseta, or in other words, conversion value increases with an appreciation of the peseta. If a constant premium level is assumed, the convertible price increases with an appreciation of the local currency versus the bond currency.

Conversion value is a function of the equity price and currency. The graph of conversion value (see Chapter 3) plots conversion value relative to the equity price and conversion ratio.

$$\text{Conversion value} = \text{Equity price} \times \text{Conversion ratio}$$

In the case of a convertible not denominated in the local currency, the graph becomes three-dimensional. It is plotted versus the equity price, currency rate, and conversion ratio (Figure 13.3). The three-dimensional graph can be described with the graphs in Figure 13.4. A constant equity price and an appreciating dollar have the effect of decreasing conversion value. A constant currency combined with an increasing equity price increases conversion value.

A fluctuation in either the equity price or the currency rate will affect conversion value. The total expected return of a convertible not denomi-

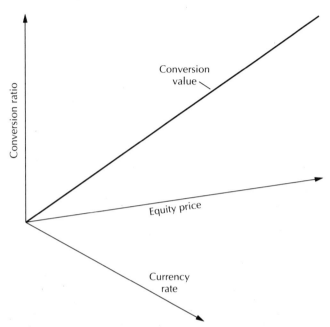

Figure 13.3 Conversion value as a function of conversion ratio, equity price, and currency.

nated in the local currency is a function of the equity price, interest rates, and currencies. The convertible is an equity, debt, and currency vehicle. A convertible's premium should also reflect the value of the potential participation in local currency appreciation.

The effect foreign currency fluctuations have on the total return of a convertible not denominated in the local currency is a function of the level of the equity price. As previously stated, foreign currency movements are reflected directly through conversion value.

$$\text{Conversion value} = \frac{\text{Equivalent equity price}}{\text{Equivalent conversion price}} \times 100$$

In the case of the Spain S.A. 4% of 200X, the peseta/U.S. dollar relationship affects conversion value.

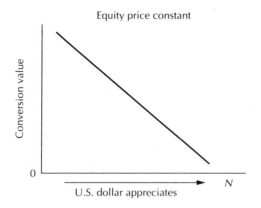

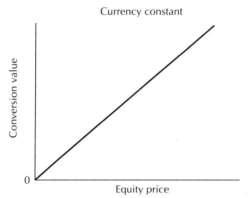

Figure 13.4 Factors affecting conversion value.

$$\text{Conversion value} = \frac{\begin{array}{c}\text{Current equity} \\ \text{price}\end{array} \div \left(\begin{array}{c}\text{Current} \\ \text{peseta/U.S.dollar rate}\end{array}\right)}{\text{Equivalent conversion price}} \times 100$$

As the equity price increases, the convertible increasingly trades with the equity component (see Chapter 8). An increase in the equity price increases the effect of currency fluctuations on conversion value. At higher equity levels, conversion value is more sensitive to movements in currency rates. In this case, the convertible generally trades at a low premium over conversion value and is more sensitive to fluctuations in the equity price and currency.

Case 3: Convertible Bonds Denominated in a Currency Other than the Investor's and Local Currency (Investor's Currency Same as the Local Currency)

	Investor's Currency	Local Currency	Bond Currency
Case 3	U.S. dollar	U.S. dollar	Sterling

A U.S. dollar–based investor purchases 1,000M America Co. 5.75% of 200X at 101 net. The bonds are denominated in pound sterling.

The evaluation of currency exposure is a two-step process. As in case 2, the convertible is subject to risk through the mathematics of conversion value. As in case 1, there is translation exposure when the bond is expressed in the investor's currency.

Currency Exposure through Conversion Value

First the convertible's exposure through conversion value will be examined. Assume that the sterling proceeds are not translated into U.S. dollars. There is no accrued interest.

America Co. 5.75% Dec. 5, 200X

Effective conversion price:	U.S.$20.00
Fixed U.S. dollar/sterling rate:	1.6500
Equivalent conversion price:	£12.12
Convertible bond price:	£1,010
Equity price:	U.S.$18.00
Current U.S.dollar sterling rate:	1.7000

$$\text{Conversion value} = \frac{\text{Equivalent equity price}}{\text{Equivalent conversion price}} \times 100$$

$$= \frac{\text{Current equity price} \div \left(\begin{array}{c} \text{Current} \\ \text{U.S.\$/£ rate} \end{array} \right)}{\text{Equivalent conversion price}} \times 100$$

$$= \frac{\text{U.S.\$18.00} \div (\text{U.S.\$1.7000/£1})}{£12.12} \times 100$$

$$= 87.36$$

$$\text{Premium} = \text{Bond price} - \text{Conversion value}$$

$$= £1,010 - £873.60$$

$$= £136.40$$

Transaction a: Bought 1,000M America Co. 5.75% of 200X at 101 net. Total investment: £1,010,000.

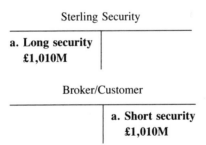

Sterling Security

a. Long security £1,010M	

Broker/Customer

	a. Short security £1,010M

Ceteris paribus, assume the U.S. dollar appreciates versus the sterling from U.S.\$1.7000/£1 to U.S.\$1.5000/£1. Conversion value must be calculated with the new U.S. dollar/sterling rate.

$$\text{Conversion value} = \frac{\text{U.S.\$18.00} \div (\text{U.S.\$1.5000/£1})}{£12.12} \times 100$$

$$= \frac{£12.00}{£12.12} \times 100$$

$$= 99$$

In this example, the premium is held constant at 13.64 points to isolate the effects of currency movements.

$$\text{Convertible bond price} = £990 + £136.40$$
$$= £1,126.40$$

The increase in the convertible price from £1,010 to £1,126.40 was caused by the fluctuation in the U.S. dollar/sterling rate. The effect of currency fluctuations on conversion value is a function of the equity price. The currency effect increases as the relative level of the equity increases. Convertibles trading closer to investment value are less sensitive to currency movements.

The investor sells the bond at £1,126.40 net.

Transaction b: Sold 1,000M America Co. 5.75% of 200X at 112.64 net. Total proceeds: £1,126,400.

Sterling Security

a. Long security	b. Sold security
£1,010M	£1,126.4M

Profit: £116.4M

Broker/Customer

b. Bought security	a. Short security
£1,126.4M	£1,010M

Loss: £116.4M

Appreciation of the U.S. dollar versus the sterling resulted in a profit of £116,400. The timing as to when the sterling proceeds are translated into U.S. dollars will determine the extent of the profit in U.S. dollar terms. Until the proceeds are translated, the investor is exposed to fluctuations in the U.S. dollar/sterling rate.

The appreciation of the U.S. dollar versus the sterling (or a depreciation of the sterling versus the U.S. dollar) increased the conversion value in sterling terms. Depreciation of the bond currency relative to the local currency increased conversion value. As in case 2, a movement in the currency alone affected conversion value. U.S. dollar–based investors favorable toward the U.S. dollar relative to the sterling can participate in the dollar's appreciation through a U.S. issuer's convertible denominated in sterling.

Currency Exposure through Translation

Assume the sterling-denominated America Co. 5.75% of 200X bonds must be translated into U.S. dollars. The second step of the currency evaluation is the translation from the bond's currency to the investor's currency (see case 1). Fluctuations in the U.S. dollar/sterling rate affect the results in U.S. dollar terms. Assume there is no accrued interest.

America Co. 5.75% Dec. 5, 200X

Convertible bond price:	£101
Equity price:	U.S.$18.00
U.S. dollar/sterling rate:	1.7000

Transaction a: Bought 1,000M America Co. 5.75% of 200X at 101 net. Total investment: £1,010,000.

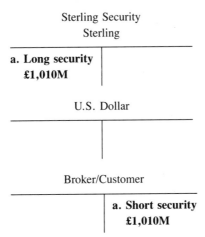

Sterling Security
Sterling

a. **Long security**
£1,010M

U.S. Dollar

Broker/Customer

a. **Short security**
£1,010M

The U.S. dollar–based investor buys sterling with U.S. dollars at U.S.$1.7000/£1 to settle the trade.

Transaction b: Bought £1,010,000 worth of sterling and sold U.S. dollars at U.S.$1.7000/£1.

Sterling Security
Sterling

a. Long security	**b. Long cash**
£1,010M	**£1,010M**

U.S. Dollar

b. Short cash	
U.S.$1,717M	

Broker/Customer

	a. Short security
	£1,010M

The convertibles have been translated into U.S. dollars.

As previously stated, only the U.S. dollar/sterling rate has changed. The U.S. dollar has appreciated versus the sterling from 1.7000 to 1.5000. A bond price of £1,126.40 was calculated with the new rate of U.S.$1.5000/£1. The investor decides to sell the convertible.

Transaction c: Sold 1,000M America Co. 5.75% of 200X at 112.64 net. Total proceeds: £1,126,400.

Sterling Security
Sterling

a. Long security	b. Long cash
£1,010M	£1,010M
	c. Sold security
	£1,126.4M

U.S. Dollar

b. Short cash U.S.$1,717M	

Broker/Customer

c. Bought security £1,126.4M	a. Short security £1,010M

Loss: £116.4M

To translate the trade into dollars, the sterling proceeds are sold for U.S. dollars at U.S.$1.5000/£1. The original foreign exchange contract is reversed.

Transaction d: Sold £1,126,400 worth of sterling and bought U.S. dollars at U.S.$1.5000/£1.

Sterling Security
Sterling

a. Long security £1,010M	b. Long cash £1,010M
d. Sold cash £1,126.4M	c. Sold security £1,126.4M

–0–

U.S. Dollar

b. Short cash U.S.$1,717M	**d. Bought cash U.S.$1,689.6M**

Loss: U.S.$27.4M

Broker/Customer

c. Bought security £1,126.4M	a. Short security £1,010M

Loss: £116.4M

A loss of U.S.$27.4M is realized in the U.S. dollar account. Since the trade is translated into U.S. dollars, the loss is reflected in the U.S. dollar account and not in the security account.

An appreciation of the U.S. dollar versus the sterling had the initial impact of increasing conversion value in sterling terms. An appreciation of the local currency versus the bond currency increased the convertible price in terms of the bond currency. The translation of the sterling proceeds into U.S. dollars resulted in an ultimate loss in U.S. dollar terms. Similarly, a depreciation of the U.S. dollar versus the sterling would result in a gain in U.S. dollar terms.

	Original Value	Subsequent Value	Percent Change	Results
U.S. dollar/ sterling	1.7000	1.5000	11.76	U.S. dollar appreciated vs. sterling, or sterling depreciated vs. U.S. dollar
Conversion value (sterling)	87.36	99.00	+13.32	Conversion value increased in sterling terms
Bond price (sterling)	101.00	112.64	+11.52	Bond price increased in sterling terms
Bond price (U.S. dollars)	1,717	1,689.6	−1.6	Bond price decreased in U.S. dollar terms

It is possible that the investor could have reduced the U.S.$27.4M loss by postponing the reversal of the foreign exchange contract. An opinion as to the direction of the U.S. dollar versus the sterling is required. A miscalculation as to the direction of the currency can result in a greater loss.

Case 4: Convertible Bond Denominated in a Currency Different from Both the Local Currency and Investor's Currency

	Investor's Currency	Local Currency	Bond Currency
Case 4	U.S. dollar	Australian dollar	Sterling

A U.S. dollar–based investor purchases the Australia Co. 6% of 200X at 104 net. The bonds are denominated in sterling, and the ordinary shares trade in Australian dollars. It is important to remember that this analysis is from a U.S. dollar perspective. There are three currencies involved, and their interrelationships impact the total return.

As in case 1, assume the U.S. dollar–based investor must translate the trade into U.S. dollars. The position is thus exposed to U.S. dollar/sterling translation exposure.

As in case 2, currency exposure is implicit in the calculation of conversion value. The currency fluctuation affecting conversion value is the Australian dollar (the local currency) versus the sterling (the bond currency).

$$\text{Conversion value} = \frac{\text{Equivalent equity price}}{\text{Equivalent conversion price}} \times 100$$

$$= \frac{\text{Current equity price} \div \left(\text{Current A\$/£ rate}\right)}{\text{Equivalent conversion price}} \times 100$$

Cross-Currency Relationship

The Australian dollar/sterling rate is a cross-currency relationship. Cross currencies are determined based on the U.S. dollar currency market. The Australian dollar/sterling rate is derived from the U.S. dollar/sterling rate and the U.S. dollar/Australian dollar rate. A movement in one currency relationship will affect the other two relationships. At any point in time, the knowledge of two of the currency values allows for the derivation of the third value.

$$\text{A\$/£} = \frac{\text{U.S.\$/£}}{\text{U.S.\$/A\$}}$$

$$\text{U.S.\$/£} = (\text{A\$/£}) \times (\text{U.S.\$/A\$})$$

$$\text{U.S.\$/A\$} = \frac{\text{U.S.\$/£}}{\text{A\$/£}}$$

A constant U.S. dollar/sterling rate and a depreciating U.S. dollar versus the Australian dollar will decrease the value of the Australian dollar/sterling rate. A decrease in the value of the Australian dollar/sterling rate indicates that fewer Australian dollars are received per one sterling. In other words, the sterling has depreciated versus the Australian dollar.

For example, say the U.S. dollar/sterling rate is 1.7340, and the U.S. dollar/Australian dollar rate is 0.8121. The Australian dollar/sterling rate is 2.1352.

$$A\$/\pounds = \frac{U.S.\$/\pounds}{U.S.\$/A\$}$$

$$= \frac{1.7340}{0.8121}$$

$$= 2.1352$$

Assume the U.S. dollar/sterling rate is 1.7340, and the U.S. dollar depreciates versus the Australian dollar from 0.8121 to 0.8500. The resulting Australian dollar/sterling rate is 2.0400.

$$A\$/\pounds = \frac{1.7340}{0.8500}$$

$$= 2.0400$$

The Australian dollar has appreciated versus the sterling from 2.1352 to 2.0400. Fewer Australian dollars are received per one sterling. Similarly, an appreciation of the U.S. dollar relative to the Australian dollar and a constant U.S. dollar/sterling rate will result in a depreciation of the Australian dollar versus the sterling.

A constant U.S. dollar/Australian dollar rate of 0.8121 and a depreciation of the U.S. dollar versus the sterling from 1.7340 to 1.8500 will increase the value of the Australian dollar/sterling rate. The sterling appreciates versus the Australian dollar. The opposite is true for an appreciation of the U.S. dollar versus the sterling and a constant U.S. dollar/Australian dollar rate.

Cross-Currency Effect on Conversion Value

The calculation for conversion value in this case uses the Australian dollar/sterling rate; a fluctuation in this rate affects conversion value. Movements in either the U.S. dollar/Australian dollar rate or the U.S. dollar/sterling rate alter the Australian dollar/sterling rate and thus affect conversion value.

In the following scenarios, assume that only one variable changes and everything else remains constant. The analysis is from a U.S. dollar perspective.

	Fluctuating Currency	Constant Currency	Translation to U.S. dollar
Scenario 1	U.S. dollar/sterling	U.S. dollar/ Australian dollar	No
Scenario 2	U.S. dollar/sterling	U.S. dollar/ Australian dollar	Yes
Scenario 3	U.S. dollar/ Australian dollar	U.S. dollar/sterling	No
Scenario 4	U.S. dollar/ Australian dollar	U.S. dollar/sterling	Yes

The purpose of the exercise is to isolate the effect of currency fluctuations on conversion value, on bond price, and, ultimately, on total profitability in U.S. dollar terms. Assume there is no accrued interest.

	Fluctuating Currency	Constant Currency	Translation to U.S. dollar
Scenario 1	U.S. dollar/sterling	U.S. dollar/Australian dollar	No

Australia Co. 6% July 9, 200X

Effective conversion price:	A$2.89
Fixed Australian dollar/sterling rate:	2.2420
Equivalent conversion price:	£1.2890

Current market data:

Convertible bond price:	£1,040
Equity price:	A$2.50
Australian dollar/sterling rate:	2.1350
U.S. dollar/Australian dollar rate:	0.8121
U.S. dollar/sterling rate:	1.7340

$$\text{Conversion value} = \frac{\text{Equivalent equity price}}{\text{Equivalent conversion price}} \times 100$$

$$= \frac{\dfrac{\text{Current}}{\text{equity price}} \div \left(\dfrac{\text{Current}}{\text{A\$/£ rate}} \right)}{\text{Equivalent conversion price}} \times 100$$

$$= \frac{\text{A\$2.50} \div (\text{A\$2.1350/£1})}{£1.2890} \times 100$$

$$= 90.84$$

$$\text{Premium} = \text{Bond price} - \text{Conversion value}$$
$$= £1,040 - £908.40$$
$$= £131.60$$

Transaction a: Bought 1,000M Australia Co. 6% of 200X at 104 net. Total investment: £1,040,000.

Sterling Security

a. Long security **£1,040M**	

Broker/Customer

	a. Short security **£1,040M**

Ceteris paribus, assume the U.S. dollar depreciates versus the sterling from 1.7340 to 1.8500. The new U.S. dollar/sterling rate and the U.S.

dollar/Australian dollar rate of 0.8121 imply an Australian dollar/sterling rate of 2.2780. The sterling has appreciated versus the Australian dollar from 2.1350 to 2.2780. More Australian dollars are received per one sterling.

$$A\$/\pounds = \frac{1.8500}{0.8121}$$

$$= 2.2780$$

Conversion value must be recalculated with the new Australian dollar/sterling rate.

Equity price:	A$2.50
Australian dollar/sterling rate:	2.2780
U.S. dollar/Australian dollar rate:	0.8121
U.S. dollar/sterling rate:	1.8500

$$\text{Conversion value} = \frac{\text{Equivalent equity price}}{\text{Equivalent conversion price}} \times 100$$

$$= \frac{\begin{array}{c}\text{Current} \\ \text{equity price}\end{array} \div \left(\begin{array}{c}\text{Current} \\ \text{A\$/\pounds rate}\end{array}\right)}{\text{Equivalent conversion price}} \times 100$$

$$= \frac{A\$2.50 \div (A\$2.2780/\pounds 1)}{\pounds 1.2890} \times 100$$

$$= 85.14$$

Conversion value decreased from £908.40 to £851.40. To calculate the bond price, the premium is held constant at 13.16 points. The effect of the currencies is isolated.

$$\text{Convertible bond price} = \text{Conversion value} + \text{Premium}$$

$$= \pounds 851.40 + \pounds 131.60$$

$$= \pounds 983.00$$

An appreciation of the sterling versus the Australian dollar resulted in a decrease in the sterling bond price from £1,040 to £983. A weaker Australian dollar decreased the sterling conversion value and bond price.

The investor decides to sell the convertible at £983 net.

Transaction b: Sold 1,000M Australia Co. 6% of 200X at 98.3 net. Total proceeds: £983,000.

Sterling Security

a. Long security £1,040M	b. Sold security £983M

Loss: £57M

Broker/Customer

b. Bought security £983M	a. Short security £1,040M

Profit: £57M

A loss of £57M results from an appreciation of the sterling versus the Australian dollar.

A constant U.S. dollar/Australian dollar rate and a depreciation of the U.S. dollar versus the sterling resulted in an appreciation of the sterling relative to the Australian dollar. An appreciation of the sterling versus the Australian dollar decreased the sterling conversion value and bond price. An appreciation of the bond currency relative to the local currency decreased conversion value and the bond price as expressed in the bond currency.

Similarly, a constant U.S. dollar/Australian dollar rate and an appreciation of the U.S. dollar versus the sterling would result in a depreciation of the sterling relative to the Australian dollar. In this instance, the sterling conversion value and bond price would increase. A depreciation of the bond currency relative to the local currency would increase the bond price in terms of the bond currency.

As in case 2, the effect currency fluctuations have on conversion value declines as the equity price declines. At relatively higher equity prices, conversion value is more sensitive to movements in currency rates.

As exhibited, a constant U.S. dollar/Australian dollar rate and a depreciation of the U.S. dollar versus the sterling resulted in a decrease in the sterling conversion value and bond price. A movement of the U.S. dollar/sterling rate also affects the bond price when translated into the investor's currency. Scenario 2 examines the translation exposure resulting from a move in the U.S. dollar/sterling rate.

	Fluctuating Currency	Constant Currency	Translation to U.S. dollar
Scenario 2	U.S. dollar/sterling	U.S. dollar/Australian dollar	Yes

Australia Co. 6% July 9, 200X

Effective conversion price:	A$2.89
Fixed Australian dollar/sterling rate:	2.2420
Equivalent conversion price:	£1.2890

Current market data:

Convertible bond price:	£1,040
Equity price:	A$2.50
Australian dollar/sterling rate:	2.1350
U.S. dollar/Australian dollar rate:	0.8121
U.S. dollar/sterling rate:	1.7340
Conversion value:	£908.40
Premium:	13.16 pts.

Transaction a: Brought 1,000M Australia Co. 6% of 200X at 104 net. Total investment: £1,040,000.

Sterling Security
Sterling

a. Long security £1,040M	

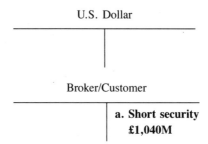

U.S. Dollar

Broker/Customer

a. Short security
£1,040M

Assume the trade is translated into U.S. dollars. The U.S. dollar–based investor enters into a contract to buy sterling with U.S. dollars at the current rate of 1.7340 for settlement date.

Transaction b: Bought £1,040M worth of sterling and sold U.S. dollars at 1.7340.

Sterling Security
Sterling

a. Long security	b. Long cash
£1,040M	**£1,040M**

U.S. Dollar

b. Short cash	
U.S.$1,803.4M	

Broker/Customer

	a. Short security
	£1,040M

The U.S. dollar/sterling rate is the only variable to change. The U.S. dollar has depreciated versus the sterling from 1.7340 to 1.8500. The original U.S. dollar/Australian dollar rate of 0.8121 and the U.S. dollar/sterling rate of 1.8500 imply an Australian dollar/sterling rate of 2.2780.

The effect on the value of the convertible is as follows. To isolate the effect of the currency, assume the premium remains at 13.16 points.

Equity price: A$2.50

Australian dollar/sterling rate: 2.2780

U.S. dollar/Australian dollar rate: 0.8121

U.S. dollar/sterling rate: 1.8500

$$\text{Conversion value} = \frac{\text{Equivalent equity price}}{\text{Equivalent conversion price}} \times 100$$

$$= \frac{\text{Current equity price} \div \left(\text{Current A\$/£ rate} \right)}{\text{Equivalent conversion price}} \times 100$$

$$= \frac{\text{A\$2.50} \div (\text{A\$2.2780/£1})}{\text{£1.2890}} \times 100$$

$$= 85.14$$

Convertible bond price = Conversion value + Premium

$$= £851.40 + £131.60$$

$$= £983$$

The depreciation of the U.S. dollar versus the sterling from 1.7340 to 1.8500 and a constant U.S. dollar/Australian dollar rate of 0.8121 resulted in appreciation of the sterling versus the Australian dollar. Conversion value decreased from £908.40 to £851.40. An appreciation of the bond currency relative to the local currency decreases conversion value.

The investor sells the bonds at £983 net.

Transaction c: Sold 1,000M Australia Co. 6% of 200X at 98.3 net. Total proceeds: £983,000.

Sterling Security
Sterling

a. Long security £1,040M	b. Long cash £1,040M
	c. Sold security £983M

U.S. Dollar

b. Short cash U.S.$1,803.4M	

Broker/Customer

c. **Bought security** **£983M**	a. Short security 1,040M

Profit: £57M

The U.S. dollar–based investor translates the sterling proceeds into U.S. dollars at a rate of U.S.$1.8500/£1. The original foreign exchange contract is reversed.

Transaction d: Sold £983M worth of sterling and bought U.S. dollars at 1.8500.

Sterling Security
Sterling

a. Long security £1,040M	b. Long cash £1,040M
d. **Sold cash** **£983M**	c. Sold security £983M

–0–

U.S. Dollar

b. Short cash U.S.$1,803.4M	d. **Bought cash** **U.S.$1,818.55M**

Profit: U.S.$15.15M

Broker/Customer

c. **Bought security** **£983M**	a. Short security £1,040M

Profit: £57M

A profit of U.S.$15.15M is realized when the position is translated into U.S. dollars. The appreciation of the sterling versus the Australian dollar resulted in a slight increase in U.S. dollar terms. The results are summarized in the following table.

	Original Value	Subsequent Value	Percent Change	Results
U.S. dollar/ sterling	1.7390	1.8500	6.69	U.S. dollar depreciated vs. sterling, or sterling appreciated vs. U.S. dollar
U.S. dollar/ Australian dollar	0.8121	0.8121	0	No change
Australian dollar/ sterling	2.1350	2.2780	6.70	Sterling appreciated vs. Australian dollar or Australian dollar depreciated vs. sterling
Conversion value (sterling)	90.84	85.14	−6.27	Conversion value in sterling terms decreased
Bond price (sterling)	1,040.0	983.0	−5.48	Bond price in sterling terms decreased
Bond price (U.S. dollars)*	1,803.4	1,818.55	+0.84	Bond price in U.S. dollar terms increased

*Assume no change in premium.

The depreciation of the U.S. dollar versus the sterling and a constant U.S. dollar/Australian dollar rate caused the sterling to appreciate versus the Australian dollar.

Initially, the sterling's appreciation versus the Australian dollar resulted in a decrease in conversion value and bond price in sterling terms. The appreciation of the bond currency versus the local currency decreases conversion value. The depreciation of the U.S. dollar relative to the sterling resulted in a slight increase in U.S. dollar terms.

The effect of the fluctuation of the U.S. dollar/sterling rate on the position in U.S. dollar terms was minor. The U.S. dollar depreciated versus sterling 6.69% while the bond price in U.S. dollar terms increased by only 0.84%. To a U.S. dollar–based investor, the sterling's relative movement is almost totally offset.

Since the Australian dollar/sterling rate is a cross-currency rate, a move in either the U.S. dollar/sterling rate or the U.S. dollar/Australian dollar rate will affect its value. In the following scenario, assume a constant U.S. dollar/sterling rate of 1.7340 and a depreciation of the U.S. dollar versus the Australian dollar from 0.8121 to 0.8500.

$$A\$/\pounds = \frac{1.7340}{0.8500}$$

$$= 2.0400$$

The sterling has depreciated versus the Australian dollar from 2.1350 to 2.0400. Fewer Australian dollars are received per sterling.

	Fluctuating Currency	Constant Currency	Translation to U.S. dollars
Scenario 3	U.S. dollar/Australian dollar	U.S. dollar/sterling	No

Australia Co. 6% July 9, 200X

Effective conversion price:	A$2.89
Fixed Australian dollar/sterling rate:	2.2420
Equivalent conversion price:	£1.2890

Current market data:

Convertible bond price:	£1040
Equity price:	A$2.50
Australian dollar/sterling rate:	2.1350
U.S. dollar/Australian dollar rate:	0.8121
U.S. dollar/sterling rate:	1.7340
Conversion value:	£908.40
Premium:	13.16 pts.

Transaction a: Bought 1,000M Australia Co. 6% of 200X at 104 net. Total investment: £1,040,000.

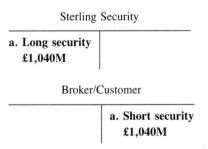

Sterling Security

a. Long security
£1,040M

Broker/Customer

a. Short security
£1,040M

The U.S. dollar depreciates versus the Australian dollar from 0.8121 to 0.8500. The new Australian dollar/sterling rate is 2.0400. The sterling has depreciated versus the Australian dollar. Due to the currency fluctuation, conversion value changes. Assume the premium remains at 13.16 points.

Equity price:	A$2.50
Australian dollar/sterling rate:	2.0400
U.S. dollar/Australian dollar rate:	0.8500
U.S. dollar/sterling rate:	1.7340

$$\text{Conversion value} = \frac{\text{Equivalent equity price}}{\text{Equivalent conversion price}} \times 100$$

$$= \frac{\text{Current equity price} \div \left(\frac{\text{Current}}{\text{A\$/£ rate}} \right)}{\text{Equivalent conversion price}} \times 100$$

$$= \frac{\text{A\$2.50} \div (\text{A\$2.0400/£1})}{\text{£1.2890}} \times 100$$

$$= 95.07$$

$$\text{Convertible bond price} = \text{Conversion value} + \text{Premium}$$
$$= \text{£950.70} + \text{£131.60}$$
$$= \text{£1,082.30}$$

Conversion value increased from £908.40 to £950.70, and the bond price increased from £1,040 to £1,082.30. A depreciation of the sterling versus the Australian dollar resulted in an increase in the sterling conversion value and bond price. The depreciation of the bond currency relative to the local currency increased conversion value and the bond price.

The investor decides to sell the convertible at 108.23 net.

Transaction b: Sold 1,000M Australia Co. 6% of 200X at 108.23 net. Total proceeds: £1,082,300.

Sterling Security

a. Long security £1,040M	b. Sold security £1,082.3M

Profit: £42.3M

Broker/Customer

b. Bought security £1,082.3M	a. Short security 1,040M

Loss: £42.3M

A profit of £42.3M results from a depreciation of the sterling versus the Australian dollar. In sterling terms, the bond price increased.

A constant U.S. dollar/sterling rate and a depreciation of the U.S. dollar versus the Australian dollar resulted in a depreciation of the sterling versus the Australian dollar. A depreciation of the bond currency relative to the local currency increased the bond price as expressed in the bond currency. The effect of currency fluctuations increases with relative increases in the equity price.

Similarly, a constant U.S. dollar/sterling rate and an appreciation of the U.S. dollar versus the Australian dollar would result in an appreciation of the sterling versus the Australian dollar. An appreciation of the bond currency relative to the local currency would decrease the bond price in terms of the bond currency.

In scenario 3, a fluctuation in the U.S. dollar/Australian dollar rate and a constant U.S. dollar/sterling rate affected the conversion value and bond price in sterling terms. Scenario 4 analyzes the effect of a fluctuating U.S. dollar/Australian dollar rate on the bond price in U.S. dollar terms.

	Fluctuating Currency	Constant Currency	Translation to U.S. dollar
Scenario 4	U.S. dollar/Australian dollar	U.S. dollar/sterling	Yes

Australia Co. 6% July 9, 200X

Effective conversion price:	A$2.89
Fixed Australian dollar/sterling rate:	2.2420
Equivalent conversion price:	£1.2890

Current market data:

Convertible bond price:	£1.040
Equity price:	A$2.50
Conversion value:	£908.40
Australian dollar/sterling rate:	2.1350
U.S. dollar/Australian dollar rate:	0.8121
U.S. dollar/sterling rate:	1.7340

Transaction a: Bought 1,000M Australia Co. 6% of 200X at 104 net. Total investment: £1,040,000.

Sterling Security
Sterling

a. Long security £1,040M	

U.S. Dollar

Broker/Customer

	a. Short security £1,040M

The U.S. dollar–based investor enters into a contract to buy sterling with U.S. dollars at the current rate of 1.7340 for settlement date.

Transaction b: Bought £1,040M worth of sterling and sold U.S. dollars at 1.7340.

Sterling Security
Sterling

a. Long security £1,040M	**b. Long cash £1,040M**

U.S. Dollar

b. Short cash U.S.$1,803.4M	

Broker/Customer

	a. Short security £1,040M

The bonds are owned in U.S. dollar terms.

The U.S. dollar has depreciated versus the Australian dollar rate from 0.8121 to 0.8500, and the U.S. dollar/sterling rate remains at 1.7340. The implied Australian dollar/sterling rate has gone from 2.1350 to 2.0400. The sterling has depreciated versus the Australian dollar. Conversion value is affected by the currency fluctuation. The premium remains at 13.16 points.

Equity price:	A$2.50
Australian dollar/sterling rate:	2.0400
U.S. dollar/Australian dollar rate:	0.8500
U.S. dollar/sterling rate:	1.7340

$$\text{Conversion value} = \frac{\text{Equivalent equity price}}{\text{Equivalent conversion price}} \times 100$$

$$= \frac{\dfrac{\text{Current}}{\text{equity price}} \div \left(\dfrac{\text{Current}}{\text{A\$/£ rate}} \right)}{\text{Equivalent conversion price}} \times 100$$

$$= \frac{\text{A\$2.50} \div (\text{A\$2.0400/£1})}{£1.2890} \times 100$$

$$= 95.07$$

$$\text{Convertible bond price} = £950.70 + £131.60$$

$$= £1,082.30$$

Conversion value increased from £908.40 to £950.70, and the bond price increased from £1,040 to £1,082.30. The depreciation of the bond currency versus the local currency has increased conversion value.

The investor decides to liquidate the position.

Transaction c: Sold 1,000M Australia Co. 6% of 200X at 108.23 net. Total proceeds: £1,082,300.

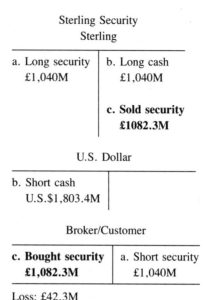

Sterling Security
Sterling

a. Long security £1,040M	b. Long cash £1,040M
	c. Sold security £1082.3M

U.S. Dollar

b. Short cash U.S.$1,803.4M	

Broker/Customer

c. Bought security £1,082.3M	a. Short security £1,040M

Loss: £42.3M

The U.S. dollar–based investor translates the sterling proceeds into U.S. dollars at a rate of U.S.$1.7340/£1. The original foreign exchange contract is reversed.

Transaction d: Sold £1,802.3M worth of sterling and bought U.S. dollars at 1.7340.

Sterling Security
Sterling

a. Long security £1,040M	b. Long cash £1,040M
d. Sold cash £1,802.3M	c. Sold security £1,802.3M

–0–

U.S. Dollar

b. Short cash U.S.$1,803.4M	**d. Bought cash U.S.$1,876.7M**

Profit: U.S.$73.3M

Broker/Customer

c. **Bought security** £1,082.3M	a. Short security £1,040M

Loss: £42.3M

A profit of U.S.$73.3M is realized when the position is translated into U.S. dollars. The depreciation of the U.S. dollar versus the Australian dollar combined with a constant U.S. dollar/sterling rate resulted in an increase in U.S. dollar terms. The results are summarized in the following table.

	Original Value	Subsequent Value	Percent Change	Result
U.S. dollar/ Australian dollar	0.8121	0.8500	4.67	U.S. dollar depreciated vs. Australian dollar, or Australian dollar appreciated vs. U.S. dollar
U.S. dollar/ sterling	1.7340	1.7340	0	No change
Australian dollar/ sterling	2.1350	2.0400	4.45	Sterling depreciated vs. Australian dollar, or Australian dollar appreciated vs. sterling
Conversion value (sterling)	908.40	950.70	+4.66	Conversion value in sterling terms increased
Bond price (sterling)*	1,040	1,082.30	+4.06	Bond price in sterling terms increased
Bond price (U.S. dollars)	1,803.40	1,876.70	+4.06	Bond price in U.S. dollar terms increased

*Assume no change in premium.

A 4.67% depreciation of the U.S. dollar versus the Australian dollar and a constant U.S. dollar/sterling rate resulted in a 4.45% depreciation of the sterling versus the Australian dollar. The sterling's depreciation relative to the Australian dollar increased conversion value by 4.66% in sterling terms. A depreciation of the bond currency relative to the local currency resulted in an increase in conversion value and the bond price as expressed in the bond currency. The U.S. dollar's depreciation versus the Australian dollar is reflected in the sterling conversion value.

The translation of the sterling bond price into U.S. dollars resulted in a 4.06% price increase. Most of the U.S. dollar's 4.67% depreciation versus the Australian dollar is reflected in the bond price in U.S. dollar terms. Although the bond price in U.S. dollar terms was not a function of the U.S. dollar/sterling rate (as in scenario 2), the price of the bond in U.S. dollar terms is a function of the U.S. dollar/Australian dollar rate.

A U.S. dollar–based investor purchasing the sterling-denominated Australia Co. 6% of 200X is exposed to U.S. dollar/Australia dollar risk. Although the investor's, local, and bond currency are all different, basically only the U.S. dollar/Australia dollar rate affects the return in U.S. dollar terms.

The Australian dollar/sterling cross-currency rate affects conversion value. The U.S. dollar/sterling rate is implicit in the Australian dollar/sterling rate, and it also affects the translation of the sterling proceeds into U.S. dollars. From a U.S. dollar perspective, the U.S. dollar/sterling rate exposure on bond price movements is minimal.

The U.S. dollar/Australian dollar rate is reflected in the sterling conversion value and bond price in U.S. dollar terms. The performance of the U.S. dollar relative to the Australian dollar affects the total return.

Pound Sterling–Based Investor

The previous analysis was from a U.S. dollar–based investor's perspective. If the investor's base currency is pound sterling, there is cross-currency exposure. Cross-currency risk as realized through translation and the mathematics of conversion value will be briefly discussed. The following analysis is from a sterling-based investor's standpoint.

Case 5: Cross-Currency Translation Exposure

	Investor's Currency	Local Currency	Bond Currency
Case 5	Sterling	French franc	French franc

A pound sterling–based investor purchases the France S.A. 6% of 200X at 98 net. The investor must translate the trade into sterling. The investor is subject to French franc/sterling translation exposure.

Convertible bond price:	FF980
Convertible price, sterling terms:	£91.10
French franc/sterling rate:	10.7570
U.S. dollar/sterling rate:	1.7350
French franc/U.S. dollar rate:	6.2000

Assume the U.S. dollar appreciates 2% versus the sterling and the French franc/U.S. dollar rate remains constant. The dollar's appreciation has the effect of decreasing the value of the French franc/sterling rate. The sterling depreciates 2% versus the French franc.

	Original Value	Subsequent Value	Percent Change	Result
Bond price	FF980	FF980	0	No change
U.S. dollar/ sterling	1.7350	1.7000	2.0	U.S. dollar appreciated vs. sterling
French franc/ U.S. dollar	6.2000	6.2000	0	No change
French franc/ sterling	10.7570	10.5400	2.0	Sterling depreciated vs. French franc
Bond price, sterling terms	£91.10	£92.98	+2.06	Bond price increases in sterling terms

The appreciation of the U.S. dollar versus the sterling and a constant French franc/U.S. dollar rate increases the bond price in sterling terms. Similarly, a depreciation of the U.S. dollar versus the sterling decreases the bond price in sterling terms.

Assume the U.S. dollar appreciates 3.2% versus the French franc and the U.S. dollar/sterling rate remains constant. The result is that the sterling appreciates 3.2% versus the French franc.

	Original Value	Subsequent Value	Percent Change	Result
Bond price	FF980	FF980	0	No change
U.S. dollar/ sterling	1.7350	1.7350	0	No change
French franc/ U.S. dollar	6.2000	6.4000	3.2	U.S. dollar appreciated vs. French franc
French franc/ sterling	10.7570	11.1040	3.2	Sterling appreciated vs. French franc
Bond price	£91.10	£88.26	−3.12	Bond price decreases in sterling terms

An appreciation of the U.S. dollar versus the French franc and a constant U.S. dollar/sterling rate decreases the bond price in sterling terms. Similarly, a depreciation of the U.S. dollar versus the French franc increases the convertible price in sterling terms.

The France S.A. 6% bonds are not exposed to currency risk through the mathematics of conversion value because the bonds are denominated in the local currency. Since the bond denomination differs from the investor's base currency, there is translation currency exposure. From a sterling-based investor's standpoint, the translation exposure arises in translating the French franc bond proceeds into pound sterling. The translation exposure is a function of the French franc/sterling rate. Fluctuations in either the U.S. dollar/sterling rate or the French franc/U.S. dollar rate affect profitability in sterling terms. Since the U.S. dollar is not directly involved, the French franc/sterling cross-currency rate causes translation exposure to be a function of two currency relationships.

Case 6: Cross-Currency Exposure Through Conversion Value

The following analysis investigates cross-currency exposure through conversion value. Assume the investor is sterling-based.

	Investor's Currency	Local Currency	Bond Currency
Case 6	Sterling	Australian dollar	Sterling

The Australian Co. 6% of 200X bonds are denominated in pound sterling. A pound sterling–based investor purchases the Australia Co. 6% of 200X at £1,040 net. Since the bond is denominated in the investor's base currency (sterling), there is no translation exposure. The Australian dollar/sterling currency exposure arises through the calculation of conversion value.

Original U.S. dollar/Australian dollar rate:	0.8121
Original U.S. dollar/sterling rate:	1.7340
Original Australian dollar/sterling rate:	2.1350
Equivalent conversion price:	£1.2890
Convertible bond price:	£1,040
Equity price:	A$2.50

$$\text{Equivalent equity price} = \frac{\text{Equity price}}{\text{A\$/£}}$$

$$= \frac{\text{A\$2.50}}{2.1350}$$

$$= \text{£1.17}$$

$$\text{Conversion value} = \frac{\text{Equivalent equity price}}{\text{Equivalent conversion price}} \times 100$$

$$= \frac{\pounds 1.17}{\pounds 1.2890} \times 100$$

$$= 90.77$$

$$\begin{matrix} \text{Premium} \\ \text{(Point method)} \end{matrix} = \begin{matrix} \text{Bond} - \text{Conversion} \\ \text{price} \quad \text{value} \end{matrix}$$

$$= \pounds 1,040 - \pounds 907.70$$

$$= \pounds 132.30$$

$$\begin{matrix} \text{Premium} \\ \text{(Percent method)} \end{matrix} = \left(\frac{\begin{matrix} \text{Bond} & \text{Conversion} \\ \text{price} & \text{value} \end{matrix}}{\text{Conversion value}} \right) \times 100$$

$$= \left(\frac{\pounds 1,040 - \pounds 907.70}{\pounds 907.70} \right) \times 100$$

$$= 14.6\%$$

Upon liquidation of the position, the U.S. dollar has depreciated versus the sterling from 1.7340 to 1.8500, and the U.S. dollar/Australian dollar rate has remained constant. The new rate implies an Australian dollar/sterling rate of 2.2780. Assuming no change in the equity price, the equivalent equity price decreases to £1.10.

Australian dollar/sterling rate:	2.2780
U.S. dollar/Australian dollar rate:	0.8121
U.S. dollar/sterling rate:	1.8500
Equity price:	A$2.50
Equivalent equity price:	£1.10

$$\text{Conversion value} = \frac{\pounds 1.10}{\pounds 1.2890} \times 100$$

$$= 85.34$$

The depreciation of the U.S. dollar versus the sterling and a constant U.S. dollar/Australian dollar results in a decrease in conversion value in sterling terms. Similarly, an appreciation of the U.S. dollar versus the sterling results in an increase in conversion value in sterling terms.

Assuming the premium remains at 13.32 points, the resulting convertible price is 98.57. A 6.7% currency movement resulted in a decrease in the convertible price from 104 to 98.57 (a 5.2% decline). Due to the mathematics, most of the U.S. dollar depreciation versus the sterling was reflected in the convertible price.

Assume that, upon liquidation, the following scenario exists. The U.S. dollar depreciates versus the Australian dollar, and the U.S. dollar/sterling rate remains the same. The implied Australian dollar/sterling rate is 2.0400. Assuming a constant equity price of A$2.50, the equivalent equity price is £1.23.

Australian dollar/sterling rate:	2.0400
U.S. dollar/Australian dollar rate:	0.8500
U.S. dollar/sterling rate:	1.7340
Equity price:	A$2.50
Equivalent equity price:	£1.23

$$\text{Conversion value} = \frac{£1.23}{£1.2890} \times 100$$
$$= 95.42$$

The depreciation of the U.S. dollar versus the Australian dollar and a constant U.S. dollar/sterling rate results in an increase in conversion value from £907.70 to £954.20. Similarly, an appreciation of the U.S. dollar versus the Australian dollar results in a decrease in conversion value in sterling terms.

The Australia Co. 6% of 200X are not denominated in the local currency; therefore, the currency risk is through the mathematics of conversion value. Since the U.S. dollar is not directly involved, the Australian dollar/sterling cross rate causes conversion value to be a function of both the U.S. dollar/Australian dollar and U.S. dollar/sterling rates. From a pound sterling perspective, fluctuations in either of the rates affect the value of the convertible bond through conversion value.

Review

The following is a review of the various currency exposures and the management of these exposures. The analysis is from a U.S. dollar perspective.

U.S. Dollar-Based Investor

	Investor's Currency	Local Currency	Bond Currency
Case 1	U.S. dollar	French franc	French franc

Exposure: Translation

Currency relationship: U.S. dollar vs. French franc

Currency Fluctuation	Effect on Convertible Price (U.S. dollar terms)
U.S. dollar depreciates vs. French franc	Gain
U.S. dollar appreciates vs. French franc	Loss

An appreciation of the French franc versus the U.S. dollar results in an increase in the bond price in U.S. dollar terms. An appreciation of the bond and local currency versus the investor's currency results in an increase in terms of investor's currency.

	Investor's Currency	Local Currency	Bond Currency
Case 2	U.S. dollar	Peseta	U.S. dollar

Exposure: Conversion value

Currency relationship: U.S. dollar vs. peseta

Currency Fluctuation	Effect on Convertible Price (U.S. dollar terms)
U.S. dollar depreciates vs. Peseta	Gain
U.S. dollar appreciates vs. Peseta	Loss

An appreciation of the peseta versus the U.S. dollar results in an increase in the U.S. dollar bond price. An appreciation of the local currency versus the bond and investor's currency results in an increase in terms of investor's currency. At relatively higher equity levels, conversion value is more sensitive to fluctuations in the currency rate.

	Investor's Currency	Local Currency	Bond Currency
Case 3	U.S. dollar	U.S. dollar	Sterling

Exposure: Conversion value
                   Translation
Currency relationship: U.S. dollar vs. sterling

Currency Fluctuation	Effect on Convertible Price	
	Sterling Terms	U.S. Dollar Terms
U.S. dollar depreciates vs. sterling	Decrease	Increase
U.S. dollar appreciates vs. sterling	Increase	Decrease

An appreciation of the pound sterling versus the U.S. dollar results in an initial decrease in conversion value in sterling terms. An appreciation of the bond currency versus the local and investor's currency results in an initial decrease in terms of the bond currency. The effect of currency fluctuations increases as the equity price increases.

The appreciation of the pound sterling versus the U.S. dollar results in an increase in conversion value when translated into U.S. dollars. An appreciation of the bond currency versus the local and investor's currency results in a final increase in conversion value in terms of the investor's currency.

	Investor's Currency	Local Currency	Bond Currency
Case 4	U.S. dollar	Australian dollar	Sterling

Exposure: Conversion value

                              Translation

Currency relationship:

      Conversion value: Australian dollar vs. sterling

      Translation: U.S. dollar vs. sterling

Currency Fluctuation	Constant Currency	Effect on Convertible Price	
		Sterling Terms	U.S. Dollar Terms
U.S. dollar depreciates vs. sterling	U.S. dollar/ Australian dollar	Decrease	None
U.S. dollar appreciates vs. sterling	U.S. dollar/ Australian dollar	Increase	None
U.S. dollar depreciates vs. Australian dollar	U.S. dollar/sterling	Increase	Increase
U.S. dollar appreciates vs. Australian dollar	U.S. dollar/sterling	Decrease	Decrease

An appreciation of the Australian dollar versus the U.S. dollar results in an increase in the bond price in both sterling and U.S. dollar terms. A fluctuation in the U.S. dollar/sterling rate has little impact on the bond price in U.S. dollar terms. An appreciation of the local currency versus the investor's currency results in an increase in terms of the bond and the investor's currency.

Pound Sterling–Based Investor

	Investor's Currency	Local Currency	Bond Currency
Case 5	Sterling	French franc	French franc

Exposure: Translation

Currency relationship: U.S. dollar vs. sterling

French franc vs. U.S. dollar

Currency Fluctuation	Constant Currency	Effect on Convertible Price, Sterling Terms
U.S. dollar appreciates vs. sterling	French franc/U.S. dollar	Increase
U.S. dollar depreciates vs. sterling	French franc/U.S. dollar	Decrease
U.S. dollar appreciates vs. French franc	U.S. dollar/sterling	Decrease
U.S. dollar depreciates vs. French franc	U.S. dollar/sterling	Increase

The sterling-based investor is exposed to cross-currency translation exposure. The appreciation of the U.S. dollar versus the sterling and a constant French franc/U.S. dollar rate increase the bond price in sterling terms. Also, the appreciation of the French franc versus the U.S. dollar and a constant U.S. dollar/sterling rate increase the bond price in sterling terms.

	Investor's Currency	Local Currency	Bond Currency
Case 6	Sterling	Australian dollar	Sterling

Exposure: Conversion value

Currency relationship: U.S. dollar vs. sterling

                             U.S. dollar vs. Australian dollar

Currency Fluctuation	Constant Currency	Effect on Convertible Price, Sterling Terms
U.S. dollar appreciates vs. sterling	U.S. dollar/Australian dollar	Increase
U.S. dollar depreciates vs. sterling	U.S. dollar/Australian dollar	Decrease
U.S. dollar appreciates vs. Australian dollar	U.S. dollar/sterling	Decrease
U.S. dollar depreciates vs. Australian dollar	U.S. dollar/sterling	Increase

The appreciation of the U.S. dollar versus the sterling and a constant U.S. dollar/Australian dollar rate increase the convertible price. Also, the depreciation of the U.S. dollar versus the Australian dollar and a constant U.S. dollar/sterling rate increase the bond price. Fluctuations in either currency affect the convertible price.

The preceding cases involved different currency exposures and were affected by U.S. dollar movements in various ways. The common factor was that the total return for each of the positions was affected by currency fluctuation. Movements in the currency are as important as movements in the equity price. International convertibles are vehicles that participate in foreign currency movements.

Foreign currency–denominated convertibles are subject to translation exposure. U.S. dollar–based investors benefit from a strengthening of the foreign currency relative to the U.S. dollar. In the case of convertibles not denominated in the local currency, conversion value is a function of the equity price, conversion ratio, and currency relationship: the graph of conversion value becomes three-dimensional. Conversion value is more sensitive to currency fluctuation at higher equity prices.

Relative percentage movements of the currencies versus the equity price determine the extent of the effect on the convertible. Capital gains and losses (from changes in the convertible price) can be offset by currency fluctuations. The total return of a convertible security is a function of the current level and future expectations of the performance of the currency. The currency risk is derived from translation, transaction, and economic exposures and through the convertible's mathematics. A thorough understanding of a company's transaction and economic exposure is essential in order to understand the total currency exposure.

14

Convertible Security Evaluation

Convertible securities should be evaluated with regard to the equity, debt, and currency components. The convertible bond's yield advantage, premium, break-even time, and currency exposure should be analyzed collectively and with respect to call protection.

Before analyzing the convertible, the investor must be comfortable with an investment in the equity. Convertibles are equity products, and the equity price is the prime factor affecting conversion value.

A convertible should also be evaluated with regard to alternative investments. The general demand for convertible securities relative to the supply of new convertible issues may alter parameters for evaluation purposes. The liquidity and leverage of an issue may determine if the convertible is a viable alternative to the equity.

The equity component of the convertible security is a function of the perceived capital appreciation potential of the underlying equity and the perceived creditworthiness of the issuer (i.e., safety of equity dividend). Convertible investments should be made in instances where the underlying equity is attractive.

Premium over conversion value expressed as a percentage provides a relative measurement of the upside potential and downside risk of a convertible security. The premium should be evaluated with regard to the yield advantage and call protection. Wider premiums are justified by:

1. greater degree of yield advantage
2. greater degree of call protection
3. volatile underlying equities
4. lower levels of interest rates

From a purist standpoint, the debt component is evaluated with regard to straight debt of comparable creditworthiness and time to maturity. Convertibles trading well above investment value are subject to greater downside risk.

Investment value is subject to changes in the level of interest rates in the market of the bond's currency. For example, if a British company issues a convertible denominated in U.S. dollars (the local currency is the pound sterling), the bond's investment value is subject to changes in the level of U.S. interest rates.

A convertible bond purchased below the strike price and held to the put date guarantees the investor the yield to put (assuming the issuer is financially viable). When the yield to put dominates the yield to maturity, the convertible is evaluated on a yield-to-put basis. The yield to put should be compared to rates in the market of the bond's currency.

The convertible's yield advantage on a current basis and on a yield-to-put basis should be evaluated with regard to the creditworthiness of the issuer. A convertible's yield is more valuable when the safety of the equity dividend is questionable.

Break-even time, although static in nature, is useful for determining relative value. In general, a break-even period of two to three years is attractive. Break-even time must be analyzed with respect to call protection. A convertible security that recoups the premium within the call protection period is attractive. A bond with a relatively high break-even time may be superior to the underlying equity if the common dividend is likely to be reduced. The concept of break-even is less important when there is little risk of call.

Convertibles denominated in foreign currency or exchangeable into ordinary shares of foreign companies (from a U.S. dollar perspective) have currency exposure. The performance of the currency is as important as the equity and debt features. The convertible may be subject to currency risk through translation exposure or the mathematics of conversion value. When exposure is through conversion value, the currency effect is greater at higher equity prices. Convertibles trading close to investment value are less sensitive to currency movements. Fluctuations in the currency may offset any gains in the convertible price realized in the bond's currency. Total returns are a function of current and future expectations of currency levels.

The following is an example of a comprehensive evaluation of the UK Plc 6% of 200X convertible bond (errors are due to rounding).

UK Plc 6%   July 6, 200X

Size of issue:	100 mil.
Country of issuer:	U.K.
Local currency:	Sterling
Bond denomination:	Sterling
Par value:	£1,000
Coupon frequency:	Annual
Bond coupon payment:	£60.00
Annual equity dividend:	£0.05
Conversion price:	£4.85
Conversion ratio:	

$$\frac{\text{Par value}}{\text{Conversion price}} = \frac{£1,000}{£4.85} = 206.19 \text{ shares/£1,000 bond}$$

Call protection:

Provisional:	Noncallable before three years on July 6, unless the average closing middle market quote of the equity share for 30 days is at least 130% of the effective conversion price
Put feature:	Holders may opt to have their convertible bonds redeemed in three years on July 6, at 127.13% of par value.

Current market data:

Convertible bond price:	105.0% of £1,000 = £1,050
Equity price:	£4.60
Current bond yield:	5.70%
Current equity yield:	1.00%
Yield to put:	9.14%

Conversion Value (Parity)

Conversion ratio method = Conversion ratio × Equity price

$$= 206.19 \text{ shares} \times £4.60$$

$$= £948.46$$

$$= 94.85\% \text{ of } £1,000$$

$$\text{Conversion price method} = \frac{\text{Current equity price}}{\text{Conversion price}} \times 100$$

$$= \frac{£4.60}{£4.85} \times 100$$

$$= 94.85\% \text{ of } £1,000$$

$$= £948.46$$

Premium over Conversion Value

Point/dollar method = Bond price − Conversion value

$$= £1,050.00 - £948.46$$

$$= £101.54$$

$$= 10.15 \text{ pts./£1,000}$$

$$\text{Percent method} = \frac{\text{Bond price} - \text{Conversion value}}{\text{Conversion value}} \times 100$$

$$= \frac{\pounds1{,}050 - \pounds948.46}{\pounds948.46} \times 100$$

$$= \frac{\pounds101.54}{\pounds948.46} \times 100$$

$$= 10.7\%$$

Yield Advantage

$$\text{Percent method} = \underset{\text{yield}}{\text{Current bond}} - \underset{\text{yield}}{\text{Current equity}}$$

$$= 5.70\% - 1\%$$

$$= 4.70\%$$

$$\text{Equity method} = \underset{\text{income}}{\text{Bond coupon}} - \underset{\text{dividend income}}{\text{Equivalent equity}}$$

$$= \underset{\text{income}}{\text{Bond coupon}} - \left(\underset{\text{ratio}}{\text{Conversion}} \times \underset{\text{dividend}}{\text{Equity}}\right)$$

$$= \pounds60.00 - (206.19 \text{ shrs.} \times \pounds0.05)$$

$$= \pounds49.69$$

$$= 4.97 \text{ pts.}/\pounds1{,}000$$

$$\text{Point/dollar method} = \underset{\text{income}}{\text{Bond coupon}} - \left(\frac{\text{Bond price}}{\text{Equity price}} \times \underset{\text{dividend}}{\text{Equity}}\right)$$

$$= \pounds60.00 - \left(\frac{\pounds1{,}050}{\pounds4.60} \times \pounds0.05\right)$$

$$= \pounds60.00 - (228.26 \text{ shrs.} \times \pounds0.05)$$

$$= \pounds60.00 - \pounds11.41$$

$$= \pounds48.59$$

$$= 4.86 \text{ pts.}/\pounds1{,}000$$

Break-Even Period (Years)

$$\text{Equity method} = \frac{\text{Premium (sterling)}}{\text{Bond coupon} - \left(\begin{array}{c}\text{Conversion} \\ \text{ratio}\end{array} \times \begin{array}{c}\text{Annual equity} \\ \text{dividend}\end{array}\right)}$$

$$= \frac{£101.54}{£60.00 - (206.19 \text{ shrs.} \times £0.05)}$$

$$= \frac{£101.54}{£49.69}$$

$$= 2.04 \text{ years}$$

$$\begin{array}{c}\text{Point/dollar} \\ \text{method}\end{array} = \frac{\text{Premium (sterling)}}{\text{Bond coupon} - \left(\dfrac{\text{Bond price}}{\text{Equity price}} \times \begin{array}{c}\text{Annual equity} \\ \text{dividend}\end{array}\right)}$$

$$= \frac{£101.54}{£60.00 - \left(\dfrac{£1,050}{£4.60} \times £0.05\right)}$$

$$= \frac{£101.54}{£60.00 - (228.26 \text{ shrs.} \times £0.05)}$$

$$= \frac{£101.54}{£60.00 - £11.41}$$

$$= 2.09 \text{ years}$$

$$\text{Percent method} = \frac{\text{Premium (\%)}}{\text{Yield advantage (\%)}}$$

$$= \frac{10.7\%}{4.7\%}$$

$$= 2.28 \text{ years}$$

$$\text{Yield-to-put method} = \frac{\text{Premium (\%)}}{\text{Yield-to-put advantage}}$$

$$= \frac{\text{Premium (\%)}}{\underset{\text{put}}{\text{Yield to}} - \underset{\text{yield}}{\text{Current equity}}}$$

$$= \frac{10.7\%}{9.14\% - 1\%}$$

$$= 1.31 \text{ years}$$

Evaluation

1. *Low premium over conversion value of 10.7%:* The convertible will participate in the movement of the equity. The investor gives up 10.7% upside potential in the equity in return for the yield advantage, put feature, and downside protection. The equity must rise to £5.09 for the conversion value to equal the convertible price paid (i.e., £1,050).

$$\text{Upside target} = \frac{\text{Bond price}}{\text{Conversion ratio}}$$

$$= \frac{£1,050}{206.19 \text{ shrs.}}$$

$$= £5.09$$

$$\text{Conversion value} = \text{Conversion ratio} \times £5.09$$

$$= 206.19 \text{ shrs.} \times £5.09$$

$$= £1,050$$

2. *Yield to put of 9.14%:* The convertible's current yield advantage is 4.70%, and the yield advantage on a put basis is 8.14%. The investment value and put feature provide downside protection.

3. *Low break-even period of two years:* The premium is recouped in a relatively short period of time.
4. *Currency exposure:* Depending on the investor's currency, there may be an opportunity to participate in fluctuation in sterling through the translation exposure.

15

Convertible Security Investment Opportunities

Convertible securities combine attributes of bonds, equities, call options, and currencies. They are considered both bull and bear market instruments. As such, convertibles attract a variety of investors with different financial objectives. The demand curve for convertible securities is greater than those for other financial instruments.

Depending on the investor's objectives, convertibles can be used as alternative investments. The conversion feature makes convertibles attractive to equity investors. Bond investors perceive convertibles as straight bonds plus an equity call option. International convertibles can be used as currency vehicles.

CONVERTIBLES AS EQUITY ALTERNATIVES

Convertible securities are defensive alternatives to investments in the underlying equity. However, in bull markets, the convertible's total return can exceed that of the equity. The conversion feature provides the convertible with its equity value, which is a function of the perceived capital appreciation potential of the underlying equity. Since convertibles are influenced by movements in the underlying equity, investors in convertibles should have a favorable opinion of the equity.

The equity investor is interested in the convertible's yield advantage, higher quality of yield, and downside protection. Income-oriented equity investors can participate in low-yielding equities' price appreciation through convertible securities. Convertibles trading at a premium increase in value at a slower rate than the underlying equity. The investor is willing to forfeit some equity upside potential for the yield and protection.

From an equity standpoint, a convertible's total return should be compared to that of the equity. The equity's total return is a function of its capital appreciation and dividend income. A convertible's total return is a function of the change in conversion value, the change in premium levels, interest income, and its put feature. The change in conversion value is based on the equity's capital appreciation. The convertible's interest income should exceed the equity's dividend income.

Changes in premium levels can be realized. An investor with a long-term perspective can profit from aberrant premium levels by swapping into the convertible from the equity when premiums are narrow and reversing the position when premiums expand. *Swapping* is the simultaneous sale of one security to purchase another security. A decision to swap into a convertible bond and out of the underlying equity should be made after a comprehensive evaluation of the convertible security has been conducted. Swapping into a convertible bond position offers the opportunity to maintain equity exposure in a company while increasing yield. Investors unsure as to the timing of a downturn in the general market (or the equity of interest) should consider a swap into the convertible bond to maintain equity exposure while establishing downside protection.

In the event of a decline in the USA Inc. share, an investor who had swapped into the convertible bond would have reduced loss exposure. The convertible bond premium expansion protects the investor from a full decline in the equity. Assume the investor swapped into 1,000M USA Inc. 7.5% of 200X and sold 28,369 shares (the equivalent number of shares embodied in 1,000M bonds). In the following scenario, the equity price declines and the premium over conversion value expands.

	Bond price	Equity price	Premium points
Purchase date	U.S.$1,030	U.S.$32.50	10.801
Later date	U.S.$940	U.S.$25.00	23.08

Loss on 1,000M convertible bond position:

1,000M bonds × (U.S.$940 − U.S.$1,030) = −U.S.$90,000

Loss on 28,369 = share equity position:

28,369 shares × (U.S.$25 − U.S.$32.50) = −U.S.$212,768

The investor reduced loss exposure by U.S.$122,768 by swapping into the convertible bonds. The convertible was the most attractive method for participating in USA Inc. shares. Due to the low premium, the bonds would have increased with the equity while providing downside protection.

The convertible position should be reversed back into the equity after the equity has declined and is believed to have begun to increase. As the equity declined, the convertible's premium expanded, providing downside protection. If the equity price recovers, the investor will take better advantage of the price appreciation through a direct investment in the equity rather than through the convertible. Convertibles trading at a premium increase at a slower rate than the equity.

CONVERTIBLES AS BOND ALTERNATIVES

Bond investors evaluate a convertible with respect to the investment value and put feature. Due to the investment value, convertibles are subject to interest rate fluctuations. Convertibles are particularly attractive bond alternatives because of the equity feature.

To a bond investor, a convertible is an equity bull market vehicle. When a portfolio is prohibited from investments in equities, convertibles can provide a source of equity market participation. If total returns on straight bonds are low, the convertible's equity feature can provide incremental returns. Straight bond investors evaluate convertibles by weighing the loss in yield against equity participation.

Due to the put feature, a convertible resembles a straight bond but with an equity call option. If the convertible's yield to put guarantees a return similar to comparable straight debt, the convertible offers the investor a cheap long-term equity call option. The bond investor is more interested in the debt component than in the size of the premium over conversion value.

Foreign currency–denominated Euroconvertibles sometimes offer an interest rate differential play. The Australia Co. issued a U.S. dollar–denominated 5.75% convertible and a sterling-denominated 6% convertible.

Australia Co. Convertible Bonds

	5.75% of 200X	6% of 200X
Denomination	U.S. dollars	Pound sterling
Local currency	Australian dollar	Australian dollar
Put date	5 years, July 9	5 years, July 9
Put price	U.S.$116.50	£124.00
Current Market Data		
Convertible bond price	U.S.$97.00	£95.00
Yield to put	10.60%	13.00%
Comparable government yield	8.50%	9.90%
Spread off government security	2.10%	3.10%

Five-year gilts yield 140 basis points over comparable U.S. treasuries. The sterling-denominated 6% bond's yield to put of 13% is 240 basis points over the U.S. dollar–denominated 5.75% bond's yield to put of 10.60%. The same credit quality term structures are compared for the two bonds. The sterling-denominated convertible offers a currency-adjusted yield advantage of 100 basis points over the U.S. dollar yield. A U.S. dollar–based investor can take advantage of the mispricing by purchasing the sterling-denominated convertible and hedging the U.S. dollar/sterling currency exposure.

CONVERTIBLES AS CURRENCY VEHICLES

Convertible securities denominated in foreign currencies or convertible into foreign equity provide the opportunity to benefit from fluctuations in currencies. A convertible's total return is a function of equity prices, interest rates, and currency rates.

Assuming there is no change in the equity price, the level of interest rates, or the conversion premium, a convertible not denominated in the local currency will increase in value with an appreciation of the local currency. For example, a U.S. dollar–based investor purchasing a convertible issued by a British company denominated in U.S. dollars will benefit from an appreciation of the sterling. The currency exposure is through the mathematics of conversion value. The effect of currency fluctuations increases as the equity price increases. Convertibles trading near investment value are less sensitive to currency movements. Ceteris paribus, the appreciation of the sterling is not realized, but the investor benefits through lower premium levels.

In addition, the investor can participate in currency movements through translation exposure. An investor can benefit from appreciation of a foreign currency versus the investor's currency by purchasing a foreign-denominated bond and ultimately translating it back into the investor's currency. A Swiss investor bullish on the U.S. dollar will participate in the dollar's appreciation relative to the Swiss franc through the purchase of a U.S. dollar–denominated convertible. Upon translation into Swiss francs, the investor receives more Swiss francs per dollar.

The total return of international convertibles is a function of current currency levels and future expectations of the levels. Investments in international convertibles, although complex, have the effect of reducing risk through diversification.

Convertible securities are equity, debt, and currency vehicles. As such, they can be utilized as alternatives to equity and debt investments. The investment objective determines the nature of the convertible to be purchased.

Type of Investor	Investment Objective	Convertible Investment
Equity	Equity participation with increase in current income	Convertibles trading at relatively low premiums with a yield advantage New issues
Equity/Bond	Income with equity participation	Convertibles trading at 30–50% premium with greater degree of yield advantage or a put
	Foreign currency participation	International convertibles
Bond	Income	Convertibles with deep discount to par value Convertibles with put features Zero-coupon convertibles

16
Convertible Hedge

WHAT IS A CONVERTIBLE HEDGE?

A *convertible hedge* involves the simultaneous purchase of a convertible security and a short sale of the underlying equity. The long convertible and short equity hedge position is effective when the convertible and the equity move in the same direction but at different rates. Hedges limit profit potential in exchange for safety. They allow for a quick shift from a bullish to a bearish trading stance and generate cash flow.

The *hedge ratio* is the number of shares sold short, expressed as a percentage of the equivalent equity embodied in the convertible. For example, a hedge position of being long 1,000M USA Inc. 7.5% of 200X versus an 80% hedge ratio is calculated as follows.

USA Inc. 7.5% Feb. 20, 200X

Conversion ratio: 28.369 shares/bond

$$\text{Equivalent equity embodied in bond} = 1{,}000M \times 28.369 \text{ shares/bond}$$

$$= 28{,}369 \text{ shares}$$

$$80\% \text{ hedge ratio} = 28{,}369 \text{ shares} \times 0.80$$
$$= 22{,}695 \text{ shares}$$

Hedge position: Long 1,000M convertible vs. short 22,695 shares

A *full hedge* is one in which the amount of equity sold short is equal to the amount of equity into which the bonds are convertible. A full hedge is a 100% hedge ratio.

$$\text{Full hedge ratio} = \text{Number of bonds} \times \text{Conversion ratio}$$
$$= 1{,}000M \times 28.369 \text{ shares}$$
$$= 28{,}369 \text{ shares}$$

For bonds trading at a premium, a full hedge is a bearish posture. For a given decrease in the equity price, the convertible bond will decline less than the equity. The premium over conversion value expands as the equity declines. The gain on the short position will exceed the loss on the long position.

A *neutral hedge* is one in which an amount of stock is sold short in order to break even for either an increase or decrease in the equity. Due to a convertible's defensive nature, it is easier for a hedge position to show a profit from a decline in the equity. The neutral hedge is intended to protect the position on the upside. For a given dollar gain on the convertible bond position, there will be an offsetting dollar loss on the short equity position. Assumptions must be made regarding future equity and premium levels, making the neutral hedge a subjective valuation.

A *partial hedge* is one in which the amount of equity sold short constitutes less than a 100% hedge. A movement in the long position is not completely offset by an identical move in the short position. A partial (biased) hedge should be established when an investor has an opinion as to the future value of the equity.

A bearish partial hedge ratio usually exceeds 70%. An increase in the number of shares shorted raises profit potential for a decrease in the equity price. The position benefits from premium expansion. A bullish hedge (i.e., usually a hedge ratio less than 50%) profits from an upward move in the equity.

In practice, the appropriate ratio is often determined through the use of theoretical option models. These models attempt to *delta-hedge* the position. A *delta* is the amount the call option price changes for a given one-point move in the underlying equity. The delta hedge ratio is used to maintain a relatively neutral stance. Once the delta hedge is established, a move in the equity price will change the delta. The hedge position is adjusted to maintain a neutral exposure.

WHY ESTABLISH CONVERTIBLE HEDGES?

A convertible hedge generates cash flow. The cash flow partially or totally offsets the financing cost. The amount of cash flow is a function of the yield advantage and the current level of interest rates.

Cash is generated from the receipt of the coupon income and the rebate on the short sale. A short seller of equity receives only a percentage of the proceeds from the sale of the borrowed stock. The equity dividend must be paid if the short position is maintained during the exdividend date. The entire position must be financed and is therefore a function of interest rates.

Source of Cash Flow	Use of Cash Flow
Coupon income	Long financing
Short sale rebate	Equity dividend

A hedge position is exposed to fluctuations in the equity price. It is also subject to interest rate risk. An increase in interest rates depresses investment value and (assuming no change in premium) the convertible price. Ceteris paribus, it is possible that the loss on the long convertible position will not be offset by a gain in the short equity position.

When foreign currencies are involved, the hedge position is exposed to currency fluctuations. The position is exposed through translation exposure and through the mathematics of conversion value.

The following example is a basic analysis that will clarify the profit potential from trading a hedge position. Bullish, bearish, and neutral hedges will be analyzed.

BULLISH HEDGE

The investor thinks USA Inc. shares will increase. A bullish partial hedge is established to take advantage of the expected premium contraction.

USA Inc. 7.5% Feb. 20, 200X

Conversion price: U.S.$35.25

Conversion ratio: 28.369 shares/bond

Current market levels:

Convertible bond price: U.S.$1030.00

Equity price: U.S.$32.50

Conversion value: U.S.$921.99

Premium: 10.801 points

Yield to put: 9.48%

The investor purchases 1,000M bonds at 103 net. Assuming a bullish 30% hedge ratio, the investor sells short 8,510 shares at U.S.$32.50. The hedge position is established at a 10.801-point premium.

$$\text{Short position} = \frac{\text{Number of bonds}}{\text{purchased}} \times \frac{\text{Conversion}}{\text{ratio}} \times \frac{\text{Hedge}}{\text{ratio}}$$

$$= 1,000\text{M bonds} \times 28.369 \text{ shares} \times 0.30$$

$$= 8,510 \text{ shares}$$

The following is a calculation of the investment in the hedge position. Assume there is no accrued interest.

$$\text{Long dollar investment} = \text{Number of bonds} \times \text{Bond price}$$

$$= 1,000\text{M bonds} \times \text{U.S.}\$1,030$$

$$= \text{U.S.}\$1,030,000$$

$$\text{Short dollar proceeds} = \frac{\text{Number of shares}}{\text{shorted}} \times \text{Equity price}$$

$$= 8,510 \text{ shares} \times \text{U.S.}\$32.50$$

$$= \text{U.S.}\$276,575$$

Convertible
Security

Long convertible U.S.$1,030,000	

Equity

	Short equity U.S.$276,575

In essence, the long convertible position is an indirect investment in the equity. For a given dollar investment, a purchase of a convertible trading at a premium costs more per share versus a direct investment in the equity. The following formula calculates the cost of the equity purchased via the convertible.

$$\frac{\text{Equivalent equity}}{\text{price}} = \frac{\text{Convertible price}}{\text{Conversion ratio}}$$

$$= \frac{\text{U.S.}\$1,030}{28.369 \text{ shares}}$$

$$= \text{U.S.}\$36.31$$

The equivalent equity long position was established at U.S.$36.31 and the partial short position at U.S.$32.50.

The position can be separated into the hedged and unhedged portions. The hedged portion of the 1,000M bonds is that against which a comparable number of shares were sold short.

$$\text{Hedged bond portion} = \frac{\text{Short equity position}}{\text{Conversion ratio}}$$

$$= \frac{8,510 \text{ shares}}{28.369 \text{ shares}}$$

$$= 300\text{M bonds}$$

The hedged portion of the position consists of the 300M bonds versus a 8,510-share short position. The number of shares sold short is equivalent to the number of shares embodied in the 300M bonds.

The unhedged portion of the 1,000M bonds is that against which no shares are sold short. The position is net long the unhedged portion.

$$\text{Unhedged bond portion} = \frac{\text{Total convertible}}{\text{position}} - \text{Hedged portion}$$

$$= 1,000\text{M bonds} - 300\text{M bonds}$$

$$= 700\text{M bonds}$$

$$\frac{\text{Equivalent unhedged}}{\text{equity position}} = 700\text{M bonds} \times \text{Conversion ratio}$$

$$= 700\text{M} \times 28.369 \text{ shares}$$

$$= 19,858 \text{ shares}$$

In essence, through the unhedged portion (700M bonds) the position is long 19,858 shares.

In addition to equity and interest rate exposure, the position is subject to premium risk. In the case of forced conversion, the premium paid over conversion value and the accrued interest are lost (see Chapter 8).

$$\text{Total dollar premium} = \text{Number of bonds} \times \text{Dollar premium}$$

$$= 1,000\text{M bonds} \times \text{U.S.\$108.01}$$

$$= \text{U.S.\$108,010}$$

If there is a forced redemption, the convertibles will lose their premium and trade at conversion value, and there will not be much change in the equity price. The loss on the long side will not be offset by a gain on the short side. It is desirable to minimize the premium in establishing a hedge position.

Upon forced conversion, the 1,000M bonds would be converted into 28,369 shares, 8,510 of which would be used to cover the short equity position. The balance of the long position, 19,858 shares, is subject to equity price risk.

Assume the USA Inc. equity and convertible prices have increased to U.S.$40 and U.S.$1,205, respectively. The investor believes the increase in price has ended. The position is reversed at a narrower premium.

Current market levels:

Convertible bond price:	U.S.$1,205
Equity price:	U.S.$40.00
Conversion value:	U.S.$1134.80
Premium:	7.02 points
Yield to put:	5.78%

The 1,000M bonds are sold at 120.50 net. A gain is realized on the long position. The 8,510-share short position is covered at U.S.$40.00. A loss is realized on the short position.

$$\frac{\text{Proceeds from sale}}{\text{of long position}} = \frac{\text{Number of bonds}}{\text{sold}} \times \frac{\text{Bond}}{\text{price}}$$

$$= 1,000\text{M bonds} \times \text{U.S.}\$1,205.00$$

$$= \text{U.S.}\$1,205,000$$

$$\frac{\text{Principal to cover}}{\text{short equity position}} = \frac{\text{Number of shares}}{\text{bought}} \times \frac{\text{Equity}}{\text{price}}$$

$$= 8,510 \text{ shares} \times \text{U.S.}\$40.00$$

$$= \text{U.S.}\$340,400$$

Convertible
Security

Long convertible U.S.$1,030,000	**Sold convertible** **U.S.$1,205,000**

Profit: U.S.$175,000

Equity

Bought equity **U.S.$340,400**	Short equity U.S.$276,575

Loss: U.S.$63,825

$$\text{Profit} = \text{Gain on long position} - \text{Loss on short position}$$
$$= \text{U.S.\$175,000} - \text{U.S.\$63,825}$$
$$= \text{U.S.\$111,175}$$

Upon reversal of the position, a profit of U.S.$111,175 is realized. The bullish hedge position benefited from the premium contraction. The gain on the long position was only partially offset by the loss in the short position.

Working the Premium to Zero

The hedge position can be enhanced by trading both the long convertible and short equity positions. By shorting additional shares at higher prices, it is possible to reduce the position's premium. If the investor's view of the equity is accurate, selling short additional shares as the equity rises will increase the average short-sale price and thus decrease the position's premium.

In this 30% bullish hedge 8,510 shares were shorted, whereas a full 100% hedge on 1,000M bonds is 28,369 shares. The investor is indirectly long 19,858 shares. It is helpful to calculate the equity price (on the upside) at which the 19,858 shares need to be sold short to bring the average price of the short sale to U.S.$36.31 (the cost basis of the equity through the convertible). In other words, as the equity price increases, the investor is able to sell additional shares short (and increase the average cost of the short position) in an attempt to work the premium to zero (i.e., to establish the position at parity). The following analysis will clarify the procedure.

$$\text{Upside equity target} = \frac{\text{Total dollar premium}}{\substack{\text{Shares needed to be} \\ \text{sold short}}} + \substack{\text{Original short} \\ \text{sale price}}$$

$$= \frac{\text{U.S.\$108,100}}{19,858 \text{ shares}} + \text{U.S.\$32.50}$$

$$= \text{U.S.\$37.94}$$

If the remaining 19,858 shares were sold short at U.S.$37.94, the average price of the short sale would be U.S.$36.31.

$$\substack{\text{Weighted} \\ \text{average of} \\ \text{short sale,} \\ 100\% \text{ hedge} \\ \text{ratio}} = \frac{\left(\substack{8,510 \\ \text{shrs.}} \times \text{U.S.\$32.50}\right) + \left(\substack{19,858 \\ \text{shrs.}} \times \text{U.S.\$37.94}\right)}{\text{Full hedge}}$$

$$= \frac{\text{U.S.\$276,575} + \text{U.S.\$753,412}}{28,369 \text{ shares}}$$

$$= \text{U.S.\$36.31}$$

A long convertible price of U.S.$1,030 and an average short sale of U.S.$36.31 reduces the position's premium to zero. Conversion value is calculated using the average short-sale equity price.

$$\text{Conversion value} = \text{Conversion ratio} \times \text{Average short sale}$$

$$= 28.369 \text{ shares} \times \text{U.S.\$36.31}$$

$$= \text{U.S.\$1,030}$$

$$\text{Position's premium} = \text{Convertible price} - \text{Conversion value}$$
$$= \text{U.S.}\$1{,}030 - \text{U.S.}\$1{,}030$$
$$= 0$$

At this point, the investor has a full hedge and no longer benefits from an increase in the equity price. The investor has "locked in" the position with an equity cost basis (through the convertible) of U.S.$36.31 and a short equity sale price of U.S.$36.31. At a full hedge, the position benefits from a decline in the equity price (see the following section).

There are two quick methods for calculating the level at which the equity must be sold to work the premium to zero. They are similar to the previous procedure yet concise.

Conversion ratio:	28.369 shares
Premium:	10.801 points
Hedge position:	
Long bonds, 1,000M:	U.S.$1,030
Short equity, 8,510:	U.S.$32.50

$$\text{Hedged bond postion} = \frac{\text{Shares short}}{\text{Conversion ratio}}$$
$$= \frac{8{,}510 \text{ shares}}{28.369 \text{ shares}}$$
$$= 300\text{M}$$

$$\text{Net long position} = \text{Long bond position} - \text{Hedged position}$$
$$= 1{,}000\text{M} - 300\text{M}$$
$$= 700\text{M}$$

$$\text{Premium risk} = \text{Hedged position} \times \text{Premium}$$
$$= 300\text{M} \times 10.801 \text{ points}$$
$$= 3{,}240.30$$

The premium risk on the hedged portion can be offset with an increase in the convertible price. The amount by which the bond price needs to increase to compensate for the premium is calculated as follows.

$$\text{Bond points to break-even} = \frac{\text{Premium risk}}{\text{Net long}}$$

$$= \frac{3{,}240.30}{700\text{M}}$$

$$= 4.63 \text{ points}$$

$$\text{Target bond price} = \frac{\text{Current bond}}{\text{price}} + \frac{\text{Bond points to}}{\text{break-even}}$$

$$= 103 + 4.63$$

$$= 107.63$$

$$\text{Target equity price} = \frac{\text{Target bond price}}{\text{Conversion ratio}}$$

$$= \frac{\text{U.S.\$1,076.30}}{28.369 \text{ shares}}$$

$$= \text{U.S.\$37.94}$$

The remaining 19,858 shares need to be sold at U.S.\$37.94 to work the premium to zero. This approach resulted in the same figure as the previous method. Following is an example of another approach that leads to the same result.

$$\text{Hedged shares} = \text{Hedged bonds} \times \text{Conversion ratio}$$

$$= 300\text{M} \times 28.369 \text{ shares}$$

$$= 8{,}510 \text{ shares}$$

$$\text{Unhedged shares} = (\text{Total bonds} \times \text{Conversion ratio}) - \text{Hedged shares}$$

$$= (1{,}000\text{M} \times 28.369 \text{ shares}) - 8{,}510 \text{ shares}$$

$$= 19{,}858 \text{ shares}$$

$$\begin{aligned}
\text{Premium risk} &= \text{Hedged shares} \times \text{Premium risk} \\
&= 8{,}510 \text{ shares} \times 10.801 \text{ points} \\
&= 91{,}916.51
\end{aligned}$$

$$\begin{aligned}
\frac{\text{Bond points to}}{\text{break-even}} &= \frac{\text{Premium risk}}{\text{Unhedged shares}} \\
&= \frac{91{,}916.51}{19{,}858 \text{ shares}} \\
&= 4.63
\end{aligned}$$

$$\begin{aligned}
\text{Target bond price} &= \text{Current bond price} + \frac{\text{Bond points to}}{\text{break even}} \\
&= 103 + 4.63 \\
&= 107.63
\end{aligned}$$

$$\begin{aligned}
\text{Target equity price} &= \frac{\text{Target bond price}}{\text{Conversion ratio}} \\
&= \frac{\text{U.S.\$1{,}076.30}}{28.369 \text{ shares}} \\
&= \text{U.S.\$37.94}
\end{aligned}$$

All of the preceding approaches arrive at the same result. The net long shares must be sold at an average price of U.S.\$37.94 in order to work the premium to zero.

There are two additional strategies for achieving zero premium by selling short additional shares. One goal is to raise the average short-sale price to U.S.\$36.31 with less than a 100% hedge ratio. For example, assume the investor wants to raise the average short sale to U.S.\$36.31 while maintaining a 75% hedge ratio. The position would have no premium risk and would retain a long bias. The hedge position would continue to benefit from an increase in the equity price.

$$75\% \text{ hedge ratio} = \frac{\text{Number of}}{\text{bonds}} \times \text{Conversion ratio} \times \frac{\text{Hedge}}{\text{ratio}}$$

$$= 1{,}000M \text{ bonds} \times 28.369 \text{ shares} \times 0.75$$

$$= 21{,}276 \text{ shares}$$

Given the current short position of 8,510 shares, an additional 12,766 shares need to be sold short to bring the total short position to 21,276 shares. The following equation calculates the price at which the 12,766 shares need to be sold to raise the average short sale to U.S.$36.31.

$$\begin{aligned}
\text{Upside equity target} &= \frac{\text{Total dollar premium}}{12{,}766 \text{ shares}} + \text{Original short sale price} \\[6pt]
&= \frac{1{,}000M \times \text{U.S.}\$108.01}{12{,}766 \text{ shares}} + \text{U.S.}\$32.50 \\[6pt]
&= \text{U.S.}\$14.02 + \text{U.S.}\$32.50 \\[6pt]
&= \text{U.S.}\$40.96
\end{aligned}$$

A short sale at U.S.$40.96 will raise the average short sale to U.S.$36.31 and increase the hedge ratio to 75%. In essence, the position is long 7,093 shares (28,369 shares − 21,276 shares). The position is set up with no premium and will benefit from increases in the equity price.

Another approach would be to sell the 19,858 shares short (to attain a full hedge) at a price exceeding U.S.$37.94 to bring the average short sale above U.S.$36.31. The establishment of a full hedge above U.S.$36.31 will lock the position in at a discount. The sale of the equity will exceed the long cost basis. The profit is the difference between the sale price and the cost basis.

For example, assume the 19,858 shares are sold short at U.S.$40.00. The average short sale is U.S.$37.75.

$$\begin{aligned}
\begin{array}{c}\text{Weighted average} \\ \text{of short sale,} \\ 100\% \text{ hedge ratio}\end{array} &= \frac{\left(\dfrac{8{,}510}{\text{shrs.}} \times \text{U.S.}\$32.50\right) + \left(\dfrac{19{,}858}{\text{shrs.}} \times \text{U.S.}\$40\right)}{28{,}369 \text{ shares}} \\[10pt]
&= \frac{\text{U.S.}\$276{,}575 + \text{U.S.}\$794{,}320}{28{,}369 \text{ shares}} \\[10pt]
&= \text{U.S.}\$37.75
\end{aligned}$$

The long equity cost basis is U.S.$36.31, and the sale price is U.S.$37.75. With a 100% hedge ratio, the position will not benefit from an increase in the equity price. Excluding accrued interest and expenses, the profit is U.S.$40,851.36.

$$\begin{aligned} \text{Profit} &= \text{(Equity sale price} - \text{Cost basis)} \times \text{Number of shares short} \\ &= \text{(U.S.\$37.75} - \text{U.S.\$36.31)} \times 28{,}369 \text{ shares} \\ &= \text{U.S.\$40,851.36} \end{aligned}$$

BEARISH HEDGE

Hedge positions can also be profitable in a bearish scenario. In fact, most hedge positions benefit from a decline in the equity price. Assume the investor believes that USA Inc. shares will decline. A bearish partial hedge is established to take advantage of the expected premium expansion.

Convertible bond price:	U.S.$1,030
Equity price:	U.S.$32.50
Conversion value:	U.S.$921.99
Premium:	10.801 points
Yield to put:	9.48%

The investor purchases 1,000M bonds at 103 net. Assuming a 90% bearish hedge ratio, the investor sells short 25,532 shares at U.S.$32.50. The hedge position is established at a 10.801-point premium. Assume there is no accrued interest.

$$\begin{aligned} \text{Short position} &= \frac{\text{Number of bonds}}{\text{purchased}} \times \frac{\text{Conversion}}{\text{ratio}} \times \frac{\text{Hedge}}{\text{ratio}} \\ &= 1{,}000\text{M bonds} \times 28.368 \text{ shares} \times 0.90 \\ &= 25{,}532 \text{ shares} \end{aligned}$$

The investor's investment in the hedge position is as follows.

$$\text{Long dollar investment} = \text{Number of bonds} \times \text{Bond price}$$
$$= 1,000\text{M bonds} \times \text{U.S.}\$1,030$$
$$= \text{U.S.}\$1,030,000$$

$$\text{Short dollar proceeds} = \frac{\text{Number of shares shorted}}{} \times \text{Equity price}$$
$$= 25,532 \text{ shares} \times \text{U.S.}\$32.50$$
$$= \text{U.S.}\$829,790$$

Convertible
Security

Long convertible U.S.$1,030,000	

Equity

	Short equity U.S.$829,790

The USA Inc. equity and convertible prices decline to U.S.$25.00 and U.S.$940, respectively. The investor believes the decline in USA Inc. shares has ended and reverses the position at a wider premium.

Current market levels:

Convertible bond price:	U.S.$940
Equity price:	U.S.$25.00
Conversion value:	U.S.$709.20
Premium:	23.08 points
Yield to put:	11.21%

The 1,000M convertible bonds are sold at 94 net. A loss is realized on the long position. The 25,532-share short position in the equity is covered at U.S.$25.00. A profit is realized on the short position.

$$\frac{\text{Proceeds from sale}}{\text{of long position}} = \frac{\text{Number of bonds}}{\text{sold}} \times \frac{\text{Bond}}{\text{price}}$$

$$= 1{,}000\text{M bonds} \times \text{U.S.\$940}$$

$$= \text{U.S.\$940,000}$$

$$\frac{\text{Principal to cover}}{\text{short equity position}} = \frac{\text{Number of shares}}{\text{bought}} \times \frac{\text{Equity}}{\text{price}}$$

$$= 25{,}532 \text{ shares} \times \text{U.S.\$25.00}$$

$$= \text{U.S.\$638,300}$$

Convertible
Security

Long convertible U.S.$1,030,000	**Sold convertible** **U.S.$940,000**

Loss: U.S.$90,000

Equity

Bought equity **U.S.$638,300**	Short equity U.S.$829,790

Profit: U.S.$191,490

$$\text{Profit} = \text{Gain on short position} - \text{Loss on long position}$$

$$= \text{U.S.\$191,490} - \text{U.S.\$90,000}$$

$$= \text{U.S.\$101,490}$$

Upon reversal of the position, a profit of U.S.$101,490 is realized. The convertible and equity moved in the same direction but at different rates.

	Price 1	Price 2	Percent Decline
Convertible price	103	94	−8.74
Equity price	32.50	25	−23.08

The bearish hedge position benefited from the premium expansion from 10.801 points to 23.08 points. The gain on the short position was only partially offset by a loss in the long position. The convertible bond outperformed the equity on the downside.

NEUTRAL HEDGE

A neutral hedge is intended to protect a hedge position from an upward move in the equity. Convertibles are defensive securities that outperform the equity on the downside. On the upside, convertibles trading at a premium tend to underperform the equity. A neutral hedge is one in which an amount of stock is sold short in order to break even on the upside.

As previously stated, delta hedges are often used for a neutral stance. Delta calculations entail sophisticated techniques. The following explanation of a neutral hedge is simplistic but intended to give a general idea of the process. In this instance, a neutral hedge is subjective in that estimates must be made of bond levels for a given equity price movement. The following example will clarify the procedure.

The current equity price is U.S.$32.50, and the current bond price is 103. Bond prices must be estimated corresponding to an equity increase of U.S.$39 or a decline of U.S.$26. One way to arrive at a bond price is by estimating where premiums have traded in the past or are likely to trade given the current environment.

Scenario	Equity Price	Percent Change	Estimated Bond Price	Percent Change	Premium
Upside	$39	20	116	12.6	4.9%
Downside	26	-20	92	-10.7	24.7%

Upside scenario:

$$\text{Gain on long} = \frac{\text{Estimated bond}}{\text{price}} - \frac{\text{Current bond}}{\text{price}}$$

$$= \text{U.S.}\$1,160 - \text{U.S.}\$1,030$$

$$= \text{U.S.}\$130$$

$$\text{Loss on short} = \frac{\text{Current equity}}{\text{price}} - \frac{\text{Upside equity}}{\text{price}}$$

$$= \text{U.S.}\$32.50 - \text{U.S.}\$39.00$$

$$= -\text{U.S.}\$6.50$$

$$\text{Ratio of gain/loss} = \frac{\text{Gain on long}}{\text{Loss on short}}$$

$$= \frac{\text{U.S. }\$130.00}{\text{U.S. }\$6.50}$$

$$= 20$$

$$\text{Hedge ratio} = \frac{\text{Ratio of gain/loss}}{\text{Conversion ratio}} \times 100$$

$$= \frac{20}{28.369 \text{ shares}} \times 100$$

$$= 70.5\%$$

The neutral hedge ratio is 70.5%. With a 70.5% hedge ratio, the position breaks even on the upside.

Upside profit/loss:

$$\text{Gain on long} = \text{U.S.}\$1,160 - \text{U.S.}\$1,030$$

$$= \text{U.S.}\$130$$

$$\text{Loss on short} = \frac{\text{Conversion}}{\text{ratio}} \times \frac{\text{Neutral}}{\substack{\text{hedge} \\ \text{ratio}}} \times \frac{\text{Change in equity}}{\text{price}}$$

$$= 28.369 \text{ shares} \times 0.705 \times (\text{U.S.}\$32.50 - \text{U.S.}\$39.00)$$

$$= -\text{U.S.}\$130$$

For an upward move in the equity price, the position assuming a neutral hedge ratio breaks even.

The neutral hedge ratio protects the position on the upside. On the downside, the neutral hedge ratio generally results in a profit.

Downside profit/loss:

$$\text{Loss on long} = \text{Estimated bond price} - \text{Current bond price}$$
$$= \text{U.S.\$920} - \text{U.S.\$1,030}$$
$$= -\text{U.S.\$110}$$

$$\text{Gain on short} = \frac{\text{Conversion}}{\text{ratio}} \times \frac{\text{Neutral}}{\text{hedge}} \times \frac{\text{Change in equity}}{\text{price}}$$
$$= 28.369 \text{ shares} \times 0.705 \times (\text{U.S.\$32.50} - \text{U.S.\$26.00})$$
$$= \text{U.S.\$130}$$

Using a neutral hedge and these estimated prices, the position breaks even on the upside and earns U.S.$20 on the downside.

Since bond prices must be estimated, the neutral hedge ratio is subjective. Often, to be protected in the case of call, the equity price on the upside is assumed to be the price that would trigger the call feature.

ANALYSIS OF HEDGE POSITIONS

In establishing a hedge position, it is important to understand the upside risk and downside risk. On the upside, the maximum loss possible if the convertibles are called is important. On the downside, if the equity price collapses, the level the convertibles must maintain to break even is important. Both scenarios will be investigated under the following assumptions.

Position	Price
Long, 1,000M bonds	U.S. $1,030
Short, (80%), 22,695 shares	U.S. $32.50

Conversion ratio:	28.369 shares
Call trigger:	130% of conversion price (U.S.$35.25)
	= U.S.$45.825
Premium:	10.801 points

Upside Risk

Assuming the convertibles are called, the following calculations are used to determine the position's maximum loss.

$$\text{Premium risk} = \text{Number of bonds} \times \text{Premium}$$
$$= 1{,}000\text{M} \times \text{U.S.}\$108.01$$
$$= \text{U.S.}\$108{,}010$$

$$\frac{\text{Loss on equity at call}}{\text{trigger price}} = \text{Call price trigger} - \frac{\text{Short-sale}}{\text{cost basis}}$$
$$= \text{U.S.}\$45.825 - \text{U.S.}\$32.50$$
$$= \text{U.S.}\$13.325$$

$$\text{Equivalent long} = \text{Number of bonds} \times \text{Conversion ratio}$$
$$= 1{,}000\text{M} \times 28.369 \text{ shares}$$
$$= 28{,}369 \text{ shares}$$

$$\frac{\text{Net long (equity)}}{\text{via convertible}} = \text{Equivalent long} - \text{Short position}$$
$$= 28{,}369 \text{ shares} - 22{,}695 \text{ shares}$$
$$= 5{,}674 \text{ shares}$$

Through the convertible, the position is essentially long 5,674 shares. This net long exposure benefits from an increase in the equity price.

$$\text{Profit via convertible} = \text{Net long} \times \text{Increase in equity}$$
$$= 5{,}674 \text{ shares} \times (\text{U.S.}\$45.825 - \text{U.S.}\$32.50)$$
$$= \text{U.S.}\$75{,}606$$

$$\text{Maximum loss} = \text{Premium risk} - \text{Profit via convertible}$$
$$= \text{U.S.\$108,010} - \text{U.S.\$75,606}$$
$$= \text{U.S.\$32,404}$$

Given the premium paid, the maximum the position can lose if the bonds are called is U.S.\$32,404. The gain on the net long partially offsets the premium that would be lost upon conversion.

Downside Risk

On the downside, the hedge position is also exposed to risk. Assuming the equity collapses from U.S.\$32.50 to U.S.\$20.00, the level the bond price must maintain to break even is important. The bond price must maintain a level that equates the loss on the long to the gain on the short.

	Quantity	Cost
Long position	1,000M bonds	U.S.\$1,030
Short position	22,695 shares	U.S.\$32.50

$$\text{Change in equity price} = \text{U.S.\$20.00} - \text{U.S.\$32.50}$$
$$= -\text{U.S.\$12.50}$$

$$\text{Gain on short position} = \text{Shares short} \times \text{U.S.\$12.50}$$
$$= 22,695 \text{ shares} \times \text{U.S.\$12.50}$$
$$= \text{U.S.\$283,687.50}$$

$$\text{Gain per bond} = \frac{\text{Gain on short}}{\text{Number of bonds}}$$
$$= \frac{\text{U.S.\$283,687.50}}{1,000\text{M}}$$
$$= \text{U.S.\$283.69}$$

$$\text{Break-even bond price} = \text{Current bond price} - \text{Gain/bond}$$
$$= \text{U.S.\$1,030} - \text{U.S.\$283.69}$$
$$= \text{U.S.\$746.31}$$

Net profit/loss:

$$\text{Gain on short} = \text{U.S.\$283,687.50}$$

$$\text{Loss on long} = \text{Number of bonds} \times \text{Change in bond price}$$
$$= 1,000M \times (\text{U.S.\$746.31} - \text{U.S.\$1,030})$$
$$= -\text{U.S.\$283,690}$$

In the case that the equity declines to U.S.\$20.00, the convertible must trade at U.S.\$746.31 for the position to break even. If the bond falls below this level, the position will lose money.

Rate of Return

Hedge positions are established to trade premium levels and to generate cash flow. The decision to set up a position is often based on the estimated standstill rate of return. The rate of return will vary based on assumptions. The following is a basic example of a rate-of-return calculation. (This is not the only way to calculate rate of return.)

	Quantity	Cost
Long position	1,000M bonds	U.S.\$1,030
Short position	18,440 shares	U.S.\$32.50

Coupon: 7.5%

Equity dividend: U.S.\$0.95

Assume that an investment of 10% of the hedged amount of the position and 50% of the unhedged portion of the position is required.

Assumptions:

Short rebate:	80%
Broker loan rate:	7.5%
Internal financing rate:	7.0%

$$\text{Long dollar} = \text{Number of bonds} \times \text{Convertible price}$$
$$= 1{,}000\text{M} \times \text{U.S.\$1,030}$$
$$= \text{U.S.\$1,030,000}$$

$$\text{Short dollar} = \text{Shares short} \times \text{Equity price}$$
$$= 18{,}440 \text{ shares} \times \text{U.S.\$32.50}$$
$$= \text{U.S.\$599,300}$$

$$\text{Hedged long} = \text{Long bonds} \times \text{Hedge ratio}$$
$$= 1{,}000\text{M} \times 0.65$$
$$= 650\text{M}$$

$$\text{Hedged dollar} = \text{Hedged bonds} \times \text{Convertible price}$$
$$= 650\text{M} \times \text{U.S.\$1,030}$$
$$= \text{U.S.\$669,500}$$

$$\text{Unhedged dollar} = \text{Long dollar} - \text{Hedged dollar}$$
$$= \text{U.S.\$1,030,000} - \text{U.S.\$669,500}$$
$$= \text{U.S.\$360,500}$$

$$\text{Actual dollar investment} = 10\% \text{ (Hedged dollars)} + 50\% \text{ (Unhedged dollars)}$$
$$= (0.10 \times \text{U.S.\$669,500}) + (0.50 \times \text{U.S.\$360,500})$$
$$= \text{U.S.\$66,950} + \text{U.S.\$180,250}$$
$$= \text{U.S.\$247,200}$$

$$\text{Borrowed amount} = \text{Long dollar} - \text{Actual investment}$$
$$= \text{U.S.\$1,030,000} - \text{U.S.\$247,200}$$
$$= \text{U.S.\$782,800}$$

$$\text{Short proceeds} = \text{Short dollars} \times \text{Rebate}$$
$$= \text{U.S.\$599,300} \times 0.80$$
$$= \text{U.S.\$479,440}$$

$$\text{Interest charge} = (\text{Borrowed amount} \times \text{Broker loan}) + (\text{Actual investment} \times \text{Internal financing rate}) - (\text{Short proceeds} \times \text{Broker loan})$$
$$= (\text{U.S.\$782,800} \times 0.075) + (\text{U.S.\$247,200} \times 0.07) - (\text{U.S.\$479,440} \times 0.075)$$
$$= \text{U.S.\$58,710} + \text{U.S.\$17,304} - \text{U.S.\$35,958}$$
$$= \text{U.S.\$40,056}$$

$$\text{Convertible income} = \text{Number of bonds} \times \text{Coupon}$$
$$= 1,000\text{M} \times \text{U.S.\$75}$$
$$= \text{U.S.\$75,000}$$

$$\text{Dividend loss on short} = \text{Shares short} \times \text{Equity dividend}$$
$$= 18,440 \text{ shares} \times \text{U.S.\$0.95}$$
$$= \text{U.S.\$17,518}$$

$$\text{Net income} = \frac{\text{Convertible}}{\text{income}} - \frac{\text{Dividend}}{\text{loss}} - \frac{\text{Interest}}{\text{charge}}$$
$$= \text{U.S.\$75,000} - \text{U.S.\$17,518} - \text{U.S.\$40,056}$$
$$= \text{U.S.\$17,426}$$

$$\text{Return on investment} = \frac{\text{Net income}}{\text{Actual investment}} \times 100$$
$$= \frac{\text{U.S.\$17,426}}{\text{U.S.\$247,200}} \times 100$$
$$= 7\%$$

On a standstill basis, the rate of return of 7% is relatively low. This calculation does not include returns from trading premium levels.

To take one step further, hedges can be established in international convertibles. In these instances, there is often foreign currency exposure. To understand the currency exposure of a hedge position, we will assume a U.S. dollar perspective in the following analysis.

The net currency exposure (whether long or short foreign currency) will determine the position's exposure. Assume that the hedge position is long and short securities denominated in the same currency.

Position	Foreign Currency Flow	Currency Exposure
Long international convertible	Need currency to settle trade	Short foreign currency
Short ordinary share	Receive currency from equity sale	Long foreign currency

In general, hedge positions established with convertibles trading at a premium will result in a net short foreign currency exposure. The long-side investment of the position tends to exceed the short side. This hedge position not only generates cash flow and provides trading opportunities with respect to premium levels, but it also offers the opportunity to profit from currency fluctuations.

If possible, positions are maintained in the currency of their denomination. Being long and short securities denominated in the same currency partially offsets the currency exposure. The net proceeds received after unwinding the hedge position (selling the convertible bond and covering the short equity position) are subject to translation exposure, as are coupon payments (and accrued interest).

A hedge position that is long a U.S. dollar–denominated convertible and short an ordinary share tends to be long foreign currency.

Position	Foreign Currency Flow	Currency Exposure
Long U.S. dollar convertible	None	None
Short ordinary share	Receive currency from equity sale	Long foreign currency

In such cases the equity position is usually translated into U.S. dollars by selling the foreign currency received from the sale of the equity for U.S. dollars. It is easier to keep the position in the same currency.

Upon unwinding the position, the purchase of the equity to cover the short position is accompanied by a purchase of the foreign currency with U.S. dollars to settle the equity trade. The original foreign currency transaction is reversed. The profit/loss from currency fluctuations is realized. Since interest payments are received in U.S. dollars, there is no currency exposure.

No matter what the currency denomination of the convertible or equity, it is always important to understand the transaction and economic currency exposures of the underlying equity. If the convertible issuer's earnings are derived in a particular currency, certain currency strategies may be more appropriate than others. It is very important to investigate the total (macro) currency exposure, whether hedging or purchasing international convertible securities outright.

The convertible hedges discussed illustrate typical positions. In general, a hedge position is established by going long a convertible and selling short the underlying equity. A "Chinese hedge" is a long equity and short convertible position. This hedge assumes the long equity position will increase at a faster rate than the short convertible position. The overall position benefits from a narrowing of premium levels. It is more often used in a bullish scenario. An important consideration is whether the convertible bond can be borrowed in order to sell short.

Hedge positions are usually established by selling short equity. The short side can be established by selling call options in lieu of equity, but the sale of call options does not provide the same downside protection. The position is protected on the downside by the amount of option premium received. On the upside, if the options are called, the short equity position is established at a cost of the premium received plus the strike price.

Hedge positions can be profitable in both bullish and bearish scenarios. They are effective when the convertible and equity prices move in the same direction but at different rates. Trading stances can be changed by adjusting the hedge ratio. The total return of the position is a function of changes in premium levels, interest rates, and currencies, as well as cash flow generated.

17

Convertible Bond Indenture

The *convertible bond indenture* (final prospectus) is a legal document that describes the privileges and specifications of the convertible bond. The amount of information disclosed depends on the legal requirements of the home country of the issuer. The prospectus' cover gives a brief description of the pertinent details of the issue. There are sections describing the convertible, the underlying equity, and the issuer. The indenture is a valuable source of information and, when available, should be obtained.

The cover page reviews the general terms of the convertible issue. The issuer's full corporate name is stated. The type of security (bond, preference share, loan stock, etc.) determines the issue's seniority with respect to the company's other financings. The size of the issue and its currency denomination are indicated.

In addition, the cover page reviews the issue's pricing with regard to its debt and equity components. Information relating to the debt feature includes the coupon rate, maturity date, interest payment dates (annual or semiannual), and face value. The pricing information regarding the conversion feature includes the conversion price and the equity closing price. The asset (usually underlying equity) into which the issue is convertible is also disclosed.

Within the indenture, the convertible's features are described in detail. It is particularly important to read this information because features vary among issues, and new features are constantly being introduced.

The convertible's income feature is described. The coupon rate, stated in gross or net terms, and interest payment dates are specified. Whether the convertible accrues interest daily or pays only on interest payment dates is disclosed. The number of days in the year (either 360 or 365) determines the accrued interest. Some issues include provisions to reset the coupon on a specific date to a level where the convertible trades at par.

The conversion rights of the convertible holder are discussed. The asset (equity, bond, commodity, cash, etc.) into which the security is convertible is specified. The convertible is usually exchangeable into the equity of the issuer, and may be exchangeable into certain classes of common stock. The indenture states whether the shares received upon conversion are entitled to the next dividend. It also states whether the shares issued are registered by governing agencies. The shares received upon conversion may not be fungible into existing shares for a period of time. These issues are important in the decision to purchase international convertibles.

Another important feature is the period during which the bonds are exchangeable. The conversion date can be continuous or periodic. In the case of forced redemption, the last day to convert with respect to the interest payment date might determine whether the accrued interest is lost upon conversion.

The conversion ratio is stated per face amount. The conversion price and closing equity price are provided to determine the premium over conversion value. Under certain circumstances, the conversion price is adjusted (e.g., for capital distribution or rights issues). Some issues have provisions to reset the conversion price on a certain date to maintain a premium level.

The redemption features are discussed. Final redemption is at maturity and usually at par value. The call feature, including call protection and the call price schedule, are explained. The nature of the issue's put feature and sinking fund is discussed. Some convertibles have rolling put features with multiple put dates.

Other miscellaneous issues—for instance, what happens in the case of default, assets available for distribution, and taxation—are also discussed in the indenture.

The indenture is a source of information regarding the nature of the issuer's business. The company's history and development are broken down by lines of business. Each segment is analyzed by its product, target markets, and customers. All subsidiaries are mentioned. Sales and profits are examined by division and geographic region.

The company's capital structure is analyzed in great detail. Current and historical income statements, balance sheets, and cash flow analyses are provided. All accounting policies are disclosed. Other important details include interest payments, taxes, capital commitments, investments, creditors, and debtors.

From the investor's standpoint, the convertible indenture is the most important source of information regarding the specifics of the convertible security and the issuer. It specifies the investor's legal rights.

18
Domestic Convertible Markets

Many countries have domestic or local convertible markets. *Domestic convertibles* are issued in the home country and are denominated in the local currency (currency of the underlying equity). They comply with local regulations and are generally sold to domestic investors.

Foreign convertibles, in contrast, are issued by a foreign borrower in another country's domestic market and local currency. For example, a Japanese borrower issues a convertible denominated in Swiss francs in Switzerland. Foreign convertibles also include domestic convertibles denominated in a foreign currency.

Countries usually have different regulations on bonds issued by domestic companies versus those of foreign borrowers. The legal distinctions may include taxation, disclosure statements, and registration requirements. Domestic convertibles are usually subject to a withholding tax unless a double-taxation treaty exists between the investor's and the issuer's home countries.

Domestic convertibles are denominated in the local currency. For example, a French company issues a convertible in France denominated in French francs. The convertibles trade and pay interest in the local currency. Depending on the investor's base currency, there will usually be foreign currency exposure related to the translation of foreign currency into the investor's base currency.

Domestic convertible securities often have features different from those of Euroconvertibles. Consequently, the methods of analyzing domestic convertibles may differ from the methods previously discussed.

In this chapter, several domestic convertible markets are evaluated. Domestic markets of the United States, Britain, Japan, France, Australia, and Canada will be analyzed. These markets were selected because they are relatively more liquid or they have unique characteristics. It should be noted that there are domestic convertible markets in more than 30 countries, and the markets selected here are just a sample.

The evaluation methods discussed are those used by participants in the respective domestic markets. Analytical methods differ because of the varying characteristics of the securities. The features and evaluation methods discussed are not necessarily the only ones found in the markets. Due to the hybrid nature of convertibles, new features are always being developed to appeal to new market participants and abide by new tax laws. In these dynamic markets, there are always exceptions to the general rules.

U.S. DOMESTIC CONVERTIBLE BONDS

Domestic U.S. convertible securities are quite similar to Euroconvertibles. The terms and evaluation methods of Euroconvertibles can be applied to domestic U.S. convertibles. U.S. domestic convertible securities come in the form of bonds and preferred shares. Convertible bonds and preferred shares will be addressed individually.

Domestic U.S. convertibles are issued at a premium to the underlying equity price. The amount of the premium determines the conversion price. The conversion ratio is derived by dividing the par value (U.S. $1,000) by the conversion price. The bond's conversion feature can be exercised up to maturity (American style).

Domestic U.S. convertible bonds typically pay interest semiannually based on a 360-day year. The price of the convertible is quoted as a percentage of par value. The bond's price does not include accrued interest.

U.S. convertibles have call features that may include absolute and provisional call protection. The provisional call protection is usually a higher percentage test (150% of the conversion price) than for Euroconvertible bonds. Put features are sometimes included among the bond's features. The yields to put tend to be less than those of Euroconvertible bonds.

Following is an analysis of a U.S. domestic convertible.

U.S. Domestic Convertible Bond

Coupon:	8.0%
Maturity:	July 15, 200X
Interest payments:	Jan. 15, July 15
Conversion ratio:	39.735 shares
Conversion price:	U.S.$25.17
Convertible bond price:	U.S.$1,050
Current bond yield:	7.62%
Equity price:	U.S.$23.00
Equity dividend:	U.S.$0.20
Current equity yield:	0.87%

Call feature: Noncallable for three years unless equity trades at 150% of conversion price for 20 consecutive days.

$$\text{Conversion value} = \text{Equity price} \times \text{Conversion ratio}$$
$$= \text{U.S.\$23.00} \times 39.735 \text{ shares}$$
$$= \text{U.S.\$913.90}$$

Premium over Conversion Value

$$\text{Point/dollar method} = \text{Bond price} - \text{Conversion value}$$
$$= \text{U.S.\$1,050} - \text{U.S.\$913.90}$$
$$= \text{U.S.\$136.10}$$

$$\text{Percent method} = \frac{\text{Bond price} - \text{Conversion value}}{\text{Conversion value}} \times 100$$
$$= \frac{\text{U.S.\$1,050} - \text{U.S.\$913.90}}{\text{U.S.\$913.90}} \times 100$$
$$= 14.89\%$$

Break-Even Period

$$\text{Equity method} = \frac{\text{Dollar premium}}{\text{Bond coupon} - \left(\dfrac{\text{Conversion}}{\text{ratio}} \times \dfrac{\text{Equity}}{\text{dividend}}\right)}$$

$$= \frac{\text{U.S.\$136.10}}{\text{U.S.\$80} - (39.735 \text{ shares} \times \text{U.S.\$0.20})}$$

$$= 1.89 \text{ years}$$

$$\text{Point/dollar method} = \frac{\text{Dollar premium}}{\text{Bond coupon} - \left(\dfrac{\text{Bond price}}{\text{Equity price}} \times \dfrac{\text{Equity}}{\text{dividend}}\right)}$$

$$= \frac{\text{U.S.\$136.10}}{\text{U.S.\$80} - \left(\dfrac{\text{U.S.\$1,050}}{\text{U.S.\$23.00}} \times \text{U.S.\$0.20}\right)}$$

$$= \frac{\text{U.S.\$136.10}}{\text{U.S.\$70.87}}$$

$$= 1.92 \text{ years}$$

$$\text{Percent method} = \frac{\text{Percent premium}}{\text{Percent yield advantage}}$$

$$= \frac{\text{Percent premium}}{\dfrac{\text{Current bond}}{\text{yield}} - \dfrac{\text{Current equity}}{\text{yield}}}$$

$$= \frac{14.89\%}{7.62\% - 0.87\%}$$

$$= 2.21 \text{ years}$$

U.S. domestic convertible bonds, like Euroconvertible bonds, are issued in registered form and are less fungible abroad. They are purchased for their equity participation, yield advantage, and downside protection. Low premiums and greater degrees of yield advantage must be evaluated with respect to call protection.

U.S. CONVERTIBLE PREFERENCE SHARES

Convertible bonds and convertible preference shares are similar securities and are evaluated with similar techniques. Convertible preference shares pay a dividend and are convertible into a predetermined number of equity shares. They are usually perpetual securities; they have no maturity dates and no stated value at maturity. Like convertible bonds, they are hybrid securities that participate in equity price appreciation with limited downside risk.

Convertible preference shares are often issued as a result of a merger or acquisition. From the issuer's standpoint, the preference share's dividend payment is not tax-deductible like a bond's interest payment. Thus, preference shares are often issued by companies who do not require the tax benefit. Investors can exclude from taxes a percentage of the dividends earned.

Convertible bonds have a senior claim to assets over convertible preference shares. Both types of securities have similar dilution protection. A preference share's par value may be U.S.$25, U.S.$50, or U.S.$100.

Relative to the underlying equity, preference shares offer equity price appreciation potential, downside protection, and a yield advantage. The dividend, expressed as an actual dollar amount, must be declared and is usually paid quarterly or semiannually. The dividend is often cumulative.

Convertible preference shares generally do not accrue the dividend on a daily basis. The preference share's price, quoted as an actual dollar amount and not as a percentage of par value, is reduced by the amount of the dividend paid on the exdividend date. Theoretically, it can be said that the preference share's price will increase to reflect the upcoming dividend payments.

Some Euroconvertible preference shares deviate from these general rules. In fact, these Euroconvertible preference shares resemble bonds more than preference shares.

Convertible preference shares are priced similarly to convertible bonds. Based on the issuer's credit rating, a dividend yield competitive to comparable paper is selected. For purposes of the following analysis, assume that competitive rates are 7.5%. Given a U.S.$50 issue price, the dividend is U.S.$3.75.

Convertible Cumulative Preference Share

Par value:	U.S.$50.00
Issue Price:	U.S.$50.00
Dividend:	U.S.$ 3.75

$$\text{Current preferred yield} = \frac{\text{Preferred dividend}}{\text{Issue price}} \times 100$$

$$= \frac{\text{U.S.\$3.75}}{\text{U.S.\$50.00}} \times 100$$

$$= 7.5\%$$

The premium over conversion value is selected at a competitive level. Assume the premium over conversion value is 25%. Given an equity price of U.S.$58.40, the resulting conversion price is U.S.$73.

$$\text{Conversion price} = \text{Equity price} \times (1 + \text{Premium})$$

$$= \text{U.S.\$58.40} \times (1 + 0.25)$$

$$= \text{U.S.\$73.00}$$

The conversion ratio is derived with respect to par value, which, in this instance, is U.S.$50.

$$\text{Conversion ratio} = \frac{\text{Par value}}{\text{Conversion price}}$$

$$= \frac{\text{U.S.\$50}}{\text{U.S.\$73}}$$

$$= 0.685 \text{ shares}$$

One preference share is convertible into 0.685 shares of equity. For a 1-point move in the equity price, the convertible (assuming no premium) will theoretically move 0.685 points.

Convertible preference shares usually have call features but not put features. The call feature may provide absolute and/or provisional protection. In this example, the preference is not callable for two years.

At that point, the issue is callable only if the equity trades at 140% of conversion price (U.S.$102.20) for 20 of 30 days. The call price starts at U.S.$52.50 (a premium to the issue price) and declines to par value (U.S.$50.00).

Convertible preference shares are evaluated similarly to convertible bonds. The following example is an analysis of a convertible preference share.

U.S.$3.75 Convertible Cumulative Preference Share

Preferred dividend:	U.S.$3.75
Conversion ratio:	0.685 shares
Equity price:	U.S.$80.00
Preferred price:	U.S.$62.00
Equity dividend:	U.S.$0.80

$$\text{Conversion value} = \text{Equity price} \times \text{Conversion ratio}$$
$$= \text{U.S.}\$80.00 \times 0.685 \text{ shares}$$
$$= \text{U.S.}\$54.80$$

Premium over Conversion Value

$$\text{Point/dollar method} = \text{Preferred price} - \text{Conversion value}$$
$$= \text{U.S.}\$62.00 - \text{U.S.}\$54.80$$
$$= \text{U.S.}\$7.20$$

$$\text{Percent method} = \frac{\text{Preferred price} - \text{Conversion value}}{\text{Conversion value}} \times 100$$
$$= \frac{\text{U.S.}\$62.00 - \text{U.S.}\$54.80}{\text{U.S.}\$54.80} \times 100$$
$$= 13.14\%$$

Yield Advantage

$$\text{Percent method} = \left(\frac{\text{Current preferred}}{\text{yield}} - \frac{\text{Current equity}}{\text{yield}} \right) \times 100$$

$$= \left(\frac{\text{Preferred dividend}}{\text{Preferred price}} - \frac{\text{Equity dividend}}{\text{Equity price}} \right) \times 100$$

$$= \left(\frac{\text{U.S.\$3.75}}{\text{U.S.\$62.00}} - \frac{\text{U.S.\$0.80}}{\text{U.S.\$80.00}} \right) \times 100$$

$$= (0.06 - 0.01) \times 100$$

$$= 5\%$$

$$\text{Equity method} = \frac{\text{Preferred}}{\text{dividend}} - \left(\frac{\text{Conversion}}{\text{ratio}} \times \frac{\text{Equity}}{\text{dividend}} \right)$$

$$= \text{U.S.\$3.75} - (0.685 \text{ shares} \times \text{U.S.\$0.80})$$

$$= \text{U.S.\$3.75} - \text{U.S.\$0.55}$$

$$= \text{U.S.\$3.20}$$

Break-Even Period

$$\text{Percent method} = \frac{\text{Percent premium}}{\text{Percent yield advantage}}$$

$$= \frac{13.14\%}{5\%}$$

$$= 2.63 \text{ years}$$

Convertible bonds and preference shares are similar securities. They participate in equity appreciation and provide downside protection. As such, both securities are evaluated in a similar fashion.

BRITISH DOMESTIC CONVERTIBLES

Domestic British convertibles have many unique attributes. Many features associated with Euroconvertibles and with some domestic markets are not found in the British domestic market. It is important to know the specific characteristics of the British market in order to make appropriate investment decisions.

Domestic British convertibles come in the form of loan stock and preference shares. They are issued at premiums to the equity price and provide incremental income. A convertible typically matures in 15 years either on one final date or on a given date over a period of consecutive years. The final date in such a series is the actual final maturity date. For example, in the case of a convertible that matures on April 30 in years 12–15, the bonds may be redeemed on April 30 in year 12, 13, 14, or 15; the final maturity date is April 30 in year 15.

Domestic British convertibles do not have call features and rarely have put features. The bond's par value is £100.

Domestic British convertibles may have a continuous or a periodic conversion feature. Some bonds may be convertible from a few days after issue date until maturity. The convertible may be exchangeable one or two days a year until maturity. The periodic conversion feature is more prevalent.

The conversion ratio is expressed as the number of shares into which the convertible is exchangeable per £100 face amount. For example, a conversion ratio of 71.428 indicates that the share is convertible into 71.428/£100. That is, one convertible loan stock or preference share is convertible into 0.71428 equity shares.

The conversion price is the cost of the equity when purchased through the convertible. When the convertible is trading at a premium, the cost of the equity via the convertible exceeds the current equity price. The conversion price changes with the convertible price.

$$\text{Conversion price} = \frac{\text{Gross convertible price}}{\text{Conversion ratio}}$$

The gross convertible price is used because, upon conversion, the accrued interest paid is forfeited. The gross price is the total cost.

Domestic British convertibles come in the form of loan stock or preference shares. All convertible prices include accrued interest (gross convertible price). Interest is usually paid semiannually and accrues based on a 365-day year. The net convertible price is the quoted price less the accrued interest. The net convertible price is used in most calculations.

Technically, there is a difference between the methods of quoting loan stock and preference shares, although the resulting principal amounts are equivalent. Loan stock is quoted as a percentage of par value (£100). Preference shares are quoted in terms of pence (p). Assume 1,000 shares of a loan stock and 1,000 preference shares are purchased.

	Quote	Principal
Loan stock	103–104	£1.04 × 1,000 shares = £1,040
Preference shares	103p–104p	104p × 1,000 shares = £1,040

For both methods, the resulting consideration is the same. The difference in quotation is a minor technicality and generally does not affect daily trading.

The investor pays 104% of par value (loan stock) or 104p (preference share) for one convertible. In either instance, the cost of £100 worth of convertibles is £1040. If an investor buys 250,000 shares, the consideration (including accrued interest) is £260,000 (250,000 × £1.04). Assuming a conversion ratio of 71.428 shares, the total number of shares controlled is 178,570 (250,000 × 0.71428).

Another difference between loan stock and preference shares is the method in which the coupon is expressed. Loan stocks have a gross coupon. A 7% loan stock trading at a net price of 103 has a current or running yield of 6.8%. Preference shares pay a coupon net of tax to U.K. investors; the current yield has to be adjusted for taxes. Assuming a tax rate of 25%, a 7% preference share trading at a net price of 103p has a gross yield of 9.06%.

$$\begin{aligned} \text{Preference share current yield} &= \frac{\left(\dfrac{\text{Net coupon}}{\text{Equity price}}\right)}{1 - \text{Tax rate}} \times 100 \\[2mm] &= \frac{7/103}{1 - 0.25} \times 100 \\[2mm] &= 9.06\% \end{aligned}$$

Domestic British convertibles are evaluated primarily with regard to yield advantage. The degree of yield advantage determines the optimal time to convert. For a given dividend growth rate, the point at which the equity yield exceeds the convertible yield is the optimal time to convert. At this point, it is no longer economical to maintain a position in the convertible. The income received from the convertible remains constant, whereas the equity dividend continues to grow.

The net present value of the net cash flows over the life of the bond is compared to the premium. If the premium paid is less than the discounted yield advantage, the convertible is considered attractive. The cost of the convertible in excess of its equity value is offset by the incremental income earned over the life of the bond. This evaluation method is possible because there is no call feature. Early conversion changes the net present value of the yield advantage.

The following is an example of an analysis of a loan stock (referred to as a bond in the example).

U.K. Domestic Convertible Loan Stock

Gross coupon:	7.0%
Maturity:	April 30, years 12–15
Interest payment date:	January 1, July 1
Par value:	£100
Conversion ratio:	71.428 shares/£100
Gross convertible bond price:	104
Net convertible bond price:	103
Equity price:	140p
Equity dividend:	4.5p

$$\text{Current bond yield} = \frac{\text{Coupon}}{\text{Net bond price}} \times 100$$

$$= \frac{7}{103} \times 100$$

$$= 6.8\%$$

$$\text{Current equity yield} = \frac{\text{Equity dividend}}{\text{Equity price}} \times 100$$

$$= \frac{4.5\text{p}}{140\text{p}} \times 100$$

$$= 3.2\%$$

Yield Advantage

$$\text{Percent method} = \frac{\text{Current bond}}{\text{yield}} - \frac{\text{Current equity}}{\text{yield}}$$

$$= 6.8\% - 3.2\%$$

$$= 3.6\%$$

The conversion price is the cost of the equity when purchased through the convertible. The conversion price changes with the convertible price.

$$\text{Conversion price} = \frac{\text{Gross convertible price}}{\text{Conversion ratio}}$$

$$= \frac{104}{71.428 \text{ shares}}$$

$$= 1.456$$

$$\text{Conversion value} = \text{Equity price} \times \text{Conversion ratio}$$

$$= \pounds1.40 \times 71.428 \text{ shares}$$

$$= \pounds100$$

Premium over Conversion Value

$$\text{Point/dollar method} = \text{Conversion price} - \text{Equity price}$$

$$= 145.6\text{p} - 140.0\text{p}$$

$$= 5.6\text{p}$$

$$\text{Percent method} = \frac{\text{Premium (points)}}{\text{Equity price}} \times 100$$

$$= \frac{5.6\text{p}}{140\text{p}} \times 100$$

$$= 4\%$$

$$\text{Percent method} = \left(\frac{\text{Conversion price}}{\text{Equity price}} - 1\right) \times 100$$

$$= \left(\frac{1.456}{1.40} - 1\right) \times 100$$

$$= 4\%$$

Break-Even Period

$$\text{Percent method} = \frac{\text{Percent premium}}{\text{Percent yield advantage}}$$

$$= \frac{4\%}{3.6\%}$$

$$= 1.1 \text{ years}$$

The convertible's yield advantage is expressed annually in Figure 18.1. Assuming a 10% dividend growth rate, the convertible has a yield advantage over the equity until the ninth year. In year 9, the convertible should be converted into the underlying equity. During those nine years, the convertible earns an additional 27.2p over the equity.

The yield advantage discounted at 10% to year 9 is 19.6p. The discounted yield advantage is compared to the actual premium. The net present value of the net cash flow of 19.6p exceeds the 5.6p premium. It is advantageous to pay the premium in order to earn the incremental yield until the bond is converted.

Assuming a 15% dividend growth rate results in optimal conversion in the sixth year (Figure 18.2). The total yield advantage after six years is 19.3p. The net cash flow discounted at 10% is 15.1p. This net present value of the cash flows exceeds the 5.6p premium.

				Year				
Dividend growth rate:	10%							
Discount rate:	10%							

	Year							
	1	2	3	4	5	6	7	8
Interest/share	.098	.098	.098	.098	.098	.098	.098	.098
Dividend/share	.045	.049	.054	.060	.066	.072	.080	.088
Net cash flow	.053	.049	.044	.038	.032	.026	.018	.010
Discounted NCF	.048	.040	.033	.026	.020	.014	.009	.005

	Year						
	9	10	11	12	13	14	15
Interest/share	.098	.098	.098	.098	.098	.098	.098
Dividend/share	.096	.106	.117	.128	.141	.155	.171
Net cash flow	**.002**	−.008	−.019	−.030	−.043	−.057	−.073
Discounted NCF	.001	−.003	−.007	−.010	−.013	−.015	−.017

Even payments are assumed for simplicity.

Figure 18.1 Discounted net cash flow: 10% dividend growth rate.

Dividend growth rate:	15%							
Discount rate:	10%							

	Year							
	1	2	3	4	5	6	7	8
Interest/share	.098	.098	.098	.098	.098	.098	.098	.098
Dividend/share	.045	.052	.060	.068	.079	.091	.104	.120
Net cash flow	.053	.046	.038	.030	.019	**.007**	−.006	−.022
Discounted NCF	.048	.038	.029	.020	.012	.004	−.003	−.010

	Year						
	9	10	11	12	13	14	15
Interest/share	.098	.098	.098	.098	.098	.098	.098
Dividend/share	.138	.158	.182	.209	.241	.277	.318
Net cash flow	−.040	−.060	−.084	−.111	−.143	−.179	−.220
Discounted NCF	−.017	−.023	−.029	−.035	−.041	−.047	−.053

Even payments are assumed for simplicity.

Figure 18.2 Discounted net cash flow: 15% dividend growth rate.

Domestic British convertibles are usually purchased for their yield advantage. They are considered both equity and bond alternatives. The optimal time to convert is when the equity yield exceeds the convertible yield. The premium paid is compared to the net present value of the net income stream received over the life of the convertible. If the discounted cash flows exceed the premium, the convertible is deemed relatively attractive.

JAPANESE DOMESTIC CONVERTIBLES

Domestic Japanese convertible bonds are similar to Euroconvertibles. Japanese domestic convertibles generally mature in 7–15 years. Upon issuance, yen convertible bonds are given a credit rating.

Japanese convertibles are issued at premiums to conversion value. The conversion price is usually set approximately 5% above the underlying equity price. Rather than using the closing equity price, the premium is usually set above an average equity price calculated over a 10–15-day period. The conversion period usually begins approximately one month after issue date and continues until maturity. Conversion value is the primary factor determining the bond's price.

Japanese convertibles do not bear high coupons; they usually offer only a slight yield advantage over the underlying equity. Interest is paid annually or semiannually. It is calculated based on a 365-day year and is usually subject to a withholding tax.

The price of a Japanese convertible does not include accrued interest. The buyer of a convertible pays the price plus accrued interest plus a commission. Sales tax is charged when the bonds are sold. The bonds are usually in bearer form. The convertibles are denominated in either ¥100M, ¥500M, or ¥1,000M units. Most are denominated in ¥1,000M units.

Most Japanese convertibles have call features. Generally, Japanese convertibles are not fully redeemed at final maturity; a portion of the issue is redeemed incrementally after an initial period of absolute call protection. For example, a 10-year convertible is not callable for 3 years, after which 5% of the issue is redeemed in years 4-9 and the remainder at final maturity. Also, the issuer often must retire a portion of the issue through a sinking fund. Put features are not common.

Japanese Domestic Convertible Bond

Coupon:	2.9%
Maturity:	August 30, 200X
Coupon payment:	March 31, September 30
Bond denomination:	¥1,000,000
Conversion price:	¥466.70
Convertible bond price:	¥1,003
Equity price:	¥445
Equity dividend:	¥3.5

$$\text{Conversion ratio} = \frac{\text{Bond denomination}}{\text{Conversion price}}$$

$$= \frac{\yen 1,000,000}{\yen 466.70}$$

$$= 2,142.70 \text{ shares}$$

$$\text{Current bond yield} = \frac{\text{Coupon}}{\text{Convertible price}} \times 100$$

$$= \frac{\yen 29}{\yen 1,003} \times 100$$

$$= 2.9\%$$

$$\text{Current equity yield} = \frac{\text{Equity dividend}}{\text{Equity price}} \times 100$$

$$= \frac{\yen 3.5}{\yen 445} \times 100$$

$$= 0.8\%$$

$$\text{Conversion value} = \frac{\text{Equity price}}{\text{Conversion price}} \times 100$$

$$= \frac{\yen 445}{\yen 466.70} \times 100$$

$$= 95.35$$

Premium over Conversion Value

$$\text{Yen method} = \text{Convertible price} - \text{Conversion value}$$
$$= ¥1,003 - ¥953.50$$
$$= ¥49.50$$

$$\text{Percent method} = \frac{\text{Convertible price} - \text{Conversion value}}{\text{Conversion value}} \times 100$$
$$= \frac{¥1,003 - ¥953.50}{¥953.50} \times 100$$
$$= 5.19\%$$

Japanese convertibles are usually not purchased for their yield advantage. However, depending on the equity market and the interest rate environment, the debt feature becomes increasingly important. As convertible bonds should, issues with greater degrees of yield advantage outperform on the downside. Investors are attracted to low-priced and low-premium issues. The low premium promotes participation in equity movements. Low-priced convertibles have less downside risk because they are trading at lower premiums over investment value.

FRENCH DOMESTIC CONVERTIBLES

Domestic French convertible bonds have unique characteristics. Often the bond's issue price, par value, and conversion price are the same. The bond's conversion price is set at a premium to the underlying equity. Par value is set at the conversion price, and the bond is priced at the conversion price.

Par value:	FF800
Conversion price:	FF800
Issue price:	FF800

By definition, the conversion ratio is one share (i.e., each bond is convertible into one share).

$$\text{Conversion ratio} = \frac{\text{Par value}}{\text{Conversion price}}$$

$$= \frac{\text{FF800}}{\text{FF800}}$$

$$= 1 \text{ share}$$

Domestic French convertible bonds generally mature in 10–15 years. The bond's price includes accrued interest. Interest is usually paid annually and is calculated on a 365-day year.

The interest payment is expressed as a percentage of par (nominal) value. For example, a 6% French domestic convertible bond with a FF800 par value has an annual interest payment of FF48.

$$\text{Interest payment} = \text{Percent payment} \times \text{Par value}$$

$$= 6\% \times \text{FF800}$$

$$= \text{FF48}$$

Call features are prevalent, and a convertible bond may have absolute or provisional call protection. The initial call price is at a premium to par value. Put features are not common.

The following example will clarify the features of a domestic French convertible bond.

6% French Domestic Convertible Bond

Interest payment:	FF48
Maturity:	10 years
Par value:	FF800
Conversion price:	FF800
Conversion ratio:	1 share
Convertible bond price:	FF855
Accrued interest:	FF5
Net convertible bond price:	FF850
Equity price:	FF740
Equity dividend:	FF10

Call protection: Absolute—3 years

Provisional—Callable after 3 years, if
equity trades at 150% of
conversion price for 20 days

$$\text{Current bond yield} = \frac{\text{Interest payment}}{\text{Net bond price}} \times 100$$

$$= \frac{\text{FF48}}{\text{FF850}} \times 100$$

$$= 5.65\%$$

$$\text{Current equity yield} = \frac{\text{Equity dividend}}{\text{Equity price}} \times 100$$

$$= \frac{\text{FF10}}{\text{FF740}} \times 100$$

$$= 1.35\%$$

$$\text{Conversion value} = \text{Equity price} \times \text{Conversion ratio}$$

$$= \text{FF740} \times 1 \text{ share}$$

$$= \text{FF740}$$

$$\frac{\text{Premium}}{\text{(Percent method)}} = \frac{\text{Net bond price} - \text{Conversion value}}{\text{Conversion value}} \times 100$$

$$= \frac{\text{FF850} - \text{FF740}}{\text{FF740}} \times 100$$

$$= 14.86\%$$

When the conversion ratio is one share, the premium can be calculated
with respect to the equity price rather than conversion value.

$$\begin{array}{l} \text{Premium} \\ \text{(Percent method)} \end{array} = \frac{\text{Net bond price} - \text{Conversion value}}{\text{Equity price}} \times 100$$

$$= \frac{\text{FF850} - \text{FF740}}{\text{FF740}} \times 100$$

$$= 14.86\%$$

$$\begin{array}{l} \text{Break-even period} \\ \text{(Percent method)} \end{array} = \frac{\text{Percent premium}}{\text{Percent yield advantage}}$$

$$= \frac{\text{Percent premium}}{\text{Current bond yield} - \text{Current equity yield}}$$

$$= \frac{14.86\%}{5.65\% - 1.35\%}$$

$$= 3.46 \text{ years}$$

Domestic French convertibles are evaluated with regard to premium and yield advantage. Low premiums and greater degrees of yield advantage are attractive. Convertibles that break even within call protection are desirable.

AUSTRALIAN DOMESTIC CONVERTIBLES

Domestic Australian convertibles come in the form of notes or preference shares. Upon maturity, the investor usually receives par value. In some instances, the convertible notes must be converted at maturity or they become perpetual debt. There are generally no call or put features.

Domestic Australian convertibles have either continuous or periodic conversion features. Some issues are convertible several days after issue until maturity. In other cases, conversion is once or twice a year. Often the notes must be converted in multiples of 100.

Many Australian convertibles are convertible into one share. In these cases, evaluation is similar to that of preferred shares. The conversion ratio is adjusted for bonus issues. The conversion price is viewed as the cost of the equity when purchased through the convertible security.

$$\text{Conversion price} = \frac{\text{Convertible price}}{\text{Conversion ratio}}$$

The Australian convertible price does not include accrued interest. Interest is usually paid semiannually. The interest payment actually has an exdate. The convertible price usually reflects the amount of the interest payment as the exdate approaches.

The evaluation procedure for domestic Australian convertible attempts to combine the equity component and the yield advantage into one value. The convertible's premium is calculated with respect to the equity price and this theoretical value. The theoretical value is the sum of the equity price and the net present value of the yield advantage over the life of the convertible. An equity dividend growth rate is assumed in order to calculate the convertible's yield advantage over the underlying equity. The net income streams are discounted (at an assumed rate) over the life of the convertible. Early conversion obviously changes the theoretical value.

The following is an example of an analysis of a domestic Australian convertible note.

Domestic Australian Convertible Note

Coupon:	12%
Maturity date:	February 28, 200X
Interest payment date:	January 31, July 31
Ex-interest date:	January 7, July 7
Note par value:	A$1.50
Conversion ratio:	1 share
Conversion dates:	January 15–31, July 15–31
Convertible note price:	A$1.70
Equity price:	A$1.65
Equity dividend:	A$0.10

$$\text{Note interest payable} = \text{Coupon rate} \times \text{Par value}$$
$$= 0.12 \times \text{A\$1.50}$$
$$= \text{A\$0.18}$$

$$\text{Current note yield} = \frac{\text{Note interest}}{\text{Note price}} \times 100$$

$$= \frac{\text{A\$0.18}}{\text{A\$1.70}} \times 100$$

$$= 10.59\%$$

$$\text{Current equity yield} = \frac{\text{Equity dividend}}{\text{Equity price}} \times 100$$

$$= \frac{\text{A\$0.10}}{\text{A\$1.65}} \times 100$$

$$= 6.06\%$$

$$\begin{array}{l} \text{Yield advantage} \\ \text{(Percent method)} \end{array} = \begin{array}{c} \text{Current note} \\ \text{yield} \end{array} - \begin{array}{c} \text{Current equity} \\ \text{yield} \end{array}$$

$$= 10.59\% - 6.06\%$$

$$= 4.53\%$$

$$\text{Equity cost via note} = \frac{\text{Note price}}{\text{Conversion ratio}}$$

$$= \frac{\text{A\$1.70}}{1 \text{ share}}$$

$$= \text{A\$1.70}$$

$$\begin{array}{l} \text{Premium} \\ \text{to equity} \end{array} = \frac{\text{Equity cost via note} - \text{Equity price}}{\text{Equity price}} \times 100$$

$$= \frac{\text{A\$1.70} - \text{A\$1.65}}{\text{A\$1.65}} \times 100$$

$$= 3\%$$

The note's theoretical value is based on the equity value and the discounted net cash flows over the life of the note. Early conversion changes the theoretical value.

Assumptions:

Discount rate:	12.00%
Dividend growth rate:	5.00%
Bond coupon:	12.00%
Current equity dividend:	A$0.10
Discounted yield advantage:	A$0.37

$$\begin{array}{l}\text{Theoretical} \\ \text{value}\end{array} = \left(\begin{array}{l}\text{Equity} \\ \text{price}\end{array} \times \begin{array}{l}\text{Conversion} \\ \text{ratio}\end{array}\right) + \text{NPV}\left(\begin{array}{l}\text{Yield} \\ \text{advantage}\end{array}\right)$$

$$= (\text{A\$1.65} \times 1 \text{ share}) + \text{A\$0.37}$$

$$= \text{A\$2.02}$$

The note's premium is evaluated with respect to the theoretical value as well as the equity price.

$$\begin{array}{l}\text{Premium to} \\ \text{theoretical} \\ \text{value}\end{array} = \frac{\text{Equity cost via note} - \text{Theoretical value}}{\text{Theoretical value}} \times 100$$

$$= \frac{\text{A\$1.70} - \text{A\$2.02}}{\text{A\$2.02}} \times 100$$

$$= -15.84\%$$

The notes are trading at a discount to the theoretical value. The cost of the equity via the convertible is less than the value of the note's conversion value and the net present value of the yield advantage.

$$\begin{array}{l}\text{Break-even period} \\ \text{(Percent method)}\end{array} = \frac{\text{Percent premium}}{\text{Percent yield advantage}}$$

$$= \frac{3\%}{4.53\%}$$

$$= 0.66 \text{ years}$$

The convertible note's break-even period relative to the equity price is eight months. Since the note is trading at a discount to theoretical value, in this instance, break-even is not applicable.

As an equity alternative, the cost of the equity via the convertible is important. It is desirable to minimize the premium paid over the equity price and theoretical value. As a debt alternative, the degree of the convertible's yield advantage is to be maximized.

CANADIAN DOMESTIC CONVERTIBLES

Domestic Canadian convertible bonds resemble U.S. domestic and Euroconvertible bonds. Canadian convertibles are issued in either bond or preferred form. The conversion price is usually set at a 10–25% premium above the underlying equity price. Par value, C$1,000, is used in conjunction with the conversion price to derive the conversion ratio. Canadian convertibles are usually convertible from issue date until maturity. Most of the convertibles have call features, and few have put features.

A Canadian convertible's bond price includes accrued interest. Interest is paid annually or semiannually and accrues based on a 365-day year. Most calculations use the bond price net of accrued interest (i.e., clean bond price).

The following example is an analysis of a Canadian convertible.

Canadian Domestic Convertible Bond

Coupon:	7%
Maturity:	June 30, 200X
Interest payment dates:	June 30, December 31
Conversion ratio:	50 shares/C$1,000 bond
Conversion price:	C$20
Convertible bond price:	C$1,060
Accrued interest:	C$10
Net convertible price:	C$1,050
Current bond yield:	6.67%
Equity price:	C$18.75
Equity dividend:	C$0.37
Current equity yield:	2.0%

$$\text{Conversion value} = \text{Equity price} \times \text{Conversion ratio}$$
$$= \text{C\$18.75} \times 50 \text{ shares}$$
$$= \text{C\$937.50}$$

$$\begin{array}{c}\text{Premium} \\ \text{(Percent method)}\end{array} = \frac{\text{Net bond price} - \text{Conversion value}}{\text{Conversion value}} \times 100$$

$$= \frac{\text{C\$1,050} - \text{C\$937.50}}{\text{C\$937.50}} \times 100$$

$$= 12\%$$

$$\begin{array}{c}\text{Break-even period} \\ \text{(Percent method)}\end{array} = \frac{\text{Percent premium}}{\text{Percent yield advantage}}$$

$$= \frac{\text{Percent premium}}{\begin{array}{cc}\text{Current bond} & \text{Current equity} \\ \text{yield} & \text{yield}\end{array}}$$

$$= \frac{12\%}{6.67\% - 2.00\%}$$

$$= 2.6 \text{ years}$$

Like most other convertibles, Canadian convertibles are evaluated with respect to premium, yield advantage, and call protection. The bonds are viewed as either equity or bond alternatives. Low premiums and higher degrees of yield advantage are attractive.

APPENDIXES

A

Examples of Convertible Evaluation

EXAMPLE 1: CONVERTIBLE BOND DENOMINATED IN LOCAL CURRENCY

Coupon:	9.5%
Date of maturity:	July 24, 200X
Size of issue:	125 million
Country of issuer:	Australia
Local currency:	Australian dollar
Bond denomination:	Australian dollar
Par value:	A$1,000
Coupon frequency:	Annual
Bond coupon payment:	A$95.00
Annual equity dividend:	A$0.21
Convertible into:	Ordinary shares of issuer
Effective conversion price:	A$8.77

Conversion ratio:

$$\frac{\text{Par value}}{\text{Effective conversion price}} = \frac{\text{A\$1,000}}{\text{A\$8.77}}$$

$$= 114.025 \text{ ordinary shares}$$

Call protection: *Absolute*—Noncallable before three years on July 24
Provisional—Noncallable before five years on July 24 unless equity is least 130% of effective conversion price for 30 days

Current Market Data

Convertible bond price:	106.75% of A\$1,000, or A\$1,067.50
Equity price:	A\$8.65
Current bond yield:	8.89%
Current equity yield:	2.43%

Conversion Value (Parity)

$$\frac{\text{Conversion ratio}}{\text{method}} = \text{Conversion ratio} \times \text{Equity price}$$

$$= 114.025 \text{ shares} \times \text{A\$8.65}$$

$$= \text{A\$986.32}$$

$$= 98.63\% \text{ of A\$1,000}$$

$$\frac{\text{Conversion price}}{\text{method}} = \frac{\text{Current equity price}}{\text{Conversion price}} \times 100$$

$$= \frac{\text{A\$8.65}}{\text{A\$8.77}} \times 100$$

$$= 98.63\% \text{ of A\$1,000}$$

$$= \text{A\$986.32}$$

EXAMPLE 1   **239**

Premium over Conversion Value

$$\frac{\text{Point/dollar}}{\text{method}} = \text{Bond price} - \text{Conversion value}$$

$$= \text{A\$1,067.50} - \text{A\$986.32}$$

$$= \text{A\$81.18}$$

$$= 8.12 \text{ points/A\$1,000}$$

$$\text{Percent method} = \frac{\text{Bond price} - \text{Conversion value}}{\text{Conversion value}} \times 100$$

$$= \frac{\text{A\$1067.50} - \text{A\$986.32}}{\text{A\$986.32}} \times 100$$

$$= \frac{\text{A\$81.18}}{\text{A\$986.32}} \times 100$$

$$= 8.23\%$$

Yield Advantage

$$\text{Percent method} = \text{Current bond yield} - \text{Current equity yield}$$

$$= 8.89\% - 2.43\%$$

$$= 6.46\%$$

$$\text{Equity method} = \frac{\text{Bond coupon}}{\text{income}} - \frac{\text{Equivalent equity}}{\text{dividend income}}$$

$$= \frac{\text{Bond coupon}}{\text{income}} - \left(\frac{\text{Conversion}}{\text{ratio}} \times \frac{\text{Equity}}{\text{dividend}}\right)$$

$$= \text{A\$95.00} - (114.025 \text{ shrs.} \times \text{A\$0.21})$$

$$= \text{A\$71.05}$$

$$= 7.105 \text{ points/A\$1,000 bond}$$

$$\text{Point/dollar} = \text{Bond coupon} - \left(\frac{\text{Bond price}}{\text{Equity price}} \times \frac{\text{Equity}}{\text{dividend}} \right)$$

$$= \text{A\$95.00} - \left(\frac{\text{A\$1,067.50}}{\text{A\$8.65}} \times \text{A\$0.21} \right)$$

$$= \text{A\$95.00} - (123.41 \text{ shrs.} \times \text{A\$0.21})$$

$$= \text{A\$69.08}$$

$$= 6.908 \text{ points/A\$1,000 bond}$$

Break-Even Period

$$\text{Equity method} = \frac{\text{Premium (Australian dollars)}}{\text{Bond coupon} - \left(\frac{\text{Conversion}}{\text{ratio}} \times \frac{\text{Equity}}{\text{dividend}} \right)}$$

$$= \frac{\text{A\$81.18}}{\text{A\$95.00} - (114.025 \text{ shrs.} \times \text{A\$0.21})}$$

$$= \frac{\text{A\$81.18}}{\text{A\$95.00} - \text{A\$23.95}}$$

$$= 1.14 \text{ years}$$

$$\text{Point/dollar method} = \frac{\text{Premium (Australian dollars)}}{\text{Bond coupon} - \left(\frac{\text{Bond price}}{\text{Equity price}} \times \frac{\text{Equity}}{\text{dividend}} \right)}$$

$$= \frac{\text{A\$81.18}}{\text{A\$95.00} - \left(\frac{\text{A\$1,067.50}}{\text{A\$8.65}} \times \text{A\$0.21} \right)}$$

$$= \frac{\text{A\$81.18}}{\text{A\$95.00} - (123.41 \text{ shrs.} \times \text{A\$0.21})}$$

$$= \frac{\text{A\$81.18}}{\text{A\$95.00} - \text{A\$25.92}}$$

$$= 1.18 \text{ years}$$

EXAMPLE 2   **241**

$$\text{Percent method} = \frac{\text{Premium (percent)}}{\text{Yield advantage (percent)}}$$

$$= \frac{8.23\%}{6.49\%}$$

$$= 1.27 \text{ years}$$

EXAMPLE 2: CONVERTIBLE BOND DENOMINATED IN A CURRENCY OTHER THAN THE LOCAL CURRENCY

Coupon:	5.25%
Date of maturity:	September 30, 200X
Size of issue:	50 million
Country of issuer:	United Kingdom
Local currency:	Pound sterling
Bond denomination:	U.S. dollar
Par value:	U.S.$1,000
Coupon frequency:	Annual
Bond coupon payment:	U.S.$52.50
Annual equity dividend:	£0.065
Convertible into:	Ordinary shares of issuer
Effective conversion price:	£3.227
Fixed exchange rate:	U.S.$1.4465/£1
Equivalent conversion price:	

$$£3.227 \times \text{U.S.}\$1.4465/£1 = \text{U.S.}\$4.668$$

Conversion ratio:

$$\frac{\text{Par value}}{\text{Equivalent conversion price}} = \frac{\text{U.S.}\$1,000}{\text{U.S.}\$4.668}$$

$$= 214.22 \text{ ordinary shares}$$
$$\text{(U.S. dollar cost basis)}$$

Call protection: *Absolute*—Noncallable before two years on Sept. 30

                        Provisional—Noncallable before three years on Sept. 30, unless ordinary share price is at least 130% of effective conversion price for 30 days

Current Market Data

Convertible bond price:	110% of U.S.$1,000, or U.S.$1,100
Equity price:	£3.00
Current U.S. dollar/sterling rate:	1.6330
Equivalent U.S. dollar equity price:	U.S.$4.90
Equivalent U.S. dollar dividend:	U.S.$0.10
Current bond yield:	4.77%
Current equity yield:	2.04%

Conversion Value (Parity)

$$\text{Conversion ratio method} = \text{Conversion ratio} \times \text{Equity price}$$

$$= 214.22 \text{ shares} \times \text{U.S.\$4.90}$$

$$= \text{U.S.\$1,049.70}$$

$$= 104.97\% \text{ of U.S.\$1,000}$$

$$\text{Conversion price method} = \frac{\text{Current equity price}}{\text{Conversion price}} \times 100$$

$$= \frac{\text{U.S.\$4.90}}{\text{U.S.\$4.668}} \times 100$$

$$= 104.97\% \text{ of U.S.\$1,000}$$

$$= \text{U.S.\$1,049.70}$$

EXAMPLE 2   **243**

Premium over Conversion Value

$$\text{Point method} = \text{Bond price} - \text{Conversion value}$$
$$= \text{U.S.\$1,100.00} - \text{U.S.\$1,049.70}$$
$$= \text{U.S.\$50.30}$$
$$= 5.03 \text{ points/U.S.\$1,000}$$

$$\text{Percent method} = \frac{\text{Bond price} - \text{Conversion value}}{\text{Conversion value}} \times 100$$
$$= \frac{\text{U.S.\$1,100.00} - \text{U.S.\$1,049.70}}{\text{U.S.\$1,049.70}} \times 100$$
$$= \frac{\text{U.S.\$50.30}}{\text{U.S.\$1,049.70}} \times 100$$
$$= 4.79\%$$

Yield Advantage

$$\text{Percent method} = \text{Current bond yield} - \text{Current equity yield}$$
$$= 4.77\% - 2.04\%$$
$$= 2.73\%$$

$$\text{Equity method} = \text{Bond coupon} - \begin{array}{c} \text{Equivalent equity} \\ \text{dividend income} \end{array}$$
$$= \text{Bond coupon} - \left(\begin{array}{c} \text{Conversion} \\ \text{ratio} \end{array} \times \begin{array}{c} \text{Equity} \\ \text{dividend} \end{array} \right)$$
$$= \text{U.S.\$52.50} - (214.22 \text{ shrs.} \times \text{U.S.\$0.10})$$
$$= \text{U.S.\$31.08}$$
$$= 3.108 \text{ points/U.S.\$1,000}$$

$$\begin{aligned}
\text{Point/dollar} \atop \text{method} &= \text{Bond coupon} - \left(\frac{\text{Bond price}}{\text{Equity price}} \times \begin{array}{c} \text{Equity} \\ \text{dividend} \end{array} \right) \\
&= \text{U.S.\$52.50} - \left(\frac{\text{U.S.\$1,100}}{\text{U.S.\$4.90}} \times \text{U.S.\$0.10} \right) \\
&= \text{U.S.\$52.50} - (224.49 \text{ shrs.} \times \text{U.S.\$0.10}) \\
&= \text{U.S.\$30.05} \\
&= 3.005 \text{ points/U.S.\$1,000}
\end{aligned}$$

Break-Even Period

$$\begin{aligned}
\text{Equity} \atop \text{method} &= \frac{\text{Premium (U.S. dollars)}}{\text{Bond coupon} - \left(\begin{array}{c} \text{Conversion} \\ \text{ratio} \end{array} \times \begin{array}{c} \text{U.S. dollar equivalent} \\ \text{dividend} \end{array} \right)} \\
&= \frac{\text{U.S.\$50.30}}{\text{U.S.\$52.50} - (214.22 \text{ shrs.} \times \text{U.S.\$0.10})} \\
&= \frac{\text{U.S.\$50.30}}{\text{U.S.\$52.50} - \text{U.S.\$21.42}} \\
&= 1.62 \text{ years}
\end{aligned}$$

$$\begin{aligned}
\text{Point/dollar} \atop \text{method} &= \frac{\text{Premium (U.S. dollars)}}{\text{Bond coupon} - \left(\frac{\text{Bond price}}{\text{Equity price}} \times \begin{array}{c} \text{U.S. dollar} \\ \text{equivalent dividend} \end{array} \right)} \\
&= \frac{\text{U.S.\$50.30}}{\text{U.S.\$52.50} - \left(\frac{\text{U.S.\$1,100}}{\text{U.S.\$4.90}} \times \text{U.S.\$0.10} \right)} \\
&= \frac{\text{U.S.\$50.30}}{\text{U.S.\$52.50} - (224.49 \text{ shrs.} \times \text{U.S.\$0.10})} \\
&= \frac{\text{U.S.\$50.30}}{\text{U.S.\$52.50} - \text{U.S.\$22.45}} \\
&= 1.67 \text{ years}
\end{aligned}$$

EXAMPLE 3   **245**

$$\text{Percent method} = \frac{\text{Premium percent}}{\text{Yield advantage (percent)}}$$

$$= \frac{4.79\%}{2.73\%}$$

$$= 1.75 \text{ years}$$

EXAMPLE 3: CONVERTIBLE BOND WITH A PUT FEATURE

Coupon:	4.5%
Date of maturity:	March 31, 200X
Size of issue:	65 million
Country of issuer:	United Kingdom
Local currency:	Pound sterling
Bond denomination:	Pound sterling
Par value:	£1,000
Coupon frequency:	Annual
Bond coupon payment:	£45.00
Annual equity dividend:	£0.136
Convertible into:	Ordinary shares of issuer
Effective conversion price:	£5.67
Conversion ratio:	

$$\frac{\text{Par value}}{\text{Effective conversion price}} = \frac{£1,000}{£5.67} = 176.37 \text{ shares}$$

Call protection: *Provisional*—Noncallable before four years on March 31, unless equity is at least 130% of effective conversion price for 30 days.

Put feature: Holders may elect to redeem their bonds in four years on March 31, at 125%

Current Market Data

Convertible bond price:	111.5% of £1,000 = £1,115
Equity price:	£5.70
Current bond yield:	4.036%
Current equity yield:	2.386%
Yield to put:	6.39%

Conversion Value (Parity)

$$\text{Conversion ratio method} = \text{Conversion ratio} \times \text{Equity price}$$

$$= 176.37 \text{ shares} \times £5.70$$

$$= £1,005.30$$

$$= 100.530\% \text{ of } £1,000$$

$$\text{Conversion price method} = \frac{\text{Current equity price}}{\text{Conversion price}} \times 100$$

$$= \frac{£5.70}{£5.67} \times 100$$

$$= 100.53\% \text{ of } £1,000$$

$$= £1,005.30$$

Premium over Conversion Value

$$\text{Point/dollar method} = \text{Bond price} - \text{Conversion value}$$

$$= £1,115.00 - £1,005.30$$

$$= £109.70$$

$$= 10.97 \text{ points/£1,000}$$

EXAMPLE 3   **247**

$$\text{Percent method} = \frac{\text{Bond price} - \text{Conversion value}}{\text{Conversion value}} \times 100$$

$$= \frac{£1,115.00 - £1,005.30}{£1,005.30} \times 100$$

$$= 10.9\%$$

Yield Advantage

$$\text{Percent method} = \text{Current bond yield} - \text{Current equity yield}$$

$$= 4.036\% - 2.386\%$$

$$= 1.650\%$$

$$\text{Equity method} = \text{Bond coupon} - \begin{array}{c}\text{Equivalent equity}\\ \text{dividend}\end{array}$$

$$= \text{Bond coupon} - \left(\begin{array}{c}\text{Conversion}\\ \text{ratio}\end{array} \times \begin{array}{c}\text{Equity}\\ \text{dividend}\end{array}\right)$$

$$= £45.00 - (176.37 \text{ shrs.} \times £0.136)$$

$$= £21.01$$

$$= 2.101 \text{ points/£1,000 bond}$$

$$\begin{array}{c}\text{Point/dollar}\\ \text{method}\end{array} = \text{Bond coupon} - \left(\frac{\text{Bond price}}{\text{Equity price}} \times \begin{array}{c}\text{Equity}\\ \text{dividend}\end{array}\right)$$

$$= £45.00 - \left(\frac{£1,115}{£5.70} \times £0.136\right)$$

$$= £45.00 - (195.6 \text{ shrs.} \times £0.136)$$

$$= £18.40$$

$$= 1.84 \text{ points/£1,000 bond}$$

$$\begin{aligned}\frac{\text{Yield to put}}{\text{method}} &= \text{Yield to put} - \text{Current equity yield} \\ &= 6.39\% - 2.386\% \\ &= 4.004\%\end{aligned}$$

Break-Even Period (Years)

$$\begin{aligned}\text{Equity method} &= \frac{\text{Premium (sterling)}}{\text{Bond coupon} - \left(\dfrac{\text{Conversion}}{\text{ratio}} \times \dfrac{\text{Equity}}{\text{dividend}}\right)} \\[2mm] &= \frac{£109.70}{£45.00 - (176.37 \text{ shrs.} \times £0.136)} \\[2mm] &= \frac{£109.70}{£45.00 - £23.99} \\[2mm] &= 5.22 \text{ years}\end{aligned}$$

$$\begin{aligned}\frac{\text{Point/dollar}}{\text{method}} &= \frac{\text{Premium (sterling)}}{\text{Bond coupon} - \left(\dfrac{\text{Bond price}}{\text{Equity price}} \times \dfrac{\text{Annual equity}}{\text{dividend}}\right)} \\[2mm] &= \frac{£109.70}{£45.00 - \left(\dfrac{£1,115}{£5.70} \times £0.136\right)} \\[2mm] &= \frac{£109.70}{£45.00 - (195.6 \text{ shrs.} \times £0.136)} \\[2mm] &= \frac{£109.70}{£45.00 - £26.60} \\[2mm] &= 5.96 \text{ years}\end{aligned}$$

$$\begin{aligned}\text{Percent method} &= \frac{\text{Premium percent}}{\text{Yield advantage (percent)}} \\[2mm] &= \frac{10.9\%}{1.65\%} \\[2mm] &= 6.6 \text{ years}\end{aligned}$$

EXAMPLE 4   **249**

$$\begin{aligned}
\text{Yield to put} \atop \text{method} \quad &= \frac{\text{Premium percent}}{\text{Yield to put advantage (percent)}} \\[2mm]
&= \frac{\text{Premium percent}}{\text{Yield to put} - \text{Current equity yield}} \\[2mm]
&= \frac{10.9\%}{6.39\% - 2.386\%} \\[2mm]
&= 2.72 \text{ years*}
\end{aligned}$$

EXAMPLE 4: EXCHANGEABLE BOND

Coupon:	6%
Date of maturity:	September 15, 200X
Size of issue:	50 million
Country of issuer:	United Kingdom
Local currency:	Pound sterling
Bond denomination:	Pound sterling
Par value:	£1,000
Coupon frequency:	Annual
Bond coupon payment:	£60.00
Annual equity dividend:	£0.055
Issuer:	Company A
Convertible into:	Ordinary shares of Company B
Effective conversion price:	£11.20 (Company B shares)

Conversion ratio:

$$\frac{\text{Par value}}{\text{Effective conversion price}} = \frac{£1,000}{£11.20}$$

$$= 89.29 \text{ ordinary shares of Company B}$$

*Assumes bond is held to put date.

Call protection: *Provisional*—Noncallable before three years on Sept 15, unless Company B's ordinary share price is at least 130% of effective conversion price

Current Market Data

Convertible bond price:	102.5% of £1,000 = £1,025
Company B equity price:	£8.67
Current bond yield:	5.85%
Current equity yield:	0.634%

Conversion Value (Parity)

$$\begin{aligned} \frac{\text{Conversion ratio}}{\text{method}} &= \text{Conversion ratio} \times \text{Equity price} \\ &= 89.29 \text{ shares} \times £8.67 \\ &= £774.10 \\ &= 77.41\% \text{ of } £1,000 \end{aligned}$$

$$\begin{aligned} \frac{\text{Conversion price}}{\text{method}} &= \frac{\text{Current equity price}}{\text{Effective conversion price}} \times 100 \\ &= \frac{£8.67}{£11.20} \times 100 \\ &= 77.41\% \text{ of } £1,000 \\ &= £774.10 \end{aligned}$$

Premium over Conversion Value

$$\begin{aligned} \frac{\text{Point/dollar}}{\text{method}} &= \text{Bond price} - \text{Conversion value} \\ &= £1,025.00 - £774.10 \\ &= £250.90 \\ &= 25.1 \text{ points/}£1,000 \end{aligned}$$

EXAMPLE 4   **251**

$$\text{Percent method} = \frac{\text{Bond price} - \text{Conversion value}}{\text{Conversion value}} \times 100$$

$$= \frac{£1,025.00 - £774.10}{£774.10} \times 100$$

$$= \frac{£250.90}{£774.10} \times 100$$

$$= 32.4\%$$

Yield Advantage

$$\text{Percent method} = \text{Current bond yield} - \text{Current equity yield}$$

$$= 5.85\% - 0.634\%$$

$$= 5.216\%$$

$$\text{Equity method} = \text{Bond coupon} - \begin{array}{c}\text{Equivalent equity}\\\text{dividend}\end{array}$$

$$= \text{Bond coupon} - \left(\begin{array}{c}\text{Conversion}\\\text{ratio}\end{array} \times \begin{array}{c}\text{Equity}\\\text{dividend}\end{array}\right)$$

$$= £60.00 - (89.29 \text{ shrs.} \times £0.055)$$

$$= £55.09$$

$$= 5.509 \text{ points}/£1,000 \text{ bond}$$

$$\begin{array}{c}\text{Point/dollar}\\\text{method}\end{array} = \text{Bond coupon} - \left(\frac{\text{Bond price}}{\text{Equity price}} \times \begin{array}{c}\text{Equity}\\\text{dividend}\end{array}\right)$$

$$= £60.00 - \left(\frac{£1,025}{£8.67} \times £0.055\right)$$

$$= £60.00 - (118.22 \text{ shrs.} \times £0.055)$$

$$= £53.50$$

$$= 5.35 \text{ points}/£1,000 \text{ bond}$$

Break-Even Period

$$\text{Equity method} = \frac{\text{Premium (sterling)}}{\text{Bond coupon} - \left(\text{Conversion ratio} \times \text{Annual equity dividend}\right)}$$

$$= \frac{£250.90}{£60.00 - (89.29 \text{ shrs.} \times £0.055)}$$

$$= \frac{£250.90}{£60.00 - £4.91}$$

$$= 4.54 \text{ years}$$

$$\text{Point/dollar method} = \frac{\text{Premium (sterling)}}{\text{Bond coupon} - \left(\dfrac{\text{Bond price}}{\text{Equity price}} \times \text{Annual equity dividend}\right)}$$

$$= \frac{£250.90}{£60.00 - \left(\dfrac{£1,025}{£8.67} \times £0.055\right)}$$

$$= \frac{£250.90}{£60.00 - (118.22 \text{ shrs.} \times £0.055)}$$

$$= \frac{£250.90}{£60.00 - £6.50}$$

$$= 4.69 \text{ years}$$

$$\text{Percent Method} = \frac{\text{Premium percent}}{\text{Yield advantage (percent)}}$$

$$= \frac{32.4\%}{5.216\%}$$

$$= 6.21 \text{ years}$$

EXAMPLE 5   **253**

EXAMPLE 5: CROSS-CURRENCY TRANSLATION EXPOSURE: POUND STERLING–BASED INVESTOR

Investor's Currency	Local Currency	Bond Currency
Sterling	French franc	French franc

A pound sterling–based investor purchases the France S.A. 6% of 200X at 98 net. The investor must translate the trade into sterling and is thus subject to French franc/sterling translation exposure.

Convertible bond price:	FF980
Convertible bond price (sterling terms):	£91.10
French franc/sterling rate:	10.7570
U.S. dollar/sterling rate:	1.7350
French franc/U.S. dollar rate:	6.2000

Assume the U.S. dollar appreciates 2% versus the sterling, and the French franc/U.S. dollar rate remains constant. The dollar's appreciation has the effect of decreasing the French franc/sterling rate: the sterling depreciates 2% versus the French franc.

	Original Value	Future Value	Percent Change	Result
Bond price	FF980	FF980	0	No change
U.S. dollar/sterling	1.7350	1.7000	2.0	U.S. dollar appreciated vs. sterling
French franc/U.S. dollar	6.2000	6.2000	0	No change
French franc/sterling	10.7570	10.5400	2.0	Sterling depreciated vs. French franc
Bond price (sterling terms)	£91.10	£92.98	+2.06	Bond price increased in sterling terms

The appreciation of the U.S. dollar versus the sterling and a constant French franc/U.S. dollar rate increases the bond price in sterling terms. Similarly, a depreciation of the U.S. dollar versus the sterling decreases the bond price in sterling terms.

Assume the U.S. dollar appreciates 3.2% versus the French franc, and the U.S. dollar/sterling rate remains constant. The result is that the sterling appreciates 3.2% versus the French franc.

	Original Value	Future Value	Percent Change	Result
Bond price	FF980	FF980	0	No change
U.S. dollar/sterling	1.7350	1.7350	0	No change
French franc/U.S. dollar	6.2000	6.4000	3.2	U.S. dollar appreciated vs. French franc
French franc/sterling	10.7570	11.1040	3.2	Sterling appreciated vs. French franc
Bond price (sterling terms)	£91.10	£88.26	−3.12	Bond price decreases in sterling terms

An appreciation of the U.S. dollar versus the French franc and a constant U.S. dollar/sterling rate decreases the bond price in sterling terms. Similarly, a depreciation of the U.S. dollar versus the French franc increases the convertible price in sterling terms.

The France S.A. 6% bonds are not exposed to currency risk through the mathematics of conversion value because the bonds are denominated in the local currency. Since the bond denomination differs from the investor's base currency, there is translation currency exposure. From a sterling-based investor's standpoint, the translation exposure arises when the French franc bond proceeds are translated into pound sterling. The translation exposure is a function of the French franc/sterling rate. Fluc-

EXAMPLE 6   **255**

tuations in either the U.S. dollar/sterling or the French franc/U.S. dollar rate affect profitability in sterling terms. Since the U.S. dollar is not directly involved, the French franc/sterling cross-currency rate causes translation exposure to be a function of two currency relationships.

EXAMPLE 6: CROSS-CURRENCY EXPOSURE THROUGH CONVERSION VALUE: STERLING-BASED INVESTOR

Investor's Currency	Local Currency	Bond Currency
Sterling	Australian dollar	Sterling

The Australian Co. 6% of 200X bonds are denominated in pound sterling. A pound sterling–based investor purchases the Australia Co. 6% of 200X at £1,040 net. Since the bond is denominated in the investor's base currency (sterling), there is no translation exposure. The Australian dollar/sterling currency exposure is through the calculation of conversion value.

Original U.S. dollar/Australian dollar rate:	0.8121
Original U.S.dollar/sterling rate:	1.7340
Original Australian dollar/sterling rate:	2.1350
Equivalent conversion price:	£1.2890
Convertible bond price:	£1,040
Equity price:	A$2.50

$$\text{Equivalent equity price} = \frac{\text{Equity price}}{\text{Australian dollar/sterling}}$$

$$= \frac{A\$2.50}{2.1350}$$

$$= £1.17$$

Conversion Value

$$\text{Conversion method price} = \frac{\text{Equivalent equity price}}{\text{Equivalent conversion price}} \times 100$$

$$= \frac{£1.17}{£1.2890} \times 100$$

$$= 90.77$$

Premium over Conversion Value

$$\text{Point method} = \frac{\text{Bond}}{\text{price}} - \frac{\text{Conversion}}{\text{value}}$$

$$= £1,040.00 - £907.70$$

$$= £132.30$$

$$\text{Percent method} = \frac{\dfrac{\text{Bond}}{\text{price}} - \dfrac{\text{Conversion}}{\text{value}}}{\text{Conversion value}} \times 100$$

$$= \frac{£1,040.00 - £907.70}{£907.70} \times 100$$

$$= 14.6\%$$

Upon liquidation of the position, the U.S. dollar has depreciated versus the sterling from 1.7340 to 1.8500, and the U.S. dollar/Australian dollar rate remains constant. The new rate implies an Australian dollar/sterling rate of 2.2780. Assuming no change in the equity price, the equivalent equity price decreases to £1.10.

Australian dollar/sterling rate:	2.2780
U.S. dollar/Australian dollar rate:	0.8121
U.S. dollar/sterling rate:	1.8500
Equity price:	A$2.50
Equivalent equity price:	£1.10

EXAMPLE 6   **257**

$$\text{Conversion value} = \frac{\pounds 1.10}{\pounds 1.2890} \times 100$$

$$= 85.34$$

The depreciation of the U.S. dollar versus the sterling and a constant U.S. dollar/Australian dollar rate results in a decrease in conversion value in sterling terms. Similarly, an appreciation of the U.S. dollar versus the sterling results in an increase in conversion value in sterling terms.

Assuming the premium remains at 13.32 points, the resulting convertible price is 98.57. A 6.7% currency movement resulted in a decrease in the convertible price from 104 to 98.57 (a 5.2% decline). Due to the mathematics, most of the U.S. dollar depreciation versus the sterling was realized through the convertible price.

Assume that, upon liquidation, the following scenario exists. The U.S. dollar depreciates versus the Australian dollar, and the U.S. dollar/sterling rate remains the same. The implied Australian dollar/sterling rate becomes 2.0400. Assuming a constant equity price of A$2.50, the equivalent equity price is £1.23.

Australian dollar/sterling rate:	2.0400
U.S. dollar/Australian dollar rate:	0.8500
U.S. dollar/sterling rate:	1.7340
Equity price:	A$2.50
Equivalent equity price:	£1.23

$$\text{Conversion value} = \frac{\pounds 1.23}{\pounds 1.2890} \times 100$$

$$= 95.42$$

A depreciation of the U.S. dollar versus the Australian dollar and a constant U.S. dollar/sterling rate results in an increase in conversion value from £907.70 to £954.20. Similarly, an appreciation of the U.S. dollar versus the Australian dollar results in a decrease in conversion value in sterling terms.

The Australia Co. 6% of 200X are not denominated in the local currency, therefore, the currency risk is through the mathematics of conversion value. Since the U.S. dollar is not directly involved, the Australian dollar/sterling cross rate causes conversion value to be a function of both the U.S. dollar/Australian dollar and U.S. dollar/sterling rates. From a pound sterling perspective, fluctuations in either rate affect the value of the convertible bond through conversion value.

EXAMPLE 7: ZERO-COUPON CONVERTIBLE BOND

Coupon:	0%
Date of maturity:	15 years
Yield to maturity:	8%
Face value:	U.S.$1,000
Conversion price:	U.S.$46.00
Conversion ratio:	6.703 shares
Zero-coupon convertible price:	U.S.$308.32
Equity price:	U.S.$40.00

Conversion Value

$$\text{Conversion ratio method} = \text{Equity price} \times \text{Conversion ratio}$$
$$= \text{U.S.\$40.00} \times 6.703 \text{ shares}$$
$$= \text{U.S.\$268.12}$$

Premium over Conversion Value

$$\text{Percent method} = \frac{\text{Bond price} - \text{Conversion value}}{\text{Conversion value}}$$
$$= \frac{\text{U.S.\$308.32} - \text{U.S.\$268.12}}{\text{U.S.\$268.12}}$$
$$= 15\%$$

EXAMPLE 8   **259**

Put Feature

Put date:	Year 5
Put price:	U.S.$456.39
Yield to put:	8%

Call Price Schedule

Year	Issue Price	Original Issue Discount	Call Price
Issue date	$308.32	0	$ 308.32
1	308.32	$ 25.16	333.48
2	308.32	52.37	360.69
3	308.32	81.80	390.12
4	308.32	113.64	421.96
5	308.32	148.07	456.39
6	308.32	185.31	493.63
7	308.32	225.59	533.91
8	308.32	269.16	577.48
9	308.32	316.28	624.60
10	308.32	367.24	675.56
11	308.32	422.37	730.69
12	308.32	481.99	790.31
13	308.32	546.48	854.80
14	308.32	616.24	924.56
Maturity date	308.32	691.68	1,000.00

EXAMPLE 8:   9.5% SYNTHETIC CONVERTIBLE

Usable bond price:	U.S.$850, or 85% of par value
Par value:	U.S.$1,000
Warrant exercise price:	U.S.$9.50
Warrant price:	U.S.$4.00
Equity price:	U.S.$10.50
Equity dividend:	U.S.$0.00

$$\frac{\text{Number of warrants}}{\text{to purchase}} = \frac{\text{Par value}}{\text{Warrant exercise price}}$$

$$= \frac{\text{U.S.\$1,000}}{\text{U.S.\$9.50}}$$

$$= 105 \text{ warrants}$$

$$\text{Synthetic convertible price} = \frac{\text{Usable bond}}{\text{price}} + \left(\frac{\text{Number of}}{\text{warrants}} \times \frac{\text{Warrant}}{\text{price}} \right)$$

$$= \text{U.S.\$850} + (105 \times \text{U.S.\$4})$$

$$= \text{U.S.\$1,270}$$

$$\text{Current yield} = \frac{\text{Coupon}}{\text{Synthetic convertible price}} \times 100$$

$$= \frac{\text{U.S.\$95}}{\text{U.S.\$1,270}} \times 100$$

$$= 7.48\%$$

$$\text{Effective exercise price} = \frac{\text{Bond price as a}}{\text{percentage of par}} \times \frac{\text{Exercise}}{\text{price}}$$

$$= 0.85 \times \text{U.S.\$9.50}$$

$$= \text{U.S.\$8.075}$$

$$\text{Intrinsic value} = \text{Equity price} - \text{Effective conversion price}$$

$$= \text{U.S.\$10.50} - \text{U.S.\$8.075}$$

$$= \text{U.S.\$2.425}$$

$$\begin{matrix} \text{Equity price} \\ \text{via bond} \\ \text{(Parity)} \end{matrix} = \text{Effective exercise price} + \text{Warrant price}$$

$$= \text{U.S.\$8.075} + \text{U.S.\$4.00}$$

$$= \text{U.S.\$12.075}$$

EXAMPLE 8   **261**

$$\text{Conversion value} = \text{Number of warrants} \times \text{Equity price}$$
$$= 105 \text{ warrants} \times \text{U.S.\$10.50}$$
$$= \text{U.S.\$1,102.50}$$

Premium over Conversion Value

$$\text{Percent method} = \left(\frac{\text{Synthetic bond price}}{\text{Conversion value}} - 1\right) \times 100$$
$$= \left(\frac{\text{U.S.\$1,270.00}}{\text{U.S.\$1,102.50}} - 1\right) \times 100$$
$$= 15\%$$

$$\text{Percent method} = \frac{\text{Parity} - \text{Equity price}}{\text{Equity price}} \times 100$$
$$= \frac{\text{U.S.\$12.075} - \text{U.S.\$10.50}}{\text{U.S.\$10.50}} \times 100$$
$$= 15\%$$

$$\text{Percent method} = \frac{\text{Synthetic convertible price} - \text{Conversion value}}{\text{Conversion value}} \times 100$$
$$= \frac{\text{U.S.\$1,270.00} - \text{U.S.\$1,102.50}}{\text{U.S.\$1,102.50}} \times 100$$
$$= 15\%$$

Break-Even Period

$$\text{Percent method} = \frac{\text{Premium percent}}{\text{Yield advantage}}$$
$$= \frac{15\%}{7.48\%}$$
$$= 2.0 \text{ years}$$

EXAMPLE 9: U.S. DOMESTIC CONVERTIBLE BOND

Coupon:	8.0%
Maturity:	July 15, 200X
Interest payments:	January 15, July 15
Conversion ratio:	39.735 shares
Conversion price:	U.S.$25.17
Convertible bond price:	U.S.$1,050
Current bond yield:	7.62%
Equity price:	U.S.$23.00
Equity dividend:	U.S.$0.20
Current equity yield:	0.87%
Call feature:	Noncallable for 3 years unless equity trades at 150% of conversion price for 20 consecutive days

Conversion Value

$$\begin{aligned}\text{Conversion ratio method} &= \text{Equity price} \times \text{Conversion ratio} \\ &= \text{U.S.\$23.00} \times 39.735 \text{ shares} \\ &= \text{U.S.\$913.90}\end{aligned}$$

Premium over Conversion Value

$$\begin{aligned}\text{Point/dollar method} &= \text{Bond price} - \text{Conversion value} \\ &= \text{U.S.\$1,050} - \text{U.S.\$913.90} \\ &= \text{U.S.\$136.10}\end{aligned}$$

$$\text{Percent method} = \frac{\text{Bond price} - \text{Conversion value}}{\text{Conversion value}} \times 100$$

EXAMPLE 9 **263**

$$= \frac{\text{U.S.\$1,050} - \text{U.S.\$913.90}}{\text{U.S.\$913.90}} \times 100$$

$$= 14.89\%$$

Break-Even Period

$$\text{Equity method} = \frac{\text{Dollar premium}}{\begin{matrix}\text{Bond} \\ \text{coupon}\end{matrix} - \left(\begin{matrix}\text{Conversion} \\ \text{ratio}\end{matrix} \times \begin{matrix}\text{Equity} \\ \text{dividend}\end{matrix}\right)}$$

$$= \frac{\text{U.S.\$136.10}}{\text{U.S.\$80} - (39.735 \text{ shrs.} \times \text{U.S.\$0.20})}$$

$$= 1.89 \text{ years}$$

$$\text{Point/dollar method} = \frac{\text{Dollar premium}}{\begin{matrix}\text{Bond} \\ \text{coupon}\end{matrix} - \left(\frac{\text{Bond price}}{\text{Equity price}} \times \begin{matrix}\text{Equity} \\ \text{dividend}\end{matrix}\right)}$$

$$= \frac{\text{U.S.\$136.10}}{\text{U.S.80} - \left(\dfrac{\text{U.S.\$1,050}}{\text{U.S.\$23}} \times \text{U.S. \$0.20}\right)}$$

$$= \frac{\text{U.S. \$136.10}}{\text{U.S. \$70.87}}$$

$$= 1.92 \text{ years}$$

$$\text{Percent method} = \frac{\text{Percent premium}}{\text{Percent yield advantage}}$$

$$= \frac{\text{Percent premium}}{\begin{matrix}\text{Current bond} \\ \text{yield}\end{matrix} - \begin{matrix}\text{Current equity} \\ \text{yield}\end{matrix}}$$

$$= \frac{14.89\%}{7.62\% - 0.87\%}$$

$$= 2.21 \text{ years}$$

EXAMPLE 10: U.S.$3.75 CONVERTIBLE CUMULATIVE PREFERENCE SHARE

Par value:	U.S.$50.00
Issue price:	U.S.$50.00
Preferred dividend:	U.S.$3.75
Conversion ratio:	0.685 shares
Equity price:	U.S.$80.00
Preferred price:	U.S.$62.00
Equity dividend:	U.S.$0.80

$$\text{Current preferred yield} = \frac{\text{Preferred dividend}}{\text{Issue price}} \times 100$$

$$= \frac{\text{U.S.\$3.75}}{\text{U.S.\$50.00}} \times 100$$

$$= 7.5\%$$

$$\text{Conversion price} = \text{Equity price} \times (1 + \text{Premium})$$

$$= \text{U.S.\$58.40} \times (1 + 0.25)$$

$$= \text{U.S.\$73.00}$$

$$\text{Conversion ratio} = \frac{\text{Par value}}{\text{Conversion price}}$$

$$= \frac{\text{U.S.\$50}}{\text{U.S.\$73}}$$

$$= 0.685 \text{ shares}$$

Conversion Value

$$\text{Conversion ratio method} = \text{Equity price} \times \text{Conversion ratio}$$

$$= \text{U.S.\$80.00} \times 0.685 \text{ shares}$$

$$= \text{U.S.\$54.80}$$

EXAMPLE 10   **265**

Premium over Conversion Value

$$\text{Point/dollar method} = \text{Preferred price} - \text{Conversion value}$$

$$= \text{U.S.\$62.00} - \text{U.S.\$54.80}$$

$$= \text{U.S.\$7.20}$$

$$\text{Percent method} = \frac{\text{Preference price} - \text{Conversion value}}{\text{Conversion value}} \times 100$$

$$= \frac{\text{U.S.\$62.00} - \text{U.S.\$54.80}}{\text{U.S.\$54.80}} \times 100$$

$$= 13.14\%$$

Yield Advantage

$$\text{Percent method} = \left(\begin{array}{c} \text{Current preferred} \\ \text{yield} \end{array} - \begin{array}{c} \text{Current equity} \\ \text{yield} \end{array} \right) \times 100$$

$$= \left(\frac{\text{Preferred dividend}}{\text{Preferred price}} - \frac{\text{Equity dividend}}{\text{Equity price}} \right) \times 100$$

$$= \left(\frac{\text{U.S.\$3.75}}{\text{U.S.\$62.00}} - \frac{\text{U.S.\$0.80}}{\text{U.S.\$80.00}} \right) \times 100$$

$$= 6\% - 1\%$$

$$= 5\%$$

$$\text{Equity method} = \begin{array}{c} \text{Preferred} \\ \text{dividend} \end{array} - \left(\begin{array}{c} \text{Conversion} \\ \text{ratio} \end{array} \times \begin{array}{c} \text{Equity} \\ \text{dividend} \end{array} \right)$$

$$= \text{U.S.\$3.75} - (0.685 \text{ shares} \times \text{U.S.\$0.80})$$

$$= \text{U.S.\$3.75} - \text{U.S.\$0.55}$$

$$= \text{U.S.\$3.20}$$

Break-Even Period

$$\text{Percent method} = \frac{\text{Premium percent}}{\text{Percent yield advantage}}$$

$$= \frac{13.14\%}{5\%}$$

$$= 2.63 \text{ years}$$

EXAMPLE 11: U.K. DOMESTIC CONVERTIBLE LOAN STOCK

Gross coupon:	7.0%
Maturity:	April 30, years 12–15
Interest payment date:	January 1, July 1
Par value:	£1,000
Conversion ratio:	71.428 shares/£100
Gross convertible loan stock:	104
Net convertible loan stock:	103
Equity price:	140p
Equity dividend:	4.5p

$$\text{Current bond yield} = \frac{\text{Coupon}}{\text{Net convertible price}} \times 100$$

$$= \frac{7}{103} \times 100$$

$$= 6.8\%$$

$$\text{Current equity yield} = \frac{\text{Equity dividend}}{\text{Equity price}} \times 100$$

$$= \frac{4.5p}{140p} \times 100$$

$$= 3.2\%$$

Yield Advantage

$$\text{Percent method} = \frac{\text{Current convertible}}{\text{yield}} - \frac{\text{Current equity}}{\text{yield}}$$

EXAMPLE 11   267

$$= 6.8\% - 3.2\%$$
$$= 3.6\%$$

$$\text{Conversion price} = \frac{\text{Gross convertible price}}{\text{Conversion ratio}}$$
$$= \frac{104}{71.428}$$
$$= 1.456$$

Conversion Value

$$\text{Conversion ratio method} = \text{Equity price} \times \text{Conversion ratio}$$
$$= £1.40 \times 71.428 \text{ shares}$$
$$= £100$$

Premium over Conversion Value

$$\text{Point/dollar method} = \text{Conversion price} - \text{Equity price}$$
$$= 145.6p - 140.0p$$
$$= 5.6p$$

$$\frac{\text{Percent}}{\text{method}} = \left(\frac{\text{Conversion price}}{\text{Equity price}} - 1 \right) \times 100$$
$$= \left(\frac{1.456}{1.40} - 1 \right) \times 100$$
$$= 4\%$$

Break-Even Period

$$\text{Percent method} = \frac{\text{Premium percent}}{\text{Yield advantage}}$$
$$= \frac{4\%}{3.6\%}$$
$$= 1.1 \text{ years}$$

	Dividend growth rate: 10% Discount rate: 10%							
	Year							
	1	2	3	4	5	6	7	8
Interest/share	.098	.098	.098	.098	.098	.098	.098	.098
Dividend/share	.045	.049	.054	.060	.066	.072	.080	.088
Net cash flow	.053	.049	.044	.038	.032	.026	.018	.010
Discounted NCF	.048	.040	.033	.026	.020	.014	.009	.005

	Year						
	9	10	11	12	13	14	15
Interest/share	.098	.098	.098	.098	.098	.098	.098
Dividend/share	.096	.106	.117	.128	.141	.155	.171
Net cash flow	.002	−.008	−.019	−.030	−.043	−.057	−.073
Discounted NCF	.001	−.003	−.007	−.010	−.013	−.015	−.017

	Dividend growth rate: 15% Discount rate: 10%							
	Year							
	1	2	3	4	5	6	7	8
Interest/share	.098	.098	.098	.098	.098	.098	.098	.098
Dividend/share	.045	.052	.060	.068	.079	.091	.104	.120
Net cash flow	.053	.046	.038	.030	.019	.007	−.006	−.022
Discounted NCF	.048	.038	.029	.020	.012	.004	−.003	−.010

	Year						
	9	10	11	12	13	14	15
Interest/share	.098	.098	.098	.098	.098	.098	.098
Dividend/share	.138	.158	.182	.209	.241	.277	.318
Net cash flow	−.040	−.060	−.084	−.111	−.143	−.179	−.220
Discounted NCF	−.017	−.023	−.029	−.035	−.041	−.047	−.053

Even payments are assumed for simplicity.

EXAMPLE 12   **269**

EXAMPLE 12: JAPANESE DOMESTIC CONVERTIBLE BOND

Coupon:	2.9%
Maturity:	August 30, 200X
Coupon payment:	March 31, September 30
Conversion price:	¥466.70
Convertible bond price:	¥1,003
Equity price:	¥445
Equity dividend:	¥3.5

$$\text{Current bond yield} = \frac{\text{Coupon}}{\text{Convertible price}} \times 100$$

$$= \frac{¥29}{¥1,030} \times 100$$

$$= ¥2.8\%$$

$$\text{Current equity yield} = \frac{\text{Equity dividend}}{\text{Equity price}} \times 100$$

$$= \frac{¥3.5}{¥445} \times 100$$

$$= 0.8\%$$

Conversion Value

$$\text{Conversion price method} = \frac{\text{Equity price}}{\text{Conversion price}} \times 100$$

$$= \frac{¥445}{¥466.70} \times 100$$

$$= 95.35$$

Premium over Conversion Value

$$\text{Yen method} = \text{Convertible price} - \text{Conversion value}$$
$$= ¥1,003 - ¥953.50$$
$$= ¥49.50$$

$$\text{Percent method} = \frac{\text{Convertible price} - \text{Conversion value}}{\text{Conversion value}} \times 100$$

$$= \frac{¥1,003 - ¥953.50}{¥953.50} \times 100$$

$$= 5.19\%$$

EXAMPLE 13: FRENCH DOMESTIC CONVERTIBLE BOND

Interest payment:	FF48
Maturity:	10 years
Par value:	FF800
Conversion price:	FF800
Conversion ratio:	1 share
Convertible bond price:	FF855
Accrued interest:	FF5
Net convertible bond price:	FF850
Equity price:	FF740
Equity dividend:	FF10

Call protection: *Absolute*—Three years

Provisional—Callable after three years, if equity trades at 150% of conversion price for 20 days

$$\text{Current bond yield} = \frac{\text{Interest payment}}{\text{Net bond price}} \times 100$$

EXAMPLE 13   **271**

$$= \frac{FF48}{FF850} \times 100$$

$$= 5.65\%$$

$$\text{Current equity yield} = \frac{\text{Equity dividend}}{\text{Equity price}} \times 100$$

$$= \frac{FF10}{FF740} \times 100$$

$$= 1.35\%$$

Conversion Value

$$\text{Conversion ratio method} = \text{Equity price} \times \text{Conversion ratio}$$

$$= FF740 \times 1 \text{ share}$$

$$= FF740$$

Premium over Conversion Ratio

$$\text{Percent method} = \frac{\text{Net bond price} - \text{Conversion value}}{\text{Equity price}} \times 100$$

$$= \frac{FF850 - FF740}{FF740} \times 100$$

$$= 14.86\%$$

Break-Even Period

$$\text{Percent method} = \frac{\text{Percent premium}}{\text{Yield advantage}}$$

$$= \frac{\text{Percent premium}}{\text{Current bond yield} - \text{Current equity yield}}$$

$$= \frac{14.86\%}{5.65\% - 1.35\%}$$

$$= 3.46 \text{ years}$$

EXAMPLE 14: AUSTRALIAN DOMESTIC CONVERTIBLE NOTE

Coupon:	12%
Maturity date:	February 28, 200X
Interest payment date:	January 31, July 31
Ex-interest date:	January 7, July 7
Note par value:	A$1.50
Conversion ratio:	1 share
Conversion dates:	January 15–31, July 15–31
Convertible note price:	A$1.70
Equity price:	A$1.65
Equity dividend:	A$0.10

$$\text{Note interest payable} = \text{Coupon rate} \times \text{Par value}$$
$$= 0.12 \times \text{A\$1.50}$$
$$= \text{A\$0.18}$$

$$\text{Current note yield} = \frac{\text{Note interest}}{\text{Note price}} \times 100$$
$$= \frac{\text{A\$0.18}}{\text{A\$1.70}} \times 100$$
$$= 10.59\%$$

$$\text{Current equity yield} = \frac{\text{Equity dividend}}{\text{Equity price}} \times 100$$
$$= \frac{\text{A\$0.10}}{\text{A\$1.65}} \times 100$$
$$= 6.06\%$$

EXAMPLE 14   **273**

Yield Advantage

$$\text{Percent method} = \frac{\text{Current note}}{\text{yield}} - \frac{\text{Current equity}}{\text{yield}}$$

$$= 10.59\% - 6.06\%$$

$$= 4.53\%$$

$$\text{Equity cost via note} = \frac{\text{Note price}}{\text{Conversion ratio}}$$

$$= \frac{\text{A\$1.70}}{\text{1 share}}$$

$$= \text{A\$1.70}$$

$$\frac{\text{Premium}}{\text{to equity}} = \frac{\text{Equity cost via note} - \text{Equity price}}{\text{Equity price}} \times 100$$

$$= \frac{\text{A\$1.70} - \text{A\$1.65}}{\text{A\$1.65}} \times 100$$

$$= 3\%$$

Assumptions:

Discount rate:	12.00%
Dividend growth rate:	5.00%
Bond coupon:	12.00%
Current equity dividend:	A$0.10
Discounted yield advantage:	A$0.37

$$\frac{\text{Theoretical}}{\text{value}} = (\text{Equity price} \times \text{Conversion ratio}) + \text{NPV(Yield advantage}$$

$$= (\text{A\$1.65} \times \text{1 share}) + \text{A\$0.37}$$

$$= \text{A\$2.02}$$

$$\begin{aligned}
\text{Premium to} \\
\text{theoretical} \\
\text{value}
\end{aligned} = \frac{\text{Equity cost via note} - \text{Theoretical value}}{\text{Theoretical value}} \times 100$$

$$= \frac{A\$1.70 - A\$2.02}{A\$2.02} \times 100$$

$$= -15.84\%$$

Break-Even Period

$$\text{Percent method} = \frac{\text{Percent premium}}{\text{Yield advantage}}$$

$$= \frac{3\%}{4.53\%}$$

$$= 0.66 \text{ years}$$

EXAMPLE 15: CANADIAN DOMESTIC CONVERTIBLE BOND

Coupon:	7%
Maturity:	June 30, 200X
Interest payment dates:	June 30, December 31
Conversion ratio:	50 shares/C$1,000 bond
Conversion price:	C$20
Convertible bond price:	C$1,060
Accrued interest:	C$10
Net convertible bond price:	C$1,050
Current bond yield:	6.67%
Equity price:	C$18.75
Equity dividend:	C$0.37
Current equity yield:	2.0%

EXAMPLE 15 **275**

Conversion Value

$$\text{Conversion ratio method} = \text{Equity price} \times \text{Conversion ratio}$$
$$= \text{C\$}18.75 \times 50 \text{ shares}$$
$$= \text{C\$}937.50$$

Premium to Conversion Value

$$\text{Percent method} = \frac{\text{Net bond price} - \text{Conversion value}}{\text{Conversion value}} \times 100$$
$$= \frac{\text{C\$}1,050 - \$937.50}{\$937.50} \times 100$$
$$= 12\%$$

Break-Even Period

$$\text{Percent method} = \frac{\text{Percent premium}}{\text{Yield advantage}}$$
$$= \frac{\text{Percent premium}}{\text{Current bond yield} - \text{Current equity yield}}$$
$$= \frac{12\%}{6.67\% - 2.00\%}$$
$$= 2.6 \text{ years}$$

B
Glossary

A

Accrued interest: The amount of interest earned since the last coupon payment. Eurobonds use a 30/360 calculation basis. Accrued interest is almost always forfeited upon conversion.

American-style option: Allows for the continuous exercise into the underlying equity.

B

Base currency: The investor's currency of denomination.

Bearer bonds: Bonds whose ownership is evidenced by physical possession of the bond.

Bond currency: The currency in which the bond is denominated and traded.

Break-even period: The amount of time required to amortize the premium of a convertible through the yield advantage over the equity. Break-even may be calculated with the equity, point, percent, or yield-to-put method.

Busted convertible: A convertible in which the equity has substantially declined below the conversion price and the premium over conversion value has expanded. Also referred to as a *broken convertible*.

C

Call option: The right to buy a certain number of shares at a predetermined price for a period of time.

Call price: The price at which the issuer has the right to redeem bonds before maturity.

Call protection: The period during which a convertible cannot be called.

Call provision: The issuer's privilege to prepay bonds before maturity at a small premium to face value.

Conversion: The exchange of a convertible security for a predetermined number of equity shares.

Conversion feature: The right, over a specific time period, to exchange a convertible security for a predetermined number of equity shares (or other asset) at a preset price.

Conversion period: The time during which the convertible can be exchanged for the underlying equity.

Conversion price: The equity price at which the bond may be exchanged.

Conversion price reset: The provision to change the conversion price at a certain date to maintain a certain premium level.

Conversion ratio: The number of shares into which a bond may be converted.

Conversion value: The current market value of equity received upon conversion.

Convertible bond indenture: A legal document that describes the privileges and specifications of the bond.

Convertible hedge: The purchase of a convertible security and a short sale of the security into which it is exchangeable.

Convertible security: Hybrid financial instruments, combining an equity feature and a debt feature, that allow the investor to participate in an equity's upside potential with limited downside risk.

Coupon: A stated rate of interest paid semiannually or annually.

Coupon reset: The provision to change the coupon on a specific date to a level where the convertibles will trade at par.

Cross-currency rates: Exchange rates not directly involving the U.S. dollar but derived from two foreign currency rates expressed versus the U.S. dollar.

D

Debt component: The convertible security's stated coupon and claim to principal.

Denomination: The minimum face amount and the currency in which bonds are traded.

Discounted yield advantage method: An evelution method that compares the net present value of the ⌐   ⌐le's cash flows to the premium over conversion ˅ ˙

Domestic co   he home country and the local cu

E

Economic expos   ⌐3.00   ιge rates on long-term macroecor

Effective conversic   00   f local currency. Used for call pro   ⌐5.00

Equity bond units: ⌐2.00   ιght bond with equity warrants.

Equivalent conversio   adjusted by the fixed exchange ι   ιle. Used to calculate the conversi   convertible is different from the l

Euroconvertible: A bon   ⌐y issued in more than one foreign country by an intei   ⌐ιal syndicate, denominated in a Eurocurrency.

Eurocurrencies: Liabilities at a bank outside the country where the currency is legal tender.

European-style option: Allows for the exercise into the underlying equity at expiration.

Exchangeable security: A security convertible into the equity of a company other than the issuer.

Exercise price: The predetermined price at which the option may be exercised. Also referred to as the *strike price*.

Expiration date: The last date to exercise an option.

F

Face value: The value of the bond at maturity. Also referred to as *par value*.

Fixed exchange rate: The exchange rate, fixed at bond issue date, used to express the effective conversion price (in equivalent terms) in the currency of the bond denomination (i.e., equivalent conversion price). Provides a fixed number of equity shares per bond.

Fixed-income-plus-option method: An evaluation method that combines the theoretical valuation of the debt component with the equity component.

Foreign convertible: A convertible issued by a foreign borrower in another country's domestic market and local currency.

Forward exchange rates: Prices at which contracts are made for the eventual exchange of currencies.

Full hedge: A hedge position in which the amount of equity sold short is equal to the amount of equity into which the bonds are convertible. Also referred to as a *100% hedge*.

G

Gearing: A measure of leverage relating the equity price to the warrant price.

Gray market: A forward market where commitments are made to trade the official bonds in the future at prearranged prices.

H

Hedge ratio: The number of equity shares sold short (against a long convertible position), expressed as a percentage of the equity embodied in the convertible.

I

In the money: Refers to an equity trading above the call option's exercise price or below the put option's exercise price.

Intrinsic value: The difference between the equity price and the exercise price. Assuming immediate exercise of the option, it is the money value of the option. Also referred to as *tangible value*.

Investment value: The price at which a convertible security would trade if it were valued strictly on its debt characteristics.

L

Local currency: The home market currency of the ordinary equity share.

M

Maturity date: The date on which bonds are redeemed at par. The issuer repays principal to the investor.

N

Neutral hedge ratio: The amount of equity sold short (against a long convertible position) to break even for either an increase or a decrease in the equity.

O

Option: The right to buy or sell a certain number of equity shares at a predetermined price for a period of time.

Option premium: The price of an option.

Original issue discount: The annual price increase of the zero-coupon convertible to maintain the yield to maturity.

Out of the money: Refers to an equity whose price is below the call option's exercise price or above the put option's exercise price.

P

Parity: The price at which the convertible security must trade to be equivalent to the market value of the equity received upon conversion. Expressed as a percentage of par value. The monetary result of parity and conversion value is the same.

Partial hedge ratio: The amount of equity sold short (against a long convertible position), less than a full (100%) hedge ratio.

Premium over conversion value: The difference between the convertible security's market price and conversion value. Expressed in point terms or as a percentage of conversion value.

Premium over investment value: The difference between the convertible security's market price and its investment value. Expressed as a percentage of investment value.

Put exercise date: The day the bonds can be tendered to the issuer before maturity.

Put feature: The bondholder's privilege to force early redemption.

Put option: The right to sell a certain number of equity shares at a given price for a period of time.

Put strike price: The predetermined price at which the bonds can be tendered to the issuer before maturity.

R

Registered bond: Bonds for which a serial number is attached to the owner.

Rolling put feature: A put feature with multiple put exercise dates.

S

Sinking fund: The issuer's ability to retire a portion of the bond issue before maturity.

Strike price: See *exercise price*.

Swapping: The simultaneous sale of one security to purchase another security.

Synthetic convertible: A usable bond plus warrant.

T

Tangible value: See *intrinsic value*.

Time value: The component of an option premium that places a value on the amount of time to expiration.

Transaction exposure: The effect of fluctuating exchange rates on revenues, expenses, and profitability.

Translation exposure: Currency risk arising from the uncertainty of converting foreign-denominated assets and liabilities into the local currency.

U

Usable bond: A bond whose principal can be given up at par value to pay for the act of exercising the warrants.

W

Warrant: A long-term right (issued by a corporation) to buy a certain number of shares at a predetermined price for a specific period of time.

Warrant premium: The additional cost of the equity when purchased through the warrant compared with a direct investment in the equity.

Y

Yield advantage: The incremental yield of the convertible security over the common, measured by either the equity, point, or percent method.

Yield to maturity: The discount rate that equates the current market price with the present value of the expected future cash inflows.

Z

Zero-coupon convertible: A convertible that pays no coupon interest payments, is issued at a deep discount to par, and is exchangeable into equity.

INDEX

Absolute call protection, 33
Accrued interest:
  calculating, 7–8
  defined, 7, 277
  forfeiture of, 16, 35
Adjusted conversion value, 66
American-style call option:
  defined, 12, 277
  and domestic U.S. convertibles, 210
  expiration, 12, 18
  value of, 70–71
  warrants and, 23
Arbitrage, 16, 102
Australian domestic convertibles:
  analysis of, 229–230
  evaluation of, 228, 229
  as an example of convertible
    evaluation, 272–274
  overview of, 228–232
  unique features of, 228–229

Base currency, 277
Bearer bonds, 6, 277
Bearish hedge, 180, 192–195
  USA Inc. convertible to illustrate,
    193–194
Biased hedge, see Partial hedge
Bond cum warrants, 81
Bond currency:
  appreciation of, 138, 144, 147
  defined, 277
  depreciation of, 128, 138, 146, 147
  and depreciation of local currency, 122
  and fixed exchange rate, 88
Bond ex warrants, 81

Bond-plus-option method, see Fixed-
    income-plus-option method
Break-even analysis, 59, 60–64
  compared to discounted yield
    advantage method, 66
  disadvantages of, 64
  equity method, 60–61
  methods compared, 64
  percent method, 62–63
  point/dollar method, 61–62
  yield-to-put method, 63–64
Break-even period:
  for British domestic convertibles,
    170–171
  and call risk, 64, 166
  computing for USA Inc. convertible,
    60–64
  defined, 60, 277
  in determining value, 166
  equity method for determining, 60–61
  methods for calculating, 60–64
  percent method for determining,
    62–63
  point/dollar method for determining,
    61–62
  reasonable, 64
  for U.S. domestic convertibles,
    211–212
  yield-to-put method for determining,
    63–64
British domestic convertibles, 216–223
  break-even period for, 170–171
  conversion value in, 168
  discounted net cash flow in, 222
  evaluating, 219

British domestic
    convertibles—*Continued*
    as an example of convertible
      evaluation, 266–268
    forms of, 217
    premium over conversion value,
      168–169, 220–221
    special market characteristics
      affecting, 217
    unique features of, 217–218
    yield advantage, 169, 219
Broken convertible, *see* Busted
    convertible
Bullish hedge:
    defined, 180
    USA Inc. convertible to illustrate,
      182–192
    working the premium to zero,
      186–192
Busted convertible:
    call risk, 51
    defined, 50, 278

Call feature:
    components of, 33–35
    in convertible preference shares,
      214–215
    defined, 9
    discounted yield advantage method, 66
    of Japanese domestic convertibles, 223
    and life of a convertible, 72
    of U.S. domestic convertibles, 210
    and value, 71, 72
    of zero-coupon convertible bonds,
      80, 81
Call option:
    compared to conversion feature, 2, 11,
      16, 70
    compared to warrants, 23, 28
    defined, 9, 17, 278
    estimating the value of, 70–71
    sale price, 19
Call price, 33, 80, 278

Call protection:
    defined, 33, 278
    in evaluating securities, 166
    in French domestic convertibles, 226
    and interest rates, 35
    provisional, 33–34, 210
    types of, 33–34
    for USA Inc. convertible, 34
    in zero-coupon convertible bonds, 80
Call provision, 278
Call redemption, 35. *See also* Early
    redemption; Redemption
Call risk:
    and break-even time, 64, 166
    and conversion value, 35
    premium over conversion value, 51
Canadian domestic convertibles:
    analysis of, 232–233
    as an example of convertible
      evaluation, 274–275
Capital appreciation, 11, 165, 174
Capital gains, 98, 163
Cash adjustments, 11
Cash flow:
    and convertible hedges, 179, 181
Chinese hedge, 204
Continuous conversion rights, 70–71, 206
Continuous options, *see* American-style
    call option
Conversion:
    defined, 11, 278
    optimal year for, 66
Conversion feature:
    accrued interest and, 16, 35
    American- *vs.* European-style
      option, 12
    attractiveness of, 173–174
    of a busted convertible, 50
    compared to call option, 2, 11,
      16, 70
    compared to warrants, 23
    and equity price appreciation, 1
    in evaluating a security, 11, 16

Conversion Feature—*Continued*
  of international Euroconvertible
    securities, 88–93
  in local *vs.* nonlocal currencies,
    88, 96
  in pricing the security, 1
  shares received upon conversion,
    93–94
Conversion period:
  defined, 8, 278
  periodic *vs.* continuous, 70–71
Conversion price:
  defined, 8, 12–13, 14, 278
  effective, 88, 92, 279
  and equity price, 12
  equivalent, 89, 90, 279
  resetting, 206
  for zero-coupon convertible bonds,
    74–75
Conversion price reset, 206, 278
Conversion ratio:
  calculating, 12, 75
  computing for USA Inc. convertible,
    12–13
  defined, 8, 12, 278
  in the equity method, 42, 61
  and fixed exchange rate, 90–91
  fluctuating, 90
  in graph form, 15
  as an indication of leverage, 13, 15
  in zero-coupon convertible bonds, 75
Conversion rights, 11
  continuous, 70–71, 206
  as outlined in convertible bond
    indenture, 206
  periodic, 70, 206
Conversion value, *see* Parity;
    Premium over conversion
    value
  adjusting, 64–66
  and bond prices, 14–15
  in a British domestic convertible, 168
  components of, 123

  costs not reflected in, 16
  cross-currency effect on, 135–152
  cross-currency exposure through,
    155–157, 255–258
  currency exposure through, 118–121,
    126–129
  defined, 9, 278
  in determining the price of Japanese
    domestic convertibles, 223
  and equity, 14
  as a function of currencies and equity
    prices, 123–126
  overview of, 13–16
  par, 15
  for synthetic convertibles, 84
  for USA Inc. convertible, 13, 52
Convertible bond(s), *see* Convertible
    securities
Convertible bond denominated in
    currency other than local,
    evaluation of, 241–245
Convertible bond denominated in local
    currency, evaluation of, 237–241
Convertible bond indenture, 205–207
  contents of, 206
  cover page, 205
  defined, 205, 278
  importance of, 206–207
Convertible bond with put feature,
    evaluation of, 245–249
Convertible debentures, 1
Convertible hedge:
  cash flow and, 179, 181
  defined, 179–181, 278
  purpose of, 179
  reasons for establishing, 181
Convertible preference shares, 1
  analysis of, 214, 215
  call feature of, 214–215
  vs. convertible securities, 216
  defined, 213
  features of, 213
  overview of, 213–216

Convertible preference shares—*Continued*
  premium over conversion value, 215
  pricing of, 213
  tax considerations, 213
  yield advantage, 215–216
Convertible securities:
  alternatives to traditional, 73–86
  attractiveness as an investment, 2
  as bond alternatives, 175–177
  call redemption of, 35
  classification of, 5–6
  conversion feature of, 1, 2, 173, 174
  currency exposure in, 97–98
  as currency vehicles, 177–178
  debt component of, 1, 2, 9, 29–32,
    49, 279
  definition, 1, 70, 278
  denominated in currency other than
    local, 241–245
  denominated in local currency,
    237–241
  domestic, defined, 5, 209, 279
  as equity alternatives, 73, 173–175
  equity bond units, 81–86
  Euroconvertibles, defined, 5–6, 279
  evaluation of, 165–172
  examples of evaluation, 237–275
  forced conversion, 35
  foreign, defined, 5, 280
  hybrid nature of, 1, 2, 8–9, 48, 56,
    70, 210
  interest rates and, 1
  in the money, 20
  investment objective and, 178
  investment opportunities, 173–178
  market terminology, 6–8
  out of the money, 20
  pricing of, 12, 14
  with a put feature, 245–249
  relationship between profitability and
    price/currency fluctuations,
    115–118
  safety features of, 48, 51

  swapping, 174–175
  synthetic, 82–86
  tax advantages of, 2
  total return, 163
    compared to equity, 174
  valuation methods for, 59–72
  value of, 29
  yield advantage, 41–44
  yield to put, 37
  zero-coupon convertible bonds, 73–81
Coupon, 6, 279
  for USA Inc. convertible, 6
Coupon reset, 12, 206, 279
Creditworthiness, 1, 11, 29, 165
Cross-currency exposure:
  through conversion value, 155–157,
    255–258
  effect on conversion value, 135–152
  from the perspective of a non-U.S.
    dollar-based investor, 109, 152
  translation exposure, 109, 153–155,
    253–255
Cross-currency rates, 99, 279
Cross-currency relationship, 133–134
Cross-currency risk, 152
Currency exposure:
  analysis from a pound-sterling
    perspective, 152–153, 161–162,
    253–255
  analysis from a U.S. dollar
    perspective, 3, 110–115,
    135–152, 158–160
  categories of, 97
  cause of, 108
  through conversion value, 118–121,
    126–129, 177
  conversion value as a function of
    currencies and equity prices,
    123–126
  for convertible bonds denominated in
    currencies other than investor's
    and local currency, 126,
    132–133

Currency exposed—*Continued*
  for convertible bonds denominated in
    currency of investor, 117–118
  for convertible bonds denominated in
    local currency, 110–115
  and convertible price fluctuations,
    115–118
  cross-currency exposure through
    conversion value, 155–157,
    255–258
  cross-currency relationship, 133–134
  cross-currency translation exposure,
    153–155
  defined, 97
  economic, 97, 102, 204, 279
  effect of currency fluctuations on
    premium, 121–123
  evaluating, 126
  foreign currency contracts to manage,
    102, 103
  foreign currency markets, 98–102
  general description of, 109–163
  of a hedge position, 181, 203–204
  management of, 102–109
  overview of types and management,
    158–163
  pound sterling-based investor,
    152–153, 253–255
  risk in, 109–110, 154
  role of, in evaluating a security,
    166–167
  transaction, 97, 102, 204, 283
  translation, 97, 129–133, 162, 177,
    181, 253–355, 283
  from a U.S. dollar perspective, 3
Currency fluctuations:
  effect on conversion value, 123–126,
    149, 162
  effect on premium, 121–123
  and equity prices, 147
  to offset capital gains/losses, 163
  relationship between profitability and,
    111, 115–118

Currency risk:
  components of, 154, 163
  evaluation of, 126

Debt component:
  defined, 279
  derivation of, 1, 2, 9, 29
  factors affecting investment value,
    31–32
  investment value, 29–31
  as a protective device, 1, 29, 49
Debt-to-equity ratio, 2
Deferred conversion dates, 12
Delta, 181
Delta hedge, 181, 195
Denomination, 6, 279
  of USA Inc. convertible, 6
Dilution, equity, 2, 74
Disclosure statements, 205, 209
Discount to conversion value, 45, 51
Discounted cash flow method,
    see Discounted yield advantage
    method
Discounted net cash flows, 65, 222
Discounted yield advantage method, 59,
    64–69
  advantages of, 69
  applications of, 64
  call/put features of, 66, 69
  compared to break-even
    analysis, 66
  defined, 64, 279
  limitations of, 68–69
  overview of, 64–69
  subjectivity of, 66, 69
  to value USA Inc. convertible, 65–66,
    67–68, 69
  when to use, 64–65, 69
Discount to par value, 51, 73
Discount rate, 30
Diversification, 177
Dividend growth rates, 66, 67, 68
Dollarizing, 107

Domestic convertibles, 3
 analysis of, 210
 Australian, 228–232, 272–274
 British, 216–223, 266–268
 Canadian, 232–233, 274–275
 defined, 5, 209, 279
 denomination of, 209
 vs. Euroconvertibles, 209, 210
 French, 225–228, 270–271
 Japanese, 223–225, 269–270
 U.S., 210–212, 262–263
Double taxation, 209
Downside risk, 1
 hedge position and, 197, 199–200
 and interest rates, 31
 neutral hedge, 197
 options, 22
 and premium, 26, 45, 51, 56
 protection against, 37

Early redemption, 9, 33, 72
Economic exposure:
 defined, 97, 279
 in foreign currency management, 102
 in hedging, 204
Effective conversion price:
 calculating, 92
 and call provision, 279
 defined, 88, 279
 uses of, 88
Equity bond units:
 advantages/disadvantages of, 82
 attractiveness of, to investors, 82
 components of, 81
 defined, 81, 279
 overview of, 81–86
 synthetic convertibles, 82–86
Equity call option, *see* Call option
Equity component, *see* Conversion
  feature
Equity cost basis, 18–19, 94
Equity dilution, 2, 74
Equity investors, 174

Equity kicker, 23
Equity method, 41
 in break-even analysis, 60–61
 conversion ratio in, 42, 61
 described, 42–43
 when to use, 44
Equity price(s):
 and conversion price, 12
 conversion value and, 14, 123–126
 currency exchange and, 102
 currency fluctuations and, 1,
  125, 147
 interest rates and, 71
 and premium over conversion value,
  49, 51
 and premium over investment value,
  57–58
Equity price appreciation:
 and premium over conversion value,
  47, 49, 51, 53
 and premium over investment value,
  57–58
 role of conversion feature in, 1
 warrants and, 28
 in zero-coupon convertible bonds, 78
Equity value, *see* Conversion value
Equivalent conversion price:
 calculating, 89–90
 and conversion ratio, 279
 defined, 89, 279
Euroconvertible bonds:
 accrued interest calculation basis
  for, 277
 defined, 5–6, 279
 forms of, 6
 interest on, 6
 reasons for issuing, 6
 special conversion features
  of, 96
 taxes on, 6
 U.S. domestic convertibles compared
  to, 210, 212
Euroconvertible preference shares, 213

Eurocurrency, 6, 87, 280
European-style call option:
  defined, 12, 280
  expiration, 12, 18
Evaluation:
  and alternative investments, 165
  Australian domestic convertible note,
    272–274
  break-even analysis, 166, 170, 172
  call protection, 166
  Canadian domestic convertible bond,
    274–275
  components to consider, 165
  conversion value, 168, 171
  convertible bond denominated in other
    than local currency, 241–245
  convertible bond denominated in local
    currency, 237–241
  convertible bond with a put feature,
    245–249
  cross-currency exposure through
    conversion value, 255–258
  cross-currency translation exposure,
    253–255
  currency exposure, 166, 172
  by equity investors, 174
  examples of, 167–172, 237–275
  exchangeable bond, 249–252
  of foreign convertibles, 166–167
  French domestic convertible bond,
    270–271
  by income-oriented equity
    investors, 174
  of an international convertible, 94–96
  investment value, 166
  Japanese domestic convertible bond,
    269–270
  justification of wider premiums, 166
  leverage as a tool, 165
  overview of, 165–172
  preliminary considerations, 165
  premium over conversion value,
    165–166, 168–169
  synthetic convertible, 259–261
  U.K. domestic convertible loan stock,
    266–268
  U.S. domestic convertible bond,
    262–263
  U.S. $3.75 convertible cumulative
    preference share, 264–266
  of a warrant, 23
  yield advantage, 169
  yield-to-put vs. yield-to-maturity, 166
  zero-coupon convertible bond, 258–259
Exchangeable security:
  defined, 1, 280
  as an example of convertible
    evaluation, 249–252
Exchange rate:
  current, 122
  fixed, 88, 89–91, 122, 280
Exercise price, see Strike price
  defined, 280
  of options, 17
  of warrants, 23
Expiration date:
  for an American-style call option,
    12, 18
  defined, 280
  for a European-style call option,
    12, 18
  of warrants, 27

Face value, 7, 9, 12, 280
Final prospectus, see Convertible bond
    indenture
Fixed exchange rate:
  in calculating effective and equivalent
    conversion prices, 89–90
  and conversion ratio, 90–91
  defined, 88, 280
  relationship to current exchange
    rate, 122
Fixed-income-plus-option model:
  defined, 59, 280
  overview of, 70–72

Fixed income securities, *see* Straight
    bonds
Forced conversion, 35. *See also*
    Mandatory redemption
Foreign convertible bonds:
    defined, 5, 280
    vs. domestic convertibles, 209
    features of, 91–93
Foreign currency contracts, 103
Foreign currency exposure, *see* Currency
    exposure
Foreign currency management:
    economic exposure in, 102
    illustration of, from a U.S. dollar
        perspective, 103–109
    overview of, 102–109
Foreign currency markets, 98–102
    currency movements in, 98–99
Foreign exchange contracts, 102
    illustration to explain the use of,
        103–108
Foreign exchange risk, 102
Foreign exchange spot rates, 99
Forward exchange rates:
    calculating, 100–101
    defined, 99–100, 280
    influence of interest rates on, 100–101
Fractional shares, 11
French domestic convertibles:
    analysis of, 225–226
    call protection in, 226
    as an example of convertible
        evaluation, 270–271
    overview of, 225–228
    unique characteristics of, 225
Full hedge, 180, 280

Gearing, 27–28, 280
Gray market, 6, 281

Hedge, *see* Convertible hedge
Hedge position(s):
    analysis of, 197–204

Chinese, 204
currency exposure of, 181, 203–204
delta, 181
downside risk, 199–200
economic exposure in, 204
establishing, 204
full, 180
importance of understanding risk in,
    197–198
interest rates and, 181
and international convertibles, 203–204
locking in, 188
net profit/loss, 200
neutral, 180
partial, 180
profitability of, 204
profit potential of, 181
rate of return, 200–204
to reduce premium, 186–192
transaction exposure and, 204
translation exposure and, 181
unwinding, 203, 204
upside risk, 198–199
working the premium to zero, 186–192
Hedge ratio, 179, 281
Historical volatility, 22
Hybrid security, 8–9, 70. *See also*
    Convertible securities, hybrid
    nature of

Implied volatility, 22
Income-oriented investors, 174
Interest:
    accrued, 7–8, 16, 35, 277
    calculating, 7, 8
    computing payment of, 7
    on Euroconvertibles, 6
    forfeiture of, 16, 35
    on USA Inc. convertible, 7
Interest rate(s):
    and bond prices, 31, 37–38
    and calls, 35
    and convertible securities, 1

Interest rates—*Continued*
  and downside risk, 31
  and equity price, 71
  and hedge position, 181
  influence on forward exchange rates,
    100–101
  and investment value, 31,
    32, 166
  protection against changes in, 12
  and puts, 37
  and zero-coupon convertibles, 76,
    79–80
Interest rate differentials, 100
International convertibles:
  evaluation of, 94–96
  hedge positions, 203–204
  overview of, 87–96
  shares received upon conversion,
    93–94
  types of, 87
International Euroconvertibles, 3
  conversion feature, 88–93
  as currency vehicles, 173,
    177–178
  distinguishing features of, 87
  hedging and, 203
  mechanics of, 87
In the money:
  defined, 20, 281
  option, 51, 71
  warrant, 24
Intrinsic value, *see* Tangible value
  defined, 19–20, 281
  graphing of, 21
  options, 19–20, 21–22,
    23–24
  warrants, 23–24, 84
Investment objective, 178
Investment opportunities:
  convertibles as bond alternatives,
    175–177
  convertibles as currency vehicles,
    177–178

convertibles as equity alternatives,
    173–175
  overview of, 173–178
Investment value, *see* Premium over
    investment value
  applying, 32
  debt component, 29–31
  defined, 29, 281
  as an evaluation tool, 166, 175
  factors affecting, 31–32
  interest rates and, 31, 32, 166
  overview of, 29–31
  and premium over conversion
    value, 49
  as a protective device, 31
  for USA Inc. convertible, 29

Japanese domestic convertibles:
  analysis of, 224–225
  call feature, 223
  conversion value, 223
  as an example of convertible
    evaluation, 269–270
  overview of, 223–225
  premium over conversion value, 225
  yield advantage, 225

Leverage:
  conversion ratio as an indication of,
    13, 15
  in evaluating convertible
    securities, 165
  gearing, 27–28
  in options, 22
  in warrants, 27
Liquidation, 108, 109
Liquidity, 165
Local currency:
  and appreciation of bond currency,
    138, 144, 147
  as a component of domestic
    convertibles, 5, 209
  conversion feature, 88, 96

Local currency—*Continued*
  defined, 281
  depreciation of, 122
  and depreciation of bond currency,
    128–129, 138, 146, 147
  example of convertible bond
    denominated in,
    237–241
Lottery, 35, 36

Mandatory redemption, 33
Marked to market, 108
Market value, 14. *See also* Conversion
  value; Parity
Maturity date, 6, 9, 33, 281
  for USA Inc. convertible, 6, 33
Mergers and acquisitions, 213
Multiplier effect, 117

Net conversion value, 13, 16, 51
Net income advantage, 66, 68
Net present value, 30, 223
Net yield advantage, 66
Neutral hedge:
  defined, 280
  downside profit/loss, 197
  overview of, 195–197
  upside profit/loss, 196–197
  upside scenario, 195–196
Neutral hedge ratio, 281

100% hedge, *see* Full hedge
Open-market purchases, 35
Opportunity cost, 62, 72
Optimal conversion date, 66
Option(s), 17–22
  attractiveness of, as an investment, 22
  call, 2, 9, 16, 17, 278
  compared to warrants, 17, 23, 28
  defined, 17, 282
  equity cost basis, 18–19
  exercising, 17
  expiration date, 18

  factors affecting option premiums,
    21–22
  in the money, 51, 71
  intrinsic value, 19–20, 21–22, 23–24
  issuing cycles, 18
  leverage, 22
  long call position, 22
  out of the money, 71
  put, 17, 20, 282
  time value, 20–21, 22, 70, 283
Option model, 70
  to determine hedge ratio, 181
Option premium:
  components of, 19
  defined, 18, 24, 282
  factors affecting, 21–22
  in the money, 51, 71
  intrinsic value, 19–20, 21–22,
    23–24, 281
  vs. premium over conversion value, 49
  time value, 20–21, 22,
    70–71, 283
  volatility of, 22
Original issue discount,
  76, 282
Out of the money:
  defined, 20, 282
  option, 71

Parity, *see* Conversion value
  defined, 14, 282
  warrant, 84
Partial hedge, 180
Partial hedge ratio, 282
Par value, 7, 12, 14, 280. *See also* Face
  value
Percent method:
  in break-even analysis, 62–63
  described, 41–42
  in determining premium over
    conversion value, 46–47
  when to use, 44, 62
Periodic conversion rights, 70, 206

Perpetual securities, 213
Point/dollar method:
  in break-even analysis, 62–63
  described, 43
  when to use, 44
Preference shares. 217, 218, 228. *See
    also* Australian domestic
    convertibles; British domestic
    convertibles
Premium:
  calculating, 25
  changes in levels of, 50, 57
  decreases in, 51
  defined, 53
  downside risk and, 26, 45, 51, 56
  effect of currency fluctuations on,
    121–123
  evaluation of, 166
  hedging to reduce to zero, 186–192
  increases in, 49–51
  and intrinsic value, 25, 84
  wider, 45, 166
  yield advantage and size of, 48
  for zero-coupon convertible bonds, 74
Premium over conversion value:
  British domestic convertibles,
    168–169, 220–221
  calculating, 45–47
  components of, 49
  convertibles trading *vs.* direct
    investment, 52–53
  costs of, 52–53
  defined, 45, 53, 282
  equity price and, 49
  expansion of as a protective device, 50
  expressing, 45
  investment value, 49
  Japanese domestic convertibles, 225
  justification, 48–49
  as a measurement of risk, 45, 165–166
  percent method in determining, 46–47
  and premium over investment
    value, 58

vs. premium of an option, 49
  reasons premiums decrease, 51
  reasons premiums increase, 49–51
  time value, 49
  in USA Inc. convertible, 46–47, 53
U.S. convertible preference
    shares, 215
U.S. domestic convertibles, 211
Premium over investment value:
  changes in, 57–58
  defined, 55
  and equity price, 57–58
  justification of, 56
  as a measurement of risk,
    56, 58
  and premium over conversion
    value, 58
  in USA Inc. convertible, 55
  yield, 56
Premium risk, 184
Price floor, 16, 31, 57
Profitability:
  and currency fluctuations, 111,
    115–118
  and hedge positions, 204
  in trading of volatile equities, 49
Provisional call protection,
    33–34, 210
Put exercise date, 36, 282
Put feature:
  defined, 9, 282
  and discounted yield advantage
    method, 66
  effect on conversion premium, 38
  evaluating convertible bond with,
    245–249
  and life of a convertible, 72
  overview of, 36–39
  as a protective device, 37
  of USA Inc. convertible, 37
  value of, 36
  of zero-coupon convertible bonds,
    80–81

Put option:
  defined, 17, 282
  in the money, 20
  sale price, 19
Put strike price, 36, 282

Rate of return, 101, 102,
    200–202
Reasonable break-even period, 64
Redemption:
  call feature, 33–35
  mandatory, 33
  put feature, 36–39
  sinking fund, 35–36
  voluntary, 33
Registered bonds, 6, 282
Risk:
  of call, 35, 51, 64, 166
  components of, 154, 163
  cross-currency, 152
  currency exposure, 109–110
  downside, 1, 22, 26, 37, 45,
      51, 56, 197
  evaluation of, 126
  foreign exchange, 102
  in hedge positions, 197–198
  premium, 184
  premium over conversion value as a
      measurement of, 165–166
  premium over investment value as a
      measurement of, 56, 58
  reducing through diversification, 177
  upside, 198–199
Rolling put feature, 38, 283

Serial sinking fund, 36
Sinking fund:
  advantages of, 36
  for busted convertibles, 51
  defined, 9, 283
  early redemption, 35
  as a form of mandatory redemption, 33
  and life of a convertible, 36

serial, 36
  types of, 35–36
Spot rates, 99
Straight bonds:
  vs. convertibles, 2, 176
  convertible securities as alternatives to,
      175–177
  in determining investment value, 29–30
  estimating value of, 30, 70–71
Straight bond value, 29
Strike price, 17, 280, 283. See also
      Exercise price
Swapping, 174, 283
  with USA Inc. convertible, 174–175
Synthetic convertibles:
  benefits of, 86
  conversion value, 84
  defined, 82, 283
  as an example of convertible
      evaluation, 259–261
  investment value, 84
  overview of, 82–86
  vs. traditional convertibles, 86

Takeovers, 52
Tangible value, 19. See also Intrinsic
      value
Taxes:
  advantages of convertible securities, 2
  and convertible preference shares, 213
  double-taxation treaties, 209
  on Euroconvertible bonds, 6
  and zero-coupon convertible
      bonds, 81
Time value:
  defined, 20, 283
  in discounted yield advantage
      method, 66
  graphing of, 22
  of options, 20–21, 22, 70–71, 283
  premium over conversion value, 49
Total return, 122, 163
  compared to equity, 174

Transaction exposure:
  applications of, 102
  defined, 97, 283
  in hedging, 204
Translation exposure:
  benefits derived from, 177
  cross-currency, 153–155, 253–255
  currency exposure through, 129–133
  defined, 97, 283
  in foreign currency-denominated
    convertibles, 162
  and hedge position, 181

USA Inc. 7.5% of 200X, 5
  bearish hedge, 193–194
  bullish hedge, 182–192
  call protection, 34
  computing the break-even period,
    60–64
  computing the conversion ratio of,
    12–13
  coupon, 6
  denomination, 6
  equity and distinguishing features
    of, 8
  face value, 7
  interest on, 7
  investment value, 29
  maturity date, 6, 33
  premium over conversion value,
    46–47, 53
  premium over investment value, 55
  put feature of, 37
  swapping, 174–175
  using the discounted yield advantage
    method to value, 65–66,
    67–68, 69
  yield advantage, 41
U.S. convertible preference shares:
  conversion evaluation, 262–266
  as an example of convertible
    evaluation, 264–266
  overview of, 210–212

premium over conversion value, 215
  yield advantage, 215–216
U.S. domestic convertible bonds:
  analysis of, 211
  break-even period, 212
  call feature of, 210
  conversion feature, 210
  vs. Euroconvertibles, 210, 212
  as an example of convertible
    evaluation, 262–263
  overview of, 210–212
  premium over conversion value, 211
U.S. Euroconvertibles, 88
Unwinding, 203, 204
Upside risk, 197, 198–199
Usable bond, 82, 283
Usable bond plus warrant, see Synthetic
    convertibles

Valuation methods:
  break-even analysis, 60–64
  discounted yield advantage, 64–69
  fixed-income-plus-option, 70–72
  overview of, 59–72
Volatility:
  and conversion premium, 51
  and conversion price, 12
  historical, 22
  implied, 22
  and option premium, 22
  premium over conversion value as a
    measure of, 45, 49, 51
  and warrant premium, 26
  of zero-coupon convertible
    bonds, 81
Voluntary redemption, 33

Warrant(s):
  as a component of equity bond
    units, 81
  conversion feature, 23
  defined, 23, 283
  and equity price appreciation, 28

Warrant(s)—*Continued*
  evaluation of, 23
  exercise price, 23
  expiration, 27
  factors affecting premium, 26–28
  in the money, 24
  intrinsic value, 23–24, 84
  as investment incentives, 23
  leverage, 27
  vs. options, 17, 23, 28
  overview of, 23–28
  parity in, 84
  price, 24
Warrant model, 70
Warrant premium:
  calculating, 25–26
  defined, 24, 283
  dynamic nature of, 26
  factors affecting, 26
  an intrinsic value, 25, 84
  volatility and, 26

Yield, 56
Yield advantage, *see* Discounted yield
    advantage method
  and bond value, 41
  in British domestic convertibles,
    169, 219
  and conversion premium, 51
  defined, 284
  equity method, 41, 42–43, 44
  in Japanese domestic convertibles, 225
  methods of calculating compared, 44
  methods of expressing, 41
  percent method, 41–42, 44
  point/dollar method, 41, 43, 44
  and size of premium, 48
  in USA convertible, 41
  in U.S. convertible preference
    shares, 215
Yield to maturity:
  defined, 31, 284

  vs. yield to put, 166
  for zero-coupon bonds, 73
Yield to put:
  calculating, 36
  defined, 36, 37
  vs. yield to maturity, 166
Yield-to-put method, 41
  in break-even analysis,
    63–64
  described, 43–44
  when to use, 44

Zero-coupon bonds:
  defined, 73
  vs. zero-coupon bonds, 74
Zero-coupon convertible bonds:
  advantages/disadvantages of,
    74, 81
  call features of, 80, 81
  call protection, 80
  conversion feature in, 78, 79
  conversion price, 74–75
  conversion ratio, 75
  defined, 284
  and equity dilution, 74
  and equity price appreciation, 78
  as an example of convertible
    evaluation, 258–259
  interest rates and, 76, 79–80
  maturity, 76
  original issue discount, 76
  overview of, 73–81
  premium, 74, 76
  price of, 74, 77
  put features of, 80–81
  tax consequences of, 81
  unique qualities of, 76
  volatility of, 81
  yields to maturity, 73, 76
  vs. zero-coupon bonds, 74
Zero premium, achieving,
    186–192